More Praise for
House as a Mirror of Self

"... A fresh, indeed unique, look at people and their dwellings ... Will be of value to environmental psychologists, designers, and, above all, to anyone who has mused about his or her own home, real or imagined."

—Robert B. Riley, Professor of Architecture and Landscape Architecture, University of Illinois at Champaign-Urbana, and editor, *Landscape Journal*

"There is a mystery at the heart of architecture that books can rarely broach, it is the 'question of spirit.' This book enters where academics normally fear to tread, a rich and insightful collection of stories about housing the human spirit; about the discovery, construction, transformation, and care of the self."

—Kim Dovey, Professor of Architecture, University of Melbourne

"This is a courageous and inviting book by a renowned scholar and environmental designer. Clare Cooper Marcus takes us on an exciting journey into the lives, minds, and feelings of real people as they disclose their joy, fear, love, hopes, and frustrations as they 'speak to,' 'speak about,' and are 'spoken to' by their homes. Cooper Marcus is a superb scholar and storyteller whose book will make vivid how 'we are our homes and our homes are us.'"

—Irwin Altman, professor of psychology and author

"Clare Cooper Marcus ... has written a thought-provoking book about the many meanings of houses ... Marcus delivers ample revelations about the enormous role home plays in the drama of our lives."

—*Body Mind Spirit* magazine

"*House as a Mirror of Self* is a thought-provoking work. Marcus teaches us that becoming aware of unresolved conflict with our environment is an important step in the 'journey to the self or soul.'"

—*San Francisco Chronicle Book Review*

House as a Mirror of Self

House
as a
Mirror of Self

Exploring the Deeper Meaning of Home

Clare Cooper Marcus

NICOLAS-HAYS

Berwick, Maine

This edition published in 2006 by
Nicolas-Hays, Inc.
P.O. Box 540206
Lake Worth, FL 33454-0206

First hardcover edition July 1995; first paperback edition 1997, Conari Press

Distributed by Red Wheel/Weiser, LLC.
65 Parker Street, Ste. 7
Newburyport, MA 01950

Cover design by Phillip Augusta

Library of Congress Cataloging-in-Publication Data
Marcus, Clare Cooper
    House as a mirror of self : exploring the deeper meaning of home / Clare Cooper Marcus.
        p.   cm.
    Includes bibliographical references.
    ISBN 10: 0-89254-124-5
    ISBN 13: 978-0-89254-124-9
        1. Object constancy (Psychoanalysis).   2. Dwellings—Psychological aspects.
        3. House furnishings—Psychological aspects.   4. Jung, C. G. (Carl Gustav), 1875-1961
        5. Psychoanalysis.   I. Title

    BF175.5.O22M37   1995
    155.9'4-dc20   95-9232

VG

This book is dedicated to Al Baum,
a dear and generous friend

CONTENTS

ACKNOWLEDGMENTS

First I must express my heartfelt thanks to the people whose stories appear in this book, and to those I spoke with whose stories did not appear. All of them provided me with invaluable insights; without their willingness to share their feelings about home, this book could not have happened.

My friends, family, and academic colleagues have all provided much-needed encouragement and support, for which I am deeply grateful. In particular I must thank my children—Jason and Lucy—embarking on environmental careers of their own; friends who have encouraged me in this work—Priscilla Thomas, Sheila Madden, Wendy Sarkissian, Sara Jaffe, Carolyn Francis, Phyllis Greenwood, Carolyn North, and Francis de Silva; many colleagues at the University of California at Berkeley; and, most especially, my dear friend, Alvin H. Baum, Jr., of San Francisco, who most generously supported me during a year's leave of absence from teaching, during which time I was able to read, write, and ponder on this topic without interruption.

Heartfelt gratitude is due also to Dr. Frances Tobriner, Jungian analyst, who journeyed with me on my own inner explorations and taught me much about the process of striving to become a whole person. This book has been as much a deepening of my own self-understanding as it has been an exploration of other people's stories about home.

It was in a University of California Extension course on the psychology of Carl Jung where this book had its early beginnings, and I must acknowledge the teacher of that class—Kathleen Whiteside-Taylor, then in her eighties and now deceased—for her enthusiasm and inspiration. Later, in a women's group lead by Berkeley counselor Anita Feder-Chernila, I found the method that helped me pursue this work, and I am deeply grateful for her sensitive instruction in the art of role-playing.

As this work progressed, I spoke on the topic of the house as a mirror of self in many professional settings. I am grateful for those who invited me to speak at the Carl Jung Institute of San Francisco; at many universities in the United States, Canada, Australia, New Zealand, Britain, Denmark, and Sweden; and at annual meetings of the Environmental Design Research Association. In all these settings, questions and comments from the audience provoked and intrigued me, pushing me into aspects of this topic I had not fully considered before. The names of those who encouraged me are too many to mention, but I must especially acknowledge my gratitude to Professor Irwin Altman of the Department of Psychology, University of Utah, and Kim Dovey, formerly a student at Berkeley and now a professor of architecture at the University of Melbourne, Australia. Both these men have written insightfully about the deeper meanings of home, and I greatly appreciate their written work, as well as many inspiring conversations we have had over the years. I am thankful, also, to the Tides Foundation of San Francisco and its executive director, Drummond Pike, for supporting this work.

There are many occasions when an author becomes bogged down. On one such occasion, I was lucky enough to meet Renate Stendhal. As both a psychotherapist and a professional editor, she had the unique capabilities to help me transform this book from a quasi-academic tome to a book with appeal to the general public. For that I am deeply grateful. Mary Jane Ryan and the team at Conari Press have guided me through the publication process with tact, sensitivity, and humor. I thank them all.

The artwork done by the people I interviewed was photographed for this book by Fran Stateler of the Department of Landscape Architecture, University of California, Berkeley. I am grateful for her professional expertise and also for that of Christophe Girot, who drew several diagrams. I must thank Glenn Robert Lym, San Francisco architect, whose book *The Psychology of Building* was an inspiration to me and who graciously permitted me to reproduce from that book his drawings of the evolution of Jung's house at Bollingen. Two photos were loaned to me by Charlotte Nolan and Christopher Grampp; all the other photos in the book are my own.

Last, but by no means least, I offer heartfelt thanks to Kaye Bock, who typed several drafts of this book in her "spare time" outside her job as graduate assistant for the Department of City and Regional Planning at the University of California at Berkeley. Her care, insights, and encouragement are deeply appreciated.

While it is normal to express one's thanks to friends, family, and colleagues in the Acknowledgments section of a book, I also feel the need to appreciate special *places* that have facilitated my explorations. As well as my own house and the houses—past and present—of those I interviewed, there are several places-of-the-soul that have inspired me to delve more deeply into the Self. Among those of profound importance in my life while writing this book are the alternative spiritual community of Findhorn in Scotland; the magical island of Iona off the west coast of Scotland; The Zen Center at Green Gulch Farm in Marin County, California; and the Santa Sabina retreat center at Dominican College, San Rafael, California.

Whereas some people write books in silent campus offices or private studies at home, I am peculiar in that I write best in cafes with a low level of human activity around me. I am especially grateful for the coffee, tea, muffins, and warm milieu of Nabolom Bakery, The Musical Offering, and Bubi's Cafe, where most of this book was written, edited, rewritten, and pondered over. I am grateful for the environmental support of these Berkeley establishments and for their tolerance of customers who, like me, spin a coffee and muffin out over two or more hours. Without these places, I doubt that I could have written this book.

FOREWORD

C. G. Jung's late-life autobiography, *Memories, Dreams, Reflections,* begins with a personal statement which is then generalized: "My life is a story of the self-realization of the unconscious. Everything in the unconscious seeks outward manifestation, and the personality too desires to evolve out of its unconscious conditions and to experience itself as a whole."

In Jung's view, the psyche is largely unconscious. The growth of consciousness is what mental life is chiefly about. What is not yet conscious is normally experienced "out there," in projection on the outer world. We find ourselves in other people, things, and places, in experiences felt to come from the outside. Only secondarily, if at all, do we recognize our own participation in our experience. When we do, we have a chance to reclaim the projection, ponder it, own it, and add it to our awareness of ourselves. It is in this way that personality grows—by a continuous cycle of projecting and reclaiming psychic contents. Through this feedback loop, unconscious potential is put out into the world and then brought back in at a realized, conscious level and integrated into the expanding personality.

Whenever we create something, we foster and stimulate this sequence of expression-feedback-integration. The expressive element may be minor and secondary to some outer objective, as when we do our work or cook. It may be the whole point, as when we deliberately use paint, clay, or movement for expressive purposes. Or it may be central but part of a larger process, as when we create an environment to suit us—when we make ourselves a home to feel at home in. Nesting, homemaking is a major means of personal expression and development. We create our immediate environment and then contemplate it and are worked on by it. We find ourselves mirrored in it, see what had been not yet visible, and integrate the reflection back into our sense of self.

Clare Cooper Marcus tells us that reading Jung's account of building his stone tower retreat on the lake at Bollingen was "the start of a new direction in my work which has absorbed me for the past twenty years." Jung says that though his scientific writing was satisfying, something was missing. He needed to concretize the psyche: "Words and paper . . . did not seem real enough to me; something more was needed. I had to achieve a kind of representation in stone of my innermost thoughts and of the knowledge I had acquired. Or, to put it another way, I had to make a confession of faith in stone."

He built the structure in four stages at intervals of four years, not by calculation but as the impulse to expand emerged in him. The work included, finally, his own paintings done on the walls, stone-carving, a well, kitchen, and provision for self-sufficient living. In retrospect, he could see that each addition expressed a development of himself, a step in the "self-realization of the unconscious."

"It is thus a concretization of the individuation process. . . . During the building work, of course, I never considered these matters. I built the house in sections, always following the concrete needs of the moment. . . . Only afterward did I see how all the parts fitted together and that a meaningful form had resulted: a symbol of psychic wholeness."

Jung expresses poetically what a dwelling can be psychologically, what Clare Cooper Marcus calls "house as a mirror of self": "At Bollingen I am in the midst of my true life, I am most deeply myself. . . . There is nothing in the Tower that has not grown into its own form over the decades, nothing with which I am not linked. Here everything has its history, and mine; here is space for the spaceless kingdom of the world's and the psyche's hinterland. . . ."

We do not usually think of our everyday residence in such grand terms, yet to the extent that they express and reflect the self the language is appropriate. "In modest harmony with nature" (the title of a Chinese woodcut) includes harmony with our own nature. A right home can do that. It can protect, heal, and restore us, express who we are now, and over time help us become who we are meant to be.

We are fortunate indeed that Clare Cooper Marcus was so gripped by her subject and persisted with it through twenty years of research. We as readers become gripped by it also. The interaction between people and their domestic contexts, a subject of overwhelming importance once she calls it to our attention, has been neglected in both architectural and psychological circles. The author moves into this interface, to the profit of both fields of study and to the benefit of the general reader. Through her magical book, we can join her in her consideration of human "place-making," and individually resonate to her study of what are universal human processes. She presents fascinating interview material about individuals in relation to their natural and created environments—about the expression and extension of self into the surround, the "personalization of space." She adds her own experiences and profound reflections about such events. Finally, she provides exercises and guidenotes for the journey, practical ways to go about occupying one's place and coming home to the self.

It seems fitting to draw a parallel between Jung's creation of his Tower and the author's twenty-year creation of her powerful book: "Only afterward did I see how all the parts fitted together and that a meaningful form had resulted: a symbol of psychic wholeness." Home is such a symbol, and this book is such a home.

—JAMES YANDELL, M.D., PH.D.
former president, C. G. Jung Institute of San Francisco

ONE

House as a Mirror of Self

That people could come into the world in a place they could not at first even name and had never known before; and that out of a nameless and unknown place they could grow and move around in it until its name they knew and called with love, and call it HOME, and put roots there and love others there; so that whenever they left this place they would sing homesick songs about it and write poems of yearning for it . . . and forever be returning to it or leaving it again!

—WILLIAM GOYEN, *The House of Breath*[1]

Why was Jean so attached to her house that to move away seemed to threaten her very being? Why did Robert buy what seemed like the perfect dwelling, only to spend as much time away from it as possible? How was it that Alan loved their house and Marion felt sick every time she parked in the driveway? Why did Peter choose a run-down apartment in a dangerous neighborhood when he could have lived anywhere? Why did Sara love her cottage, Jeff his houseboat, Michael his city loft? What is behind these profound feelings about house and home? These are the kinds of questions that have intrigued and fascinated me most of my life. I set out looking for answers and was often stunned by what I learned.

This is a book about people and their homes. It is not about architecture per se, or decorating styles, or real estate, but about the more subtle bonds of feeling we experience with dwellings past and present. Some people have profound memories of a special childhood home and unconsciously reproduce aspects of its form or essence in a house of adulthood. Others find their current dwelling-place curiously uncomfortable, yet know that it has nothing to do with the usual concerns for privacy, security, or personal space. Some people, on experiencing the stress of divorce or death of a loved one, find their bondedness to home to be dramatically changed.

A home fulfills many needs: a place of self-expression, a vessel of memories, a refuge from the outside world, a cocoon where we can feel nurtured and let down our guard. A person without a fixed abode is viewed with suspicion in our society, labeled "vagrant," "hobo," "street person." The lack of a home address can be a serious impediment to someone seeking a job, renting a place to live, or trying to vote. Those of us lucky enough to have a home may rarely reflect on our good fortune.

At the base of this study is a very simple yet frequently overlooked premise: As we change and grow throughout our lives, our psychological development is punctuated not only by meaningful emotional relationships with people, but also by close, affective ties with a number of significant physical environments, beginning in childhood. That these person-place relationships have been relatively ignored is partly due to the ways in which we have chosen to "slice up" and study the world. Psychologists whose domain is the study of emotional development view the physical environment as a relatively unimportant backdrop to the human dramas of life. Those who *are* interested in people-environment relations—geographers, anthropologists, architects, and those in the newly emerging field of environmental psychology—have for the most part ignored issues dealing with emotional attachment.

Home can mean different things to different people. Those far away from their place of upbringing may refer to England, or China, or "back east" as home. For immigrants to a new country, there may be a long period of adjustment revolving around the issue of just where home *is*. In young adulthood, many vacillate between thinking of home as where they now live, and thinking of it as where they grew up. For many people living in cities, home may be the village where they were born or the cabin they go to on vacation. City dwellers in Nairobi, Kenya, for example, refer to their ancestral farm or village as home and expect to be buried there when they die. Apartment dwellers in Stockholm, Sweden, often consider home to be the second home, where they spend weekends and vacations on the coast or in the forest. Ties to the land and nature, and memories of extended family, prove stronger than the mere number of days spent in a particular dwelling.

Much of my academic career has focused on low-income housing. I was intrigued to discover what the residents of public housing projects felt about the physical environment in which they lived, all the more so when the design of that environment had received an award from the American Institute of Architects. Did professional appraisal and resident experience coincide?

I was interested in this question because most people of low or modest income have little choice about where they live, while the designers of the housing projects rarely have the time, training, or inclination to ask them about their preferences. I authored a couple of books that attempted to fill this gap, using a format that designers could consult at the drawing board.

As I continued this work, I became vaguely dissatisfied. I was learning and communicating a lot about *house* (kitchen design, room layout, privacy needs, inadequate storage, and so on), but little about *home.* During my early years as a graduate student and young faculty member at Berkeley, I moved ten times in ten years. Each time, the actual physical move was followed by weeks, sometimes months, of getting used to the new place. Hanging pictures, moving houseplants around, rearranging furniture, I gradually created a home in each new setting. I reflected on my own feelings about moving and settling into a new place and realized that my door-to-door surveys in housing projects were only skimming the surface of what house and home mean to the human heart. I searched in the library but found little guidance: Psychologists, anthropologists, architects, planners—few had delved into the deeper emotional meanings of home. Novelists and playwrights, filmmakers and poets had more profound insights. Reading Swiss psychologist Carl Jung's autobiography, *Memories, Dreams, Reflections,* was a turning point. Here was a deeply reflective man who had built his own house and linked its form with aspects of his own psychological development. This was the start of a new direction in my work, which has absorbed me for the past twenty years.

Since the mid-1970s, I have talked with more than sixty individuals about their homes, most of them living in the San Francisco Bay Area. The people I spoke with were young and old, owners and renters, men and women. The dwellings they lived in ranged from urban mansions, rented apartments, cottages, and suburban homes, to converted factories, houseboats, mobile homes, convents, and domes in the forest. Some people were wealthy enough to own two houses but felt at home in neither of them. Others lived in great contentment in a single room or an illegal self-built shack. What all these people had in common was a strong emotional relationship with their homes, either positive or negative. Some felt profoundly at home; others felt distressingly alienated. What I was interested in discovering through the real-life stories of a wide variety of people was why people felt the way they did about their homes.

The people I talked with were from a range of backgrounds, but all had a number of things in common: They all had strong feelings about where they lived and were able—and willing—to share these feelings with me; and they all had some degree of economic freedom about how and where they lived. In this particular study, I was interested in people who had a certain amount of choice: Given some degree of freedom, where did people select to live? What kind of dwelling did they choose? How did they relate to their furniture and possessions? If they disliked where they lived, what would be an ideal home? I did not talk with the very poor, with residents of housing projects, or with homeless people; for some of them, my questions might have seemed strange, superfluous, even insulting. Nor did I talk with the very rich, or those who employed professional interior designers. I was interested in the average, middle-of-the-road house- or apartment-dweller who had created their own homes, whatever they might now feel about it. Each story is unique, and yet there is a touch of Everyman/woman in all of them.

It is not necessarily comfortable to talk about feelings with a relative stranger. Two things made this easier for the people I spoke with. First, I made no attempt to select a random sample, so people were not contacted via an unexpected phone call or formal letter. All of them volunteered to speak with me, having heard of my work, either through a friend or through a lecture or informal talk where I spoke about it. Thus, if people knew they would be very uncomfortable talking about feelings, they didn't volunteer. Those who did—regardless of gender, educational level, or socioeconomic status—had some capacity for expressing their feelings.

Another reason why people were able to talk freely—often emotionally and poetically—about their feelings for home was, I think, the particular method I used. Even with the best rapport, it is not easy for people to launch into an answer to the question: How do you feel about your home? How I stumbled upon a better approach is a story in itself.

In the early 1970s, I wrote a paper entitled "The House as a Symbol of the Self." It was a "think-piece," partially inspired by the work and theories of Carl Jung, and was published in several academic readers. While I was gratified by letters from people telling me that they had been inspired by this article, I was impatient to move on, to find out from "real people" whether some of the ideas in this paper had validity. Academic colleagues tried to make helpful suggestions regarding controlled experiments, but that was not the route I wanted to follow. Meanwhile, I was busy raising two small children and put the project on the back burner.

By the mid-1970s, I found myself going through the emotional turmoil of a divorce. For support and guidance, I joined a women's group run by a therapist using the Gestalt approach. A year later, two Roman Catholic sisters, Pat and Joanna, joined the group. Pat had recently moved to California from Tucson, Arizona, where she had lived in a convent close to the desert. One evening, she began to talk about how much she missed the desert where she had gone each day to pray and meditate. Since a basic technique of Gestalt therapy is role play-ing, the therapist running the group suggested that Pat talk to the desert and tell it her feelings. The resulting dialogue between Pat and the desert was poetic and deeply moving. Scales fell from my eyes! If Pat could speak so eloquently to—and as—the desert (an inanimate setting), why couldn't I ask people to do the same with their houses?

I interviewed a few members of the women's group who had strong feelings about their homes, using this role-playing approach. The results were more than I had hoped for. I had finally found a method with which I could proceed. In order to learn to use this approach in a responsible way, I went into training with Anita Feder-Chernila, a Gestalt counselor leading the women's group referred to above. My motivation was not to *become* a therapist, but to utilize role playing as a means of uncovering feelings in a way that would not be damaging to my informants.

Each story in this book was told to me while sitting in the person's own home. I found this to be a necessary part of putting people at ease. In order to have them begin to focus on their emotions, I first would ask that the person put down his or her feelings about home in a picture; I supplied a large pad of paper, crayons, and felt pens. If they objected with "Oh—I can't draw," I reassured them that this was not a test in drawing, but rather an opportunity for them to focus on their feelings without speaking. Some people did childlike house diagrams with words or colors indicative of feelings. Others produced mandala-like symbols, semiabstract images, or artistic renderings. For most people, it seemed that this experience of beginning to explore feelings in a visual image while I absented myself from the room was extremely helpful in allowing them to focus before starting to talk.

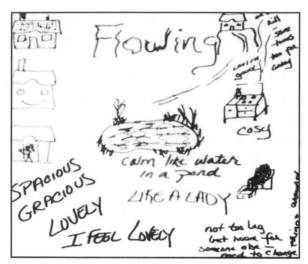

While this was going on, I would wander around the house or apartment, taking photos and notes about how the setting seemed to me. Then, after fifteen to twenty minutes, I would return and ask the person to describe, somewhat objectively, what they had put on paper. For example, a young woman who was happy with her recently purchased woodsy house described how she had first drawn an image of a pond with the phrase, *calm like water in a pond* and then had added small, smiling houses and the words *cosy, spacious, gracious,* and *lovely.*

After the person had described what they had put down, I would place the picture on a cushion or chair about four feet away and would ask them to speak to the drawing as if it *were* their house, starting with the words, "House—the way I feel about you is . . ." At an appropriate moment, I would ask them to switch places with the house, to move to the other chair and speak back to themselves as if they were the house. In this way, I facilitated a dialogue between person and house, which often became quite emotional, sometimes generated laughter, and occasionally brought forth statements beginning, "Oh, my God . . . ," as some profound insight came into consciousness.

A recently divorced woman, for example, spoke to the house she had left and had never liked; the house, in turn, was glad she was gone, since it had never felt cared for. A retired man shared his feelings of profound attachment to a home which mirrored that of a beloved grandfather. A woman who lost her home to fire grieved as if for a deceased lover. A middle-aged man rejected home, family, and job as he went through a crisis of identity.

If, as sometimes happened, the dialogue aroused deep emotion or unexpected insights, I made sure before I left that the person had a close friend, partner, spouse, or therapist with whom to continue the conversation. In some cases, I did two or three interviews with the same person over a seven- to ten-year period; in this way, particularly fascinating insights were gained as to the different meanings of home at different stages in a person's life. For example, a professional woman who hated the house her husband had remodeled reflected very different feelings about home when I interviewed her in her own cozy apartment five years after a divorce.

To protect the privacy of those I interviewed, some requested that I not use their real names. In a few cases, details of location have been changed for a similar reason. The many extensive quotes throughout this book are the verbatim words of those I talked with, tape-recorded, and transcribed. Many interviews lasted two hours or more, hence the quotes represent a small proportion of what any individual actually said. I have attempted to recount these stories as accurately as possible. Where a sentence or two has been omitted from a particular quote in order to facilitate smooth-flowing text, I have *not* observed the standard academic practice of three-dot ellipses (. . .) to indicate that something is missing.

The more stories I listened to, the more it became apparent that people consciously and unconsciously "use" their home environment to express something about themselves. On a conscious level, this is not a new insight. We have all had the experience of visiting new friends in their home and becoming aware of some facet of their values made manifest by the environment—be it the books on their shelves, art (or the lack of it) on the walls, the degree to which the house is open or closed to the view of visitors, and so on. All of these represent more or less conscious decisions about personal expression, just as our clothes or hairstyle or the kind of car we drive are conscious expressions of our values. What is more intriguing and less well recognized is that we also express aspects of our *unconscious* in the home environment, just as we do in dreams. Adolescents may leave their rooms in disarray as an unconscious gesture of defiance against their parents. A woman may buy a home, unconsciously emulating the style of a much-loved deceased relative. Or a man may be mystified as to why he rented a house that is completely inappropriate for his needs, only to discover later that it is a copy of a childhood home that is still reverberating in his unconscious.

For Sigmund Freud, the unconscious was like some dangerous wilderness, and symbols manifested in dreams contained impulses or conflicts the conscious mind needed to conceal. Carl Jung had a very different perception of the unconscious. For him, it had both a personal and a collective component and was "like the night sky, an infinite unknown, studded with myriads of tiny sparks of light that can become the sources of illumination, insight, and creativity for the person in the process of individuation."[2] Jung postulated the notion of individuation, or striving toward inner wholeness. Learning to read messages from the unconscious made manifest in dreams, waking insights, and creative endeavors assists us on our journey toward integration. There is no doubt that Jung's view of the unconscious and of our psychological development has deeply influenced my work.

A core theme of this book and the stories within it is the notion that we are all—throughout our lives—striving toward a state of wholeness, of being wholly ourselves. Whether we are conscious of it or not, every relationship, event, mishap, or good fortune in our lives can be perceived as a "teaching," guiding us toward being more and more fully who we are. Although this has been widely written about, especially by Jungians, what this book adds to the debate is the suggestion that the places we live in are reflections of that process, and indeed the places themselves have a powerful effect on our journey toward wholeness.

In the course of our lives, other people enter, and sometimes leave, the field of our psychic awareness. We pay attention to some, invest deep emotion in some, and selectively pay little attention to others. This seems so obvious; we know we could not survive without this selectivity. The world is too populated and too complex.

What is less obvious is that the same thing happens, I believe, with the objects and places in our lives. We selectively pay attention and invest them with emotion as it serves the deeper, largely unconscious process of individuation, or becoming who we truly are. Objects, like people, come in and out of our lives and awareness, not in some random, meaningless pattern ordained by fate, but in a clearly patterned framework that sets the stage for greater and greater self-understanding. We all play roles in each other's dramas: sometimes as lead, sometimes as supporting actor. To continue the theatrical analogy, a play or drama also needs a set and props. In our own lives, we select the sets and props of different "acts" (or periods of life) in order—often unconsciously—to display images of ourselves and to learn by reflection of the environment around us.

The key seems to be in the personalization of space: More and more, I found in the stories I heard that it is the movable objects in the home, rather than the physical fabric itself, that are the symbols of self. Even the prisoner, shut away by society because of a crime, is permitted to bring into prison certain effects that are personally meaningful (posters, pinups, family pictures). Even when stripped of all symbols of selfhood, all possibilities of choice, we do concede that the personalization of place is an inalienable right. Conversely, when society wishes to mold a group of individuals into a whole (military personnel), or the attention of the group is deliberately focused away from personal needs (religious orders), the personalization of space is consistently precluded.

Several generations ago, most of us might have inherited a house from our parents or grandparents; or moving with the frontier, we might have fashioned a dwelling out of Nebraska sod or woodlot logs in Illinois. Nowadays, we seek a home to rent or buy from what is available. Our motives for choosing a particular place are driven by what we can afford, its neighborhood location, and its style and level of upkeep, but also by the symbolic role of the house as an expression of the social identity we wish to communicate. We have become more self-conscious about home as a vehicle for communication and display. The neighbors, our visitors, and ourselves are the intended recipients of this communication. If you have any doubts about the extent to which homes communicate, think about the number of TV shows that began with the camera panning over the exterior of a home—*Dallas, Dynasty, All in the Family, The Waltons, The Cosby Show, Roseanne,* and the list goes on. Though barely conscious of it, we are always making judgments about who these people are, their probable income, place in the society, cultural values, and so on.

⌜While the house as symbol of our place in society has been discussed and researched by social scientists, the house interior and its contents as a mirror of our inner psychological self have received much less attention. It is *this* that is the subject of this book.⌟

Thus, throughout our lives, whether we are conscious of it or not, our home and its contents are very potent statements about who we are. In particular, they represent symbols of our ego-selves, for in the first half of life, our primary psychological task is to develop a strong and comfortable personality with which we meet and

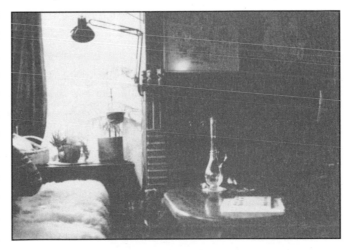

For many people, their furniture, pictures, and other moveable objects are more powerful expressions of self than is the house-structure itself (Priscilla's house).

function in the world. Starting with childhood, our explorations in and around home allow us to develop a sense of self as individuals. A child constructing a den or clubhouse under the hedge is doing far more than merely manipulating dirt and branches. He or she is having a powerful experience of creativity, of learning about self via molding the physical environment.

In adolescence, posters fixed to the bedroom wall, photos displayed, clothes left in disarray—all may make a statement to parents: This is who *I* am! I am my own person, even if I'm not quite sure yet what that is.

Moving into young adulthood, relationships and career may be at the forefront of our consciousness, but in the establishment of our first home-away-from-home, we begin to express who we are as distinct individuals, apart from our family of birth. Some people have a hard time doing this, and unconsciously repeat some unresolved conflict with mother or father in the ways they do—or do not—create a home for themselves.

Marriage or a decision to live with a partner raises many issues of potential conflict as barely conscious values regarding privacy, territory, self-expression, and so on come to the surface. Problems within a relationship may be acted out via the domestic environment, since focusing on issues of decor or use of rooms is—for some people—less threatening than direct confrontation. If a relationship ends in separation or divorce, all kinds of emotions come to the surface regarding possessions, furniture, house, and property, since statements about the marriage have often become concretized in these material objects.

As we mature psychologically, particularly in the second half of life, pressing questions other than those surrounding relationships, family, and success begin to emerge: Why am I alive? What is my purpose? Is there a meaning to my life? In beginning to address such questions, some people experience subtle, and then profound, changes in their feelings about home or in their connection to possessions. The acknowledgment of our relationship to a higher Self, or soul, has begun to take hold. Throughout this book, *self* in lowercase refers to the ego-self, whereas *Self* with a capital *S* refers to the higher or transpersonal self.

So far as I was able, I attempted to approach this material via what philosopher Martin Heidegger called "pre-logical thought." This is not "illogical" or "irrational," but rather a mode of approaching being-in-the-world that permeated early Greek thinkers at a time before the categorization of our world into mind and matter, cause and effect, in-here and out-there had gripped and mesmerized the

Western mind. I firmly believe that a deeper level of person/environment interaction can be approached only by means of a thought process that attempts to eliminate observer and object. If I dared, I would communicate what I have learned via a poem; I would let this work be dreamed through me. But because I don't yet have the courage to leap from academic to poet, I must perforce attempt to communicate in linear, verbal thought, a relationship (self/dwelling) which I sense is preverbal, almost mystical. Although I have attempted to approach this work in a state of meditative thinking, I have also attempted to facilitate a comparable state of being in my informants. Perhaps a better word would be *co-researchers,* since my insights—such as they are—emerged from a resonance between their words and my thoughts. I allowed what they wanted to articulate to come forth.

After many years of conducting these dialogues, it has become clear to me that I am doing more than collecting data on people/environment feelings; these encounters were to a greater or lesser degree therapeutic for the informants. Some people registered an "A-ha!" experience as something they said helped them understand an aspect of their life for which the house-self dynamic provides a clue or metaphor.

Anita, for example, was looking for a house to buy. She had lived for fourteen years in a rented cottage in a modest neighborhood, where she raised two daughters after a divorce. The landlord decided to sell the cottage; the family had to move. Anita searched for a house and, although there were plenty on the market and she had the money for a down payment, nothing "clicked." She asked me to do an interview with her to see if that would help.

After some discussion of her wishes for a new house, I sensed that the problem had something to do with her not having acknowledged her feelings for the house she was living in. I asked her to close her eyes and took her on a tour of her living room, touching all her favorite things. She started to cry. I asked her to tell the house what it meant to her. A dialogue ensued in which she expressed her happiness of the past fourteen years and her grief at leaving. Through her tears, she laughed as the house replied that it would be happy to have various repairs carried out, which Anita had not been willing or able to do.

When it seemed appropriate, I asked Anita to describe the house she'd like to move to. She described it in some detail. A week later, she called in some excitement to say she had found a house just like the one she had described and was in the process of buying it.

This is an example of an interview being unintentionally therapeutic. Just as with the loss of a relationship or a job, the loss of a house needs to be acknowledged and grieved before our consciousness opens up to new possibilities.

When I began this work, I had no idea what I would discover. All I sensed at the beginning was that there were multiple layers of meaning in our feelings of attachment to house and home. As I listened to story after story, themes began to emerge and repeat themselves. It became clear that some kind of developmental explanation made sense; that from childhood to old age, our relationship to the physical environment of home goes through subtle shifts and changes, mirroring shifts of attention from outer accomplishment to deeper inner concerns.

Starting with our early years, chapter 2, "The Special Places of Childhood," recounts the memories of young adults thinking back to their first experiences of "house making" in the dens, forts, cubbies, and clubhouses they found or created in those magic years of middle childhood between the ages of six and twelve. Older adults, having established homes, reflect on how they have re-created some patterns from a much-loved home or homes of childhood in their current environment.

In chapter 3, "Growing Up: Self-Expression in the Homes of Adulthood," I explore the accounts of people who have learned to truly express who they are via their choice of a house: by remodeling a dwelling as family needs change; by building, buying, or refinishing furniture; by changing the decor after the end of a relationship; and by coming to terms with the inevitable tensions between clutter and tidiness.

In chapter 4, "Always or Never Leaving Home," we encounter several people who have become more or less stuck in their relationship to home, either by seemingly excessive bonding to one house or its contents, or by never being able to settle down in one place. In both situations, it seems that an unresolved issue regarding their relationship to home in childhood, or to one parent in that home, is at the core of this adult dilemma.

"Becoming More Fully Ourselves: Evolving Self-Image as Reflected in Our Homes" is the subject of chapter 5. Here we encounter the stories of people who, finding themselves in a home environment that no longer reflects who they are, make a dramatic change and move to a setting in which they feel more comfortable. These moves range all the way from a shift from a suburban to an urban location, to leaving a religious institution, to selling a house and moving abroad. All represent attempts to surround the self with a setting that is reflective of newly emerging values.

The next two chapters deal with the often complex and emotional issues that revolve around two people establishing a home together. In chapter 6, "Becoming Partners: Power Struggles in Making a Home Together," we meet several couples who have come to terms with differing preferences regarding furnishing style, decor, or house type, and several others who have separated or divorced over these same issues or over what they symbolize. In particular, the issue of traditional gender roles is discussed, for many "house conflicts" come down to the issue of who has the power to make decisions, who is considered the primary homemaker, and what each individual feels about this.

Many people now are working for a full- or part-time salary in the home. This adds another dimension to the issue of sharing a house with a spouse, partner, or children. Also fraught with emotion is the situation in which one person moves into a house or apartment where his or her partner has been living alone or with a previous spouse. In chapter 7, "Living and Working: Territory, Control, and Privacy at Home," questions of how space in a home is divided up and who has access to, or control over, which rooms is explored via the stories of several couples who have grappled with these problems.

Chapter 8, "Where to Live? Self-Image and Location," discusses the notion of "settlement identity," or how we carry with us, often from childhood, a preference for a particular type of location. This is not about preference for a particular style of house or type of furniture, but about *where* we prefer our home to be—in a rural area, a new suburban subdivision, an old established suburb, an inner-city neighborhood, a small town, and so on. Sometimes a person becomes very dissatisfied with his or her home but doesn't realize that it's the location, rather than the house per se, that is the problem. Occasionally, a person will place himself in a highly unsuitable location as if to force into consciousness a psychological problem which is symbolized by this dissonance. Or a couple will separate because the chosen location

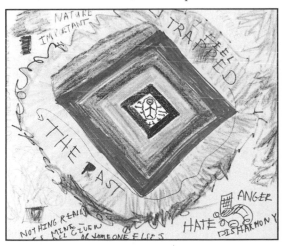

The feelings of a woman who hated the house where she lived. It had been decorated and furnished by her husband's first wife.

reflects the inner needs of one but not the other. Although much has been written on the social status and symbolism of different kinds of neighborhoods and locales, the focus in this chapter, as in the whole book, is on the psychological or inner meaning of the issue.

In chapter 9, "The Lost House: Disruptions in the Bonding with Home," we hear accounts of people who have lost their home through divorce or have stayed on in the family home without their partner; feelings about home when a partner dies; the traumatic experience of loss of home through natural disaster; and the profound experience of home-memories in old age.

Finally, in the last chapter, "Beyond the House-as-Ego: The Call of the Soul," we hear the stories of a number of individuals who have, to varying degrees, moved beyond the need to express some aspect of ego-self in the style, furnishing, decor, or location of home. Having involved themselves in meeting the demands of family, marriage, child rearing, work, and society, they find themselves turning more and more inward to focus on the process of individuation. Now begins in earnest the process of integrating the excluded parts of oneself—unacceptable impulses and feelings (*the shadow* in Jungian terms)—and the "other" as manifested in attributes of the opposite sex (in Jung's terms, the man opening to his feminine side or *anima,* the woman to her masculine side or *animus*). Above all, this turning inward and journey toward wholeness involves creating a bridge to the higher Self, or soul, which has always been there at the core of our being, but whose presence has often been overlooked in our hastiness to make our way in the world.

If the stages of our life and psychological development are best expressed as a journey, this state of reconnection with soul is best described by the metaphor *coming home.* People who have spoken or written about this transformative process have often likened it to waking up, returning from exile, returning to a place they once knew, or coming back to their true home. Ironically, this awakening may come about by leaving an actual home and finding our inner home symbolized in the interconnectedness of nature, in the natural processes of the seasons, or the behavior of other animal species. Thus, for some people, this process of soul-awakening is nurtured by time outdoors, away from the ego-symbolism of the home environment. For others, however, a newly awakened sense of the higher Self may be nurtured by contemplation or meditation within the house, contacting that still core of the psyche where time and space are seemingly transcended. Whatever the outer setting for these transformative experiences, the house as a mirror of the ego-self takes on less importance. Stating who we are in the world retreats in importance; seeking answers to the meaning of life becomes more pressing.

Having listened to many, many accounts of people's feelings about their homes—positive, negative, and ambivalent—there is no doubt in my mind that we all, to some degree, display in the physical environment messages from the unconscious about who we are, who we were, and who we might become. Unable to comprehend all that is encapsulated in the psyche, we need to place it "out there" for us to contemplate, just as we need to view our physical body in a mirror. To assist the reader who might like to learn more from their own house or home, brief do-it-yourself exercises appear at the end of each chapter. The house is indeed a mirror of the self if we can learn to interpret what we see, comprehend what it means, and act on what it seeks to communicate.

"Make yourself at home," we say to the guest whom we invite into our dwelling. In this world of busyness, overscheduling, and external pressures, it is an invitation we need also to extend to ourselves: Make yourself at home. In British English we have an expression—"And what is *that* when it's at home?"—meaning, what is that when it is most truly itself. Perhaps, too, we all need to ask that question of ourselves: Who am I when I'm at home? When I am feeling most grounded, most centered, most at peace, most "at home"? Who is the "I" who lives there? This book will guide you toward an answer. It is intended to inform, to inspire, to raise questions, to raise consciousness. Enjoy the process—and welcome home!

TWO

The Special Places of Childhood

Oh, there were empty houses and houses half-constructed where, as children, we stamped about on the bare winter-pale wood sending up clouds of sawdust into the half-formed rooms, where the wall-frames rose up like thin unfleshed arms and the roof was partly sky, summer-blue, endless as our visions of childhood and life without death.

—Janet Frame, *Living in the Maniototo*[1]

Do you remember smelling new-mown grass or fresh-baked bread, the special odor of Play-Doh or a Crayola crayon, and being instantly swept back to a scene from your childhood? Have you, perhaps, felt the texture of a particular tree or of a brocade-covered couch, heard the sound of a distant train or of a nearby steam radiator and suddenly found yourself for an instant in your grandmother's home or in a secret childhood hideaway? Our senses have a way of reconnecting us, without warning, to memories of times and places long ago, and in particular to memories of childhood.

"First houses are the grounds of our first experience," writes Australian novelist David Malouf. "Crawling about at floor level, room by room, we discover laws that we will apply later to the world at large; and who is to say if our notions of space and dimension are not determined for all time by what we encounter there, in the particular relationship of living-rooms to attic and cellar . . . of inner rooms to the verandas that are open boundaries?"[2]

Childhood is that time when we begin to be conscious of self, when we start to see ourselves as unique entities. It is not surprising that many of us regard that time as an almost sacred period in our lives. Since it is difficult for the mind to grasp a time period in abstract, we tend to connect with it through memories of the *places* we inhabited. For most of us, a return in later life to a dwelling or landscape where we spent our childhood years can be a highly charged experience, the more so if we find the place has changed—a house demolished, a favorite play place built over. We hold on to childhood memories of certain places as a kind of psychic anchor, reminding us of where we came from, of what we once were, or of how the physical environment perhaps nurtured us when family dynamics were strained or the context of our lives fraught with uncertainty. For each of us, it was in the environments of childhood that the person we are today began to take shape.

In my own case, the stress of growing up in a country at war and in a fragmented family prompted me to seek solace in nature. This connection to wildflowers, birds, trees, and the landscape continues to enrich my life half a century later.

I grew up during World War II in England. In 1940, my father left for military service, and my mother, older brother, and I moved from our vulnerable London house to a small dwelling in the country. Here—apart from the occasional air raid or V-2 rocket that overshot London—we lived in relative safety for the remainder of the war. *Relative* is the operative word, since during 1940–41, enemy invasion of our island-home appeared imminent, and images of soldiers falling silently by parachute from the night sky pervaded my dreams. In waking fantasies, I imagined myself defending the family with a machine gun, sitting astride our roof and picking off enemy soldiers as they marched in helmets and boots toward our house. My brother, Paul, and I did our bit to help the war effort. I raised vegetables, chickens, and rabbits to supplement the family's food rations. An aunt taught me the principles of gardening. I don't remember who built the rabbit hutches or chicken coop, or how—at that early age—I knew what to do. I do remember that I gave the rabbits the names of war heroes (Monty, Gort, Wavell) and opera heroines (Carmen, Tosca), and that I tried not to get too attached to them. Once every few weeks, a neighbor performed the fatal act, and I had to disassociate the delicious dinnertime casserole from my furry friends. My brother helped to bring in the harvest at a nearby farm, and decided he did not want to be a veterinarian after he watched a horse being castrated. Together, he and I scavenged the local woods for firewood, collected blackberries and mushrooms, worked with adult neighbors in making camouflage netting, and loaned our children's books to friends for one penny at a time to raise money for the Spitfire Fund.

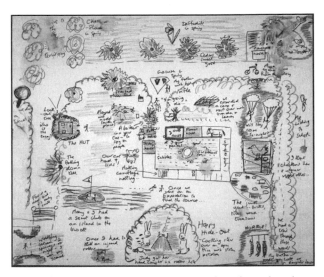

The special places of that period of my life remain vivid in my memory. Although I have few distinct recollections of the inside of our house, or even how certain rooms connected with each other, I have precise memories of the outdoor environments over which we children ranged.

There was a brook where we loved to play. One hot summer, my friend Mary and I "swam" in its water to cool off and, not having brought a towel with us, ran back and forth on a narrow plank bridge to dry ourselves in the sun. Glancing across at a nearby wood named Grimstone Furze, we saw an old farmworker (all the young men had gone to the war) leaning on a gate and staring incredulously at these two naked, cavorting nine year olds. We ran, terrified and ashamed, and lay panting in the tall meadow grass until he went away. Decades later, I returned and found the brook and the bridge just as I remembered them. As I stood on the bridge, the iridescent colors of a kingfisher streaked across the water, and I was jolted back to another memory. One day, looking for birds' eggs, my brother's friend Bert put his hand down a hole in the riverbank. As he drew it out, the female kingfisher, who had been sitting on her nest, came out too, perched on his hand, paralyzed with fear. Her feathers shone like multicolored jewels before, recovering, she flew away.

Other memories of that time are of the formal gardens of the Rothschild estate. My father worked at Rothschild's bank in London, and it was this connection that had brought us to this particular place. We were given a cottage to live in, rent-free, for the duration of the war. Seventy gardeners had been employed to keep up the estate grounds before the war; by 1940, that number was reduced to two. The

flower beds, rock gardens, borders, statuary, and lawns had become wildly overgrown, creating a paradise for exploring children. Particularly memorable were our encounters with "The Birth of Venus," a huge statuary tableau in a formal pool which Anthony de Rothschild's father had had transported at great expense from Italy. We were fascinated with the naked figure of Venus, standing proudly on a scallop-shell, borne aloft by dolphins. Scooping up the spongy pond weed that had covered the surface of the round pool, we fashioned it into missiles and tried to target her private parts. One fall, a large wad of weed hit her in the pubic region and, stuck fast by an early frost, remained there all winter. When I recently revisited the gardens—now administered by the National Trust—I found the pool clean and sparkling, but Venus still sporting a slightly discolored patch on the mound that bears her name.

I marvel now at the extraordinary territorial range enjoyed by my brother, myself, and our friends: perhaps two miles across the fields to the hilltop copse where we picked wild plums; half a mile to the ruins of an old mansion, a pile of rubble we called "The Mountain"; a quarter mile to the lily pond where we played ice hockey on our bikes one frigid winter. With little vehicular traffic to worry about due to wartime gasoline rationing, and none of the current urban fears of crime, kidnapping, or molestation, we ranged over farmland, woods, streams, overgrown quarries, and formal gardens.

These rich environmental experiences of childhood—ironically provided via wartime evacuation from a dull London suburb—have affected my life profoundly. I now teach students of design and planning, and frequently emphasize the needs of children, that powerless population group whose development is most affected by the setting in which they are raised. Especially, I urge students to think about children's territorial range and ability to explore the world on their own. It is this gradual, ever-widening extension of "home" that tends to preoccupy much of our human experience in the crucial middle years of childhood and which in today's urban settings is becoming frighteningly diminished.

Secret Homes: Hiding Places in Childhood

As infants, we relate primarily to mother or other primary caregiver. We are dependent on this other being for food, care, nurturance, protection, and love. As we start to mature into early childhood, we begin to explore the space we occupy; we touch and throw and hit and crawl to discover the nature of the "stuff" around us. Gradually, and with greater assurance, we begin to explore the world outside the protection of home. First under the watchful eye of an adult, and then alone in a setting that adults may have created partially for our safe use (yard, garden, play area), we dig, break sticks, pick up leaves, watch insects, climb trees, and create river systems in the sandbox. We learn what the world is made of; we learn how we can manipulate it to satisfy our questioning minds, our sensing fingertips, our excitement-seeking emotions. We play at now-you-see-me-now-you-don't, at first through peekaboo, and then by running ahead in the park and bouncing out from behind a bush, then by playing hide-and-seek with our friends, and, finally, by creating a secret place (cubby, clubhouse, den, hideout) which our parents may not ever know about.

Part of the process of growing up is learning to do without our parents, to move bit by bit away from their nurturance and watchful eyes, and to test ourselves in those parts of the environment that are "not home." We act out the inevitable process of separation via games and activities in the environment. One way in which children do this is to create their own homes-away-from-home, like homesteads on the frontier. Such place-making activities are almost universal in childhood, regardless of culture, social context, or gender. They are part of the process of growing up. For some people, that place of initial separation and autonomy, that secret home-away-from-home, lingers in adult life as a powerful and nostalgic memory.

For myself, two places stand out among many secret settings we found or made. One was "The Hut," built by my brother and his friends out of poles and flattened-out army gasoline cans, in a wood near our house. It had a "thatched" roof of branches and leaves, a perimeter fence and gate, and a lookout platform in a yew tree. From this vantage point, we would watch for "The Enemy." Inside, on a stove made from an old lavatory cistern, we would boil water for tea. The other place, my friend Mary and I named "Happy Hideout." It was a wildly overgrown depression between two fields which had once been a small quarry. We would spend whole days here in the summertime, setting off the rabbit traps placed by the local gamekeeper and cooking a lunch of stolen potatoes over a small campfire.

Perhaps The Hut represented a "masculine" need for boundaries, territory, and defensible space, whereas the other (where only girls played) fulfilled a more "feminine" need to nurture. We always cooked something and always sprung the iron traps with a big stick so no animals would be killed while we were there. The Hut has long since disappeared, vulnerable to the weather and natural decay. Happy Hideout is still there. On several nostalgic visits to that part of England, I have seen the cluster of trees that mark its location but have resisted the temptation to explore it more closely. I prefer to retain my memories and not discover—with adult perceptions—a perhaps rather ordinary place.

Recalling Child-Created Dwellings

In teaching young designers, I have found that having them draw and write about their own memories of significant environments is a powerful exercise. Such memories tend to be especially evocative when recalling the middle years of childhood, approximately from six to twelve. There are few people, recalling this period of their life, who do *not* remember some kind of secret place they found or made.

A young man who was training to be a landscape architect described his secret home: "There was an old shack on the hill behind Huber Park that was about to fall apart. About half the wall boards and most of the roof were missing. There was nothing to sit on but the rough board floor. It was totally surrounded by lush greenery, much of which extended inside through the missing wall planks. It really seemed to be out in the jungle. In reality, it was only about thirty feet or less from an asphalt path. A friend and I would sneak back there. We had to push the bushes and blackberry vines aside to gain entrance. Once inside, I remember it as being lush and cool—a very tranquil setting. My friend and I had a code word for it. We called it 'The Palace.' This word was part of a larger code which we designed to speak secretly about going to this place to smoke cigarettes." It is significant that many special places of childhood are given names; they often form part of a "secret" language and set apart those activities which coexist with the adult world. The designation of special names is an important component of childhood appropriation of space, the beginnings of a lifetime experience with place-making.

Such environments secretly appropriated by children and recalled nostalgically in adulthood are frequently outside the house. Some people, however, recall spaces *inside;* these are more likely to be women who, as girls, often had less territorial freedom than boys. A young woman recalls *her* special place: "The walk-in closet in the bedroom was my favorite hideaway. It had doors that could be opened from both the inside and the outside and a light within. The closet was large enough for three people to fit in, but I often liked to close the doors and lock myself in to play house or read books."

Sometimes it is not a person-made space that is rediscovered and claimed, but a particularly evocative natural setting. A young woman who lost her mother in early childhood describes a secret place at the back of her house, bounded by trees and a small stream: "I remember the mud shining and wet, slicked down after a rain. It smelled special too—extremely musty, damp, and secretive. Together, the mud, the dark, and the running water encircled me. My feelings about being thus enclosed are ambiguous. Because much of my early life was so traumatic, I deeply appreciated feeling 'cared for' by this place. But sometimes, I was afraid of my lack of control over it. For instance, I vividly remember when my good friend Laura and I were exploring the creek. We picked our way over the big stones until we reached a big tunnel. Poking my head inside the tunnel, I saw a painted skeleton on the wall. I screamed and tried to run but couldn't because of the swift current and all the big rocks."

A young woman who grew up near the back bay in Newport Beach,

"the back bay"

Childhood memory of a hiding place on the back bay, Newport Beach.

California, also recalls a secret place in the natural landscape, shared with friends and remembered as "ours": "A grassy bank on 'our' side of the bay led from the houses down to shallow water. The grass was tall enough for me to hide in most of the year, and there was a deep ravine down by the water, which was a perfect location for our club, usually a very secretive organization of play friends—three of them. I can remember the rich smell of salt and warm sun intensifying the smell of the grass. The smell to most people was offensive—stagnant water—but to us it was paradise because it was 'ours.'

"The mud was the consistency of clay and was fantastic for molding objects that could be left to dry in the sun, such as secret club objects and things to use in the fort and of course our 'food'—ceremonial cakes, elaborately decorated with wildflowers and shell remnants pressed in the mud. Sometimes a whole day would pass and the sun would start to set and we could hardly believe it was gone."

One significant function of childhood hiding places is the creation of a place to be *private*—be it a blanket "fort" in the playroom, a tree house at the bottom of the garden, or an area of flattened-out grass in the middle of a meadow. If our dwellings in adulthood are those settings where we are most at liberty to be ourselves, where we don't have to put up any facades, then this process clearly begins in childhood. Such strivings for a place to be private become especially urgent in the years just prior to puberty. A young woman describes the family garage:

"We used to play in the rafters in the garage, because it was a secretive, cozy place among the brass trunks. We played there on rainy days because it was a warm spot near the roof, especially when the dryer was on. Our cat had several litters of kittens up there, which was a real attraction for us. I remember liking it up there because it was a two-story place, and our house was only one story. I felt that I was above everything, hidden and secretive. This spot was even more attractive to me later in the sixth and seventh grades, when I would retreat and write in my diary or read Nancy Drew books for hours."

A place to be private and let down one's facade does not necessarily have to be secret. A young woman who grew up in a middle-class neighborhood of San Francisco describes the importance of her bedroom: "I loved my room because of the large window and the view out to the backyards. I rearranged it so that my bed was by the window and I lay in my bed, gazing at the stars. I felt philosophical and wondered about the universe, UFOs, and the existence of other forms of life. I felt very much at peace with myself and my surroundings. I tried to pick out constellations. I would write 'Good morning world' backward on the window through the dew."

Whether these places were called forts, dens, houses, hideaways, or clubhouses, whether they were in the home or

were found, modified, or constructed, they all seem to serve similar psychological and social purposes—places in which separation from adults was sought, in which fantasies could be acted out, and in which the very environment itself could be molded and shaped to one's own needs. This is the beginning of the act of dwelling, or claiming one's place in the world.

Making a Home-Away-from-Home

Some people recall their hiding places as indeed a microcosm of home—a place to prove that a child, too, can create a house and play at adult roles. A young woman describes a special place in the yard of her suburban New Jersey home:

"There was a brick well around the base of the tree, topped with a wooden bench that I turned into a play kitchen. There was enough room inside the well for me and the tree. I would stand inside and 'cook' on the wooden counter and then serve my dishes to my imaginary friends who sat around the counter. Upstairs, the tree house was my living room with a 'panoramic view of the city'—really just my backyard. I liked playing house a lot, but only when I was alone, because that way I could be mother, father, brother, sister, dog, cousin, and everyone else. I played with my brother in the tree house, but never in my 'kitchen'—that was my secret game."

When a space is made *for* you, it is often not the same; tree houses built by doting fathers or grandfathers rarely have the appeal of "owner-built" homes. A young man, studying architecture, recalls early building experiences on a hillside near his California suburban home:

"The wooded hillside provided a natural play area. Soon after moving in, I carried leftover building materials up the hill and built a tree house, which afforded a fine view of the house and backyard but which could not be seen from below. At first my private domain, my brothers and friends eventually started building their own forts (as we called them) out of scrap materials under and around my tree house. We soon had quite an extensive structure up there, but we were constantly tearing down, expanding, rebuilding. The fun of having this fort was in constantly changing it, and not just enjoying it as it was. Whenever a new house was built in the neighborhood, my brothers, friends, and I would scout the building site for discarded materials and haul them up the hill. After a few years of using this structure, my father, delighted with the arrangement we had created, decided to construct a fort for us. However, this structure was carefully designed and built out of more permanent materials by an adult, and, while we enjoyed it for a short time, the simple fact that it had been built in a manner not meant for alteration quickly led us to abandon it for our old fort, where we could easily and continually manipulate our environment."

These poignant memories of fort-building reveal an early recognition of the human need to claim space by changing the environment. In adult life, this need is expressed in a range of activities from building one's own home or rearranging the furniture, to repainting a rented room, to pinning up posters at the office. It is a need that parents and teachers may recognize yet mistakenly "support" by creating places *for* their children. An architect who grew up in a Dallas suburb described how in his childhood, his father hired a professional landscape architect to redesign their backyard:

"The play yard I shared with my brother and sister was made 'beautiful' and 'ordered.' A playhouse with operable windows, shutters, window box, and Dutch door was built. It was white with a shake shingle roof and (I don't believe it!) an angled redwood deck. Out from the deck was a marble-chip play area. Over the marble chips, hanging from a fine tree, was a rope swing with a metal disk for a seat. Ivy had been planted all around with metal edges. This house was furnished with odds and ends and toys.

"I remember this play area with mixed emotions, but primarily one of childhood misunderstanding. Somehow, I could not fathom why I had not been consulted, because I was convinced I could have done a much better job. After all, when you fall off the swing onto a bed of jagged marble chips, or try to run across them barefooted, it becomes readily apparent what a mistake the designer has made. Consequently, I tried other means to manipulate the environment. While playing fireman one day, I had the hose and a hammer (my hatchet) and, because the 'whole town' was burning down, I clang-clanged over to the rear door of the garage and broke out every pane of glass, stuck in the hose, and turned on the water full blast! What I 'put out' was my dad, who proceeded to 'set fire' to my backside."

For many children, their hiding place is the only corner of the environment that they, personally, are able to build, maintain, and modify, and often the question of "property rights" surfaces. Rules and boundaries become especially important as the settings we make or modify become expressions of who we are. A young woman recalls her New Jersey childhood: "'The Hill' was a pile of dirt which apparently had been dumped by builders into the woods across the street from my friend Kathy's house. Kathy, her younger brother, two younger sisters, myself, and other neighborhood children often played there. I was about ten; the others were all younger. We pretended that the hill and the area around it was our 'town.' We all made 'houses' by raking up leaves into long piles which represented walls.

"I remember that we were quite possessive about our 'houses.' We each had a territory staked out by piles of leaves and other junk. There were continuous battles about where one person's 'house' ended and another's began. I also remember that it was a major offense to steal something from someone else's 'house.' I suppose the hill itself was a focal point in our environment. Nobody ever claimed the top of it for themselves. Our 'houses' crept up the flanks, but the hill was more a communal place or rallying spot. It didn't belong to any one individual."

Sometimes the "territorial imperative" can lead to mock battles and destruction of property. An architectural student wrote evocatively of his childhood play on some wasteland near the edge of a small California town:

"During this time, we got really into building forts. I was small, so I couldn't do too much, but they let me help. We

Memories of a secret house in a tree.

would divide into smaller groups, and each group would build their own fort. It would take weeks; we would drag materials from the railroad yard, from our houses, from anywhere we could find them, dig holes into the hill, and erect our forts. After they were up, they became clubhouses for the kids who built them and were the center of activity for a while. Territorial pressures would build up and would finally erupt into a spontaneous rock fight; actually, now that I think of it, they weren't that spontaneous because I remember we would stockpile rocks for a few days and then as the taunts flew we would get into a fight. Invariably, the victors would be the ones whose fort held up. The battles took a heavy toll on the structures; most of them would be total wrecks because when we ran out of rocks we would run and tear each other's fort down. After the fight, the site would be abandoned, new alliances would be formed, and a new site somehow selected, and the process would begin all over again."

Exploration and Overcoming Fear

While many childhood memories relate to places found or built—homes-away-from-home—most of us also recall some environments that scared us, a setting we returned to, and dared ourselves to enter, to overcome our fears. It might have been the neighborhood "haunted house," a spooky place in the basement, a dark alley, or part of the schoolyard where a bully might confront us. For myself, it was a wooden building with slatted walls, where my older brother would lure me to peek through to see dripping carcasses of recently slaughtered cattle hanging in bloody silence. I was terrified but nevertheless dared myself to return periodically. The rush of adrenaline and the desire to be brave and master our fears are compelling experiences in childhood.

David, an architecture student in one of my classes, described his most vividly remembered place of childhood—a dark, scary culvert—where his experiences were in marked contrast to those in the neat and bland yard of his suburban home:

"I lived across the Trinity River from the downtown business district in Dallas. The culvert was for drainage out of a low spot in a wide, grassy easement. The easement was at least a few thousand yards wide, and I knew it must stretch all the way to New York (at the age of seven, my refined sense of distance had not quite bloomed).

"The culvert was a favorite 'hidden' place for me to go. It was dark in the tunnel—darker the farther you dared go in. I knew the Giant Spiders lived there; I just didn't know how far in. About ten feet in, there was a second culvert branching off. It was smaller and had metal reinforcing bars covering the opening.

The home of the Giant Spiders.

These had been pulled back (by the spiders?) and were twisted and rusted."

"It was a quiet place where I could retreat from everything. Over a short span of years, I grew with this place. I conquered the spiders eventually and traveled great distances through the tunnels. I was alone there but secure, knowing the tunnels connected me with hundreds of others. I was nearly always silent, surrounded by gurgling, trickling water, deep resonant earth sounds, and rustling leaves."

For this young man, his place was a setting both for testing his courage and for quiet retreat. We venture forth as we all must do to test our boundaries, to overcome fears, to find out what the outer space of our world contains. As parents, we set limits for our children yet know that at some stage these will be transgressed, for every child in his or her own way needs to "conquer the spiders."

Chris, a student of landscape architecture, grew up on a fruit farm in New England. He recalls a special feeling for a forested area beyond his father's orchards, where he once got lost but later returned to overcome his fears.

"When I was eight, Chip, Matt, and I went for a hike up in the woods. After playing cowboys and Indians for an hour or so, we realized we were lost. First thing we did was run to every clearing we thought we saw. This proved to be exhausting and fruitless. After a while, we popped out onto a rock ledge about thirty feet high and a hundred feet long. We started off again, in a more stressed state, and an hour later ended up at the same ledge. At this point, Matt started to cry and Chip looked very worried. I remembered not being worried but feeling like I should be because they were. At this point, we figured out that if we lined up certain trees, we could form a straight line and continuously do this until we reached something manmade. Ten minutes later, we wandered out into the orchard feeling like we had just found the source of the Nile. The next day, I went back into those woods to find my lost six-shooter. I didn't find it, but I did get lost again and was able to find my way out easily using our newfound technique. From that point on, I've always had confidence about finding my way through a forest, and those woods became one of my favorite walking places."

Why Look Back?

The near universality of remembered childhood places and the emotion of these recollections many years later suggest that they represent experiences that go far beyond the actual act of making or finding a secret place, or overcoming our fear of Giant Spiders. Our hiding places are a physical expression of our emerging ego-self, separate from parents and family. They are our first tentative experiments in the experience of dwelling, in appropriating and personalizing a special place, and—unconsciously—reflecting on what we have made.

Beyond the experiences of place-making linked to our needs for expressing our ego-selves in the world, many people have poignant memories of connections with nature. These connections, I would suggest, are our first experiences of the significance of the transpersonal or spiritual self. For those of my students who grew up in rural areas, or who had the good fortune to be taken on wilderness trips by their family or spend time at a camp or in nature, memories of bonding with the natural world are particularly poignant. A city planner now working to protect the natural environment wrote with feeling about the wooded landscape of an outdoor education center in Ohio, first visited in the fifth grade:

"I don't know why I felt or continue to feel so strongly about this place. It may have been one of the first significant places that I was able to 'bond' with. I think it's important for people to have such a place, even if it is thousands of miles away, where they know the place will take them back and nurture them no matter how long they have been absent. That is how I feel about the glen. Whenever I return to Ohio, usually once a year or less, I insist on returning and renewing myself there."

It is significant that this man, and many other men and women with powerful memories of bonding with nature in childhood, has chosen a career that involves designing and protecting similar places for the next generation.

There is no doubt that for most of us, the childhood dwelling and its environs is the place of first getting in touch with who we are as distinct personalities. Indeed, we may have a clearer and more accurate sense of our true selves at that time than in later years, when the demands of societal and familial expectations create masklike overlays on the psyche, hence the critical importance of looking back at childhood places as sources of understanding more deeply who we are.

It is probably significant that I have ended up teaching design students and, among other things, facilitating their understanding of the roots of their connections with the physical environment. I was not aware of the strength of my own feelings for the plants and trees of my childhood until, quite recently, visiting a friend's summer cottage in southern Sweden, I was overwhelmed by what I saw, smelled, and touched in the landscape around me, especially the wildflowers, all of which I could still name like members of my family. Here is part of what I recorded in my journal at the time:

"Hedge parsley, buttercups, ragged robin, heartsease, speedwell, vetch, and dandelion. Lilac and hawthorn in bloom; split leaves of ash and elderberry. Chestnut trees lit up like vast candelabra; copper beeches sweeping the grasses below in gentle broom waves.

"I feel at home, at ease, among familiar trees and plants. The waving grass heads greet me like an old friend. If I erased architecture and language, I could be in southern England, in the fields and meadows of my childhood. I am in my rightful 'ecological niche.' Here are the wildflowers I came to know as a child. Here are the many cousins of umbiliferae or leguminosea I pressed between blotting paper and left for weeks under a heavy pile of encyclopedias. . . . Why do these familiar flowers, grasses, and trees bring back such memories? Why, after twenty years of residence in California, do I feel only partially 'at home'? I walk there with friends and learn the names of manzanita, blue gum, bay, and redwood—yet they are like labels in a museum. I see them, yet they evoke no feelings. A glass pane of time and space separates me from them. These were not the trees I climbed, the bark I felt with childish fingers, the flowers I collected, the blossoms I smelled, the pollen on my nose. Despite friends and family, house and career, this place will never be truly 'home.'

"The sounds and smells and, above all, the vegetation of a country childhood seem like the soft pillow and quilt of our infant crib, writ large upon the landscape. Here were the trees that nurtured us, the shrubs that gave us fruit and berries, the flowers we called brothers and sisters. These were our family beyond the family, timeless scenery, imprinted in that time of acute vulnerability and openness to the world. The human family is mobile and mortal; the botanical family of childhood returns each season, indifferent to our coming and going. But we are not indifferent to it—our green womb of homecoming."

A Jungian scholar, Edward Edinger, has proposed that those who, in adult life, go further in the process of individuation—becoming their own unique selves—have almost always had meaningful experiences of the unconscious in childhood. "Often secret places or private activities are involved which the child feels are uniquely his and which strengthen his sense of worth in the face of an apparently hostile environment. Such experiences, although not consciously understood . . . leave a sense that one's personal identity has a transpersonal source of support."[3]

In the fascinating account of his life, Swiss psychologist Carl Jung describes an experience when he was about twelve, in the village where he grew up: "Nature seemed to me full of wonders, and I wanted to steep myself in them. Every stone, every plant, every single thing seemed alive and indescribably marvelous. I immersed myself in nature, crawled, as it were, into the very essence of nature and away from the whole human world. . . . At about this time, I was taking the long road to school . . . when suddenly for a single moment I had the overwhelming impression of having just emerged from a dense cloud. I knew all at once: now I am *myself!* . . . Previously I had existed too, but everything had merely happened to one. Now I happened to myself."[4]

For some children, a hiding place becomes a crucial retreat from painful family stress.

Growing up in a different setting, American writer Richard Merrifield comes to a similar conclusion regarding the significance of nature as our wider home. "In childhood we do not know what 'co-extensive' means, but it is the special marvel of that time. It meant the feel of sand underfoot, the cool branch of a maple, the taste of being along a hot wayside . . . We were like plants that had grown hands and feet, or animals just risen from plant existence at a creek's edge. It was as if we ourselves were Nature, as indeed we were, and might even be again if we could drop our innocence and return to that sublime sophistication."[5]

Reproducing Special Childhood Places in Adulthood

I came to the United States as an immigrant thirty years ago in my midtwenties. After marriage and the acquisition of a house in Berkeley, California, I began to create an English garden in front of our house, a very different garden from most of those in the neighborhood. At the back, a large vegetable bed became my private preserve; I like to work there alone. Gardening permits me to reproduce the place and activity that gave me the most profound experience of centeredness and nurturance during those impressionable and sometimes fearful years of a wartime childhood. I am seeking that numinous connection with earth and nature, first experienced in childhood, as the age-old tasks of sowing, tending, and harvesting are repeated in their appropriate seasons.

This phenomenon—creating a garden that repeats some aspects of an earlier, fondly remembered place—may be more common than we think. For re-creating some aspects of a childhood garden is more possible for most of us than re-creating the home itself. In a study for her master's degree in landscape architecture, Berkeley student Helena Worthen looked at more than a hundred gardens in new suburban tracts east of San Francisco Bay and found that many people "did not understand where they were. . . . People planted gardens which made them feel at home. . . . They weren't interested in discovering which plants were ecologically best suited to their gardens. A man from Oregon wanted roses, gladioli, and a blue spruce, because that was what he had grown up with. A teenaged girl, who loved 'Hawaii Five-0' created a tropical jungle out front. A woman of Italian extraction planted the same vegetables her mother had grown. . . . A pleasantly daffy elderly man was cultivating a 'Grevillea robusta' which he claimed was a silver birch. . . . 'Oh, I'm sure it's a birch,' he said. 'I'm from Illinois and all we had were roses and silver birches.'"[6]

Clearly, for this man, the tree *had* to be a silver birch because such a tree enabled him to feel linked to the places of his formative years. In people's stories of houses and homes recounted to me, repetition and re-creation of the ambience of childhood is a frequently recurrent theme. Two accounts—those of Priscilla and Joe—stand for many similar life-stories.

Priscilla: The Contrast of Old and New

For Priscilla, living alone in a rustic, one-bedroom rented cottage in the Berkeley hills, both her home and the surrounding neighborhood contain positive echoes of a New England childhood forty years before. When asked to describe her feelings for her current home, she says: "I feel a lot of comfort around me. Harmonious colors. Good feelings under my feet, rugs, pillows, all full of life, warmth. Things that I grew up with as a child, I've brought back with me; I've put them into my nest. Like this lamp and pictures I had a great feeling for. The old chair in the kitchen which I brought back from my mother's house two years ago. I really have a good feeling of continuity. I love having things which have been in the family, which have been used before, and which I can see again in a different light in a different environment, and feel as if they've been around for a long time. They have a voice, a life of their own."

I asked Priscilla to go back, in her imagination, to the home of her childhood—it was just outside Boston in a place which was then semirural but is now a suburb.

"Just thinking about the house is putting some sort of vibration in my body. I lived there from the time I was born until I left for college. So it had very strong roots for me. And in that house, too, the furniture and the furnishings were old pieces. They were pieces which had come from my father's mother. There was a sense of rootedness about the furniture, dark furniture, beautiful fabrics, old beautiful rugs. A feeling of heaviness too. As a child, I suppose that I felt tremendous security from all of these things which had been around for a while. My feeling about that house is that it was a wonderful place to be *from!* I feel very separate from it now, although I've taken some of the things from that house and put them into my own environment, which is lighter. I love the fact of bringing some of those things into my life now, by having contrasting environments, contrasting fabrics . . . a contrast of old and new."

For Priscilla, then, an important theme in her home is one of *continuity*—of having things in her house that have been used before, that she grew up with as a child, and that she "can see in a different light." When recalling with some emotion the house she

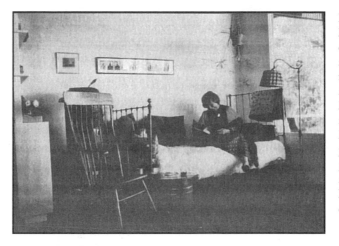

Priscilla's living room contained many items from her mother's and her grand-mother's houses, providing pleasing memories of a New England childhood.

grew up in, she remembers that there were pieces there, too, which had come from her grandmother's house. The objects with which she decorates her current home environment are ever-present, material reminders of the positive, nurturing environment she experienced as a child, particularly from her mother.

Significantly, when Priscilla decided—shortly after her fiftieth birthday—to leave this much-loved cottage and buy a small house of her own, her choice was to move to Ashland, Oregon, because, among other things, the small town and the vegetation reminded her of her New England upbringing. This need to return to our environmental roots seems especially pressing for many people in the second half of life, as old age appears on the horizon.

Joe: Echoes of a Missouri Childhood

Joe, a middle-aged university professor of forestry, lives with his wife and two teen-aged children in a modest stucco house in an older suburb of a university city. The house stands on a small, thirty-five-foot-wide lot with a short setback and no street trees; the whole block of similar houses is quite visible and exposed.

At the time of our dialogue, Joe's house was in the process of a major conversion. The house was being extended at the back to include an enlarged kitchen and an additional bedroom. Planning regulations allow only 50 percent coverage of the lot; with this addition, the house would cover 49.8 percent. Joe applied for an exception to cover more, but had been turned down. If he had had his way, the house would have covered virtually the whole lot. Reflecting on his profession in forestry, I naively expected that he might be interested in having a garden or at least some trees around his house. That he was interested in neither seems to be a reflection of his own childhood environment and what he absorbed from that time of a "suitable" image of home:

"I have never enjoyed what I call yard work, and I have one of the worst yards in the neighborhood. I don't look forward to those days when I mow the lawn. I don't anticipate the roses blooming or anything like that. I think this probably came out of my childhood. My family was never involved in these activities, and I didn't learn to gain any pleasure from them.

"I grew up with my parents and older brother in an apartment in Missouri. It was much more spacious and private than this house, but had virtually no outdoor space. We had a small patch of grass in front of the apartment building. It was my job to mow it. As a child, I didn't see I was getting any benefit out of keeping it trim. I have always felt a strong separation of urban and rural space. I think I would have been very content to live in a medieval city with a wall that said: This is the city and this is the non-city. I feel very content in cities like Chicago or New York; they are not trying to be anything else but cities. On the other hand, I get a lot of pleasure from being out in the country or the wilderness. I have never felt a strong incentive to mix the two. It doesn't bother me that there aren't any trees along this street. My appreciation of the outdoors evolved from a childhood in which my family did a lot of camping. We never used a garden or even urban parks. When we were outdoors, it was completely away from our home, in the mountains or wilderness. I didn't grow up with any intermediate outdoor space. I see this home as part of the same pattern; if I want to do something outside, I would never think of doing it in my backyard."

Responding to the wish of his mother to have a doctor-son, Joe began his university studies as a premed student. But two summers working for the Forest Service in Montana convinced him that a career in forestry was more to his liking. Curiously, it was again a powerful house memory from childhood that influenced the direction his career ultimately took.

"My mother came from a large family of five children. They lived in a big house with a very large yard. They had a big vegetable garden, and she talked about it a lot when I was a child. I saw it quite often because my grandparents lived there until I was seven; it was in the same town where we lived in the apartment.

My fond memories of that house, as much as anything else, turned me away from a regular career in the Forest Service.

"The Forest Service moves their personnel quite often; it's seldom you stay in one place more than three years. I realized that if I stayed in the service, we would always live in government housing. It's not that they aren't *nice* houses. Many district rangers in Montana live in much larger houses than this one—and much newer. So it's not to do with the *quality* of the house, but that you can't own it. All the rangers I knew in Montana felt a certain reluctance to do anything to those houses because they didn't own them.

"So I finally woke up one day and said, 'Well, what are my options if I want to stay in forestry and I don't want to be moved around, and I want to make changes to my home.' And it occurred to me that being a college professor could be a very good lifestyle. I could stay in forestry, go out in the field to do my research, but not be forced to move around."

And so, in a curious way, Joe's current living environment is a fascinating mixture of influences from both his parent's and his grandparent's homes. From his parents, he inherited a preference for urban living, for an apartment-like dwelling with little intermediate outdoor space. From his grandparents' house (and his mother's recollection of *her* childhood in that home), he inherited a desire to own a dwelling that he could change and improve and that he would not have to move from. In his modest but expanding stucco house with no yard, he has achieved an amalgam of these two significant places of childhood.

Memory or Fantasy?

As we recall memories from our childhood, or listen to those of our friends, we may start to question: Did this really happen? Was there really a place like that?

A woman architect I met talked about a recurring memory of an attic—of creeping up into it, exploring it, knowing it was forbidden territory. She couldn't be sure if it was a real place, or if she had once had a particularly vivid dream of an attic that kept reverberating in her mind. In some ways, I told her, it doesn't matter; if the image keeps recurring, we can be sure it is the unconscious trying to tell us something, nudging us to explore, perhaps, what is in the attic. Eventually, this woman built herself a real attic by adding a second story to her suburban home. Accessed by a ladder, this space was hers alone, forbidden territory to her husband and children. Here she daydreamed, watched shadow patterns on the skylight, and eventually started a meditation practice. The attic was the opening to her spiritual journey. Whether she had ever, in reality, visited an attic in her childhood was irrelevant.

The unconscious often chooses houses, buildings, and secret rooms as symbols. The basement or cellar is often a metaphor for the unconscious, of something hidden that needs to be explored, whereas the attic or roof or opening to the sky often reflects a desire to explore transpersonal realms or spiritual directions.

If we start to consider the messages from the unconscious made manifest through our dreams, we have even more striking evidence of the house-as-self symbol. In his autobiography, Carl Jung describes vividly a dream of himself as a house, and his explorations within it:

"It was in a house I did not know, which had two storeys. It was 'my house.' I found myself in the upper storey, where there was a kind of salon furnished with fine old pieces in rococo style. On the walls hung a number of precious old paintings. I wondered that this should be my house, and thought, 'not bad.' But then it occurred to me that I did not know what the lower floor looked like. Descending the stairs, I reached the ground floor. There everything was much older, and I realized that this part of the house must date from about the fifteenth or sixteenth century. The furnishings were medieval; the floors were of red brick. Everywhere it was rather dark. I went from one room to another thinking, 'Now I really must explore the whole house.' I came upon a heavy door and opened it. Beyond it, I discovered a stone stairway that led down into the cellar. Descending again, I found myself in a beautifully vaulted room which looked exceedingly ancient. Examining the walls, I discovered layers of brick among the ordinary stone blocks, and chips of brick in the mortar. As soon as I saw this I knew that the walls dated from Roman times. My interest by now was intense. I looked more closely at the floor. It was on stone slabs, and in one of these I discovered a ring. When I pulled it, the stone slab lifted, and again I saw a stairway of narrow stone steps leading down into the depths. These, too, I descended, and entered a low cave cut into rock. Thick dust lay on the floor, and in the dust were scattered bones and broken pottery, like remains of a primitive culture. I discovered two human skulls, obviously very old and half-disintegrated. Then I awoke."[7]

Jung's own interpretation of the dream is as follows: "It was plain to me that the house represented a kind of image of the psyche—that is to say, of my then state of consciousness, with hitherto unconscious additions. Consciousness was represented by the salon. It had an inhabited atmosphere, in spite of its antiquated style.

"The ground floor stood for the first level of the unconscious. The deeper I went, the more alien and the darker the scene became. In the cave, I discovered remains of a primitive culture, that is the world of the primitive man within myself—a world which can scarcely be reached or illuminated by consciousness. The primitive psyche of man borders on the life of the animal soul, just as the caves of prehistoric times were usually inhabited by animals before man laid claim to them."[8]

Jung describes here the multilevel house seen as the symbol-of-self with its many levels of consciousness; the descent downward into lesser-known realms of the unconscious is represented by the ground floor, cellar, and vault beneath it. A final descent leads to a cave cut into bedrock, a part of the house rooted in the very earth itself. This seems very clearly to be a symbol of the collective unconscious, part of the self-house and yet, too, part of the universal bedrock of humanity.

Often our childhood home recurs in dreams as we work through unresolved emotional issues from that time. American author Louise Bogan recalls a dream about the house where she first began to read:

"Why do I remember this house as the happiest in my life? I was never really happy there. But now I realize that it was the house wherein I began to read, whole-heartedly and with pleasure. It was the first house where bookshelves appeared as a part of the building. It is a house to which I return, in a recurrent dream . . . I go back to the house as I now am. I put into it my chairs, my pictures, but most of all my books . . . I rearrange the house from top to bottom: new curtains on the windows, new pictures on the walls. But somehow the old rooms are still there—like shadows seeping through. Indestructible. Fixed."[9]

Our memories and dreams are our personal "library"; they can be powerful motivations and inspirations, rich resources for later creative thinking. The haunting compositions of red walls, pools, and falling water by Mexican designer Luis Barragan, for example, retain the magic, almost surrealistic quality that permeates his memories of his native village. Here he recalls this childhood environment: "My earliest childhood memories are related to a ranch my family owned near the village of Mazamitla. It was a *pueblo* with hills, formed by houses with tile roofs and immense eaves to shield passersby from the heavy rains which fall in that area. Even the earth's color was interesting because it was red earth. In this village, the water distribution system consisted of great gutted logs, in the form of troughs, which ran on a support structure of tree forks, five meters high, above the roofs. This aqueduct crossed over the town, reaching the patios, where there were great stone fountains to receive the water. The patios housed the stables, with cows and chickens, all together. Outside, in the street, there were iron rings to tie the horses. The channeled logs, covered with moss, dripped water all over town, of course. It gave this village the ambience of a fairy tale."[10]

The students of design whom I teach are at the start of their careers and, unlike Barragan, have rarely had anything built. But they, too, frequently recognize in their design work significant echoes imprinted in childhood. When they write, at my request, their own environmental autobiographies, I ask them to reflect on these place-memories and to notice if there are any connections to places they have designed on paper as adults. A young woman from Taiwan, puzzled by the repetition of a particular entry arrangement in everything she designed, discovered upon reflection that this was an echo of the entry to the country house of a much-loved grandfather. A young man, training to be a landscape architect, found that he always specifies very low maintenance plant materials in his work, and recalled his anger at having to be responsible for the upkeep of the family's large, high-maintenance yard when his father died. An architecture student with many fond memories of a grandfather who established a famous hydrotherapy spa in Southern France found himself compelled to do sketches and studies of water, and eventually wrote an eloquent thesis entitled "Captive Waters."

Though you may not be a designer in a formal, professional sense, we are all designers of the immediate milieu in which we live. We choose plants or pictures, fabrics, or furniture. We arrange and rearrange the near environment of our

A childhood environment remembered.

home, be it a room in a student dormitory or a house on its own lot. We feel nurtured by this place that seems to permit us to be ourselves, to relax into our innermost being. As you look around at the place where you now live, consider what aspects of it evoke memories of childhood, or, if that was a period of life that holds bad memories for you, how does your current home contrast with or reject that setting of early upbringing?

If you are thinking of redecorating, renovating, buying or renting, or having a house designed for you, or if you are just curious about your own environmental memories and how they affect your current preferences about home, the following exercises may be enlightening.

A reflection on your own special places of childhood can be a powerfully evocative experience. Although you may not be seeking actively to reproduce such settings, there will surely be aspects of privacy, enclosure, view, form, materials, sounds, textures, and so on that were imprinted on you at that time. It can be a richly creative experience to bring these place-memories into consciousness, to understand their roots, and, if so inclined, to re-create them in some form in your current environment. I have conducted this first exercise with many hundreds of students, and all have apparently found it a richly rewarding experience.

HOME AND CHILDHOOD:
EXERCISES YOU CAN DO YOURSELF

Recalling a Special Childhood Place

Buy yourself a pad or block of drawing paper and a box of crayons. Set aside at least an hour when you can be by yourself in a relaxed, reflective mood. Settle down in your favorite armchair, your bed, or a hammock in the garden—wherever you feel most "at home." Close your eyes, relax, and pay attention to your breathing. Imagine that you can picture your breath flowing in and out of your lungs like a silver stream. Now start to remember the places where you lived, explored, or spent time as a child. Let your mind wander through homes of your childhood—your own, those of friends or relatives, perhaps places where you spent vacations. Think about special places indoors and outdoors: places where you spent time with friends or alone, places you made your own by naming them, changing them, or just spending time there. Start to focus on just *one* place (you can explore others on another day!). What did it feel like? What were its boundaries? What made it special? Was it a place that adults didn't know about or visit? How did you keep it secret or private? Are there any special smells, or tastes, or sounds associated with this place? What did you do there? Thinking back on it now, as an adult, what particular feelings does it evoke?

When you have thought about this place long enough, take the drawing pad and crayons and create some kind of visual image of it. Don't worry if you're not an "artist"! Just put down in colors, shapes, images—perhaps a few words—all that you can about

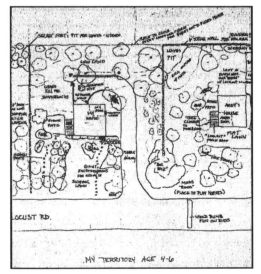

A childhood environment remembered.

this place. You may be surprised! Sometimes the act of drawing—especially with the kinds of crayons you probably used as a child—triggers memories and details long since forgotten.

When you've finished this picture, put it up somewhere in your home where you'll see it every day—in your bedroom or on the door of the refrigerator. If you feel drawn to writing, at some point you might want to describe it in your journal. If you feel like talking about it, choose a place that is private and a time that is open-ended and share your place-memories with a close friend or intimate partner. Let them ask you questions. If there are sad, painful, or frightening memories associated with this place, try not to avoid them by focusing only on good memories.

This exercise may give you insights into:

- How you use or feel about your current home
- Issues of importance to you in a new or projected home
- How your unique experience of home may differ from that of your spouse or partner or children

Making a Home Comfortable for Children or for the Child Within

The notion that each one of us carries a child inside us has spawned much useful debate in the field of psychology and is worth thinking about in this context. How does *your* home nurture the inner child? If you have a real-life child or children, you may also want to think about the environments *they* inhabit, both indoors and outdoors. According to Stuart Miller, in an article entitled "Designing the Home for Children," when adults reflect back on those aspects of their own childhood environments that seem important and positive, a number of qualities emerge:

- **a place of nurturance:** This may have little to do with architecture or location but it has a lot to do with human love, warmth, and caring. However, these feelings may well be associated with the quality of a bedroom or kitchen being secure, cozy, and comfortable; with a fireplace, radiator, the warmth of sunlight, or a down comforter; with symbols of permanence and familiarity; with the proximity of parents' or siblings' bedrooms; with memories of mealtimes. Where are the places of nurturance in your child's life or in the life of your inner child? Is there anything you might do to the physical environment to enhance this experience?

• **a place of sociability:** Memories of this aspect of home often have to do with playing games, sharing a meal, watching TV together, talking, working on chores together, or doing homework while a parent prepares dinner. These might take place in the kitchen, the basement, the garden, the family room, or a bedroom. These remembrances, often fixed in a place, have to do with the family as a unit—the family being any grouping of adults and children that thinks of itself as a family. Are there particular places where you and your children share an activity together? Is there anything you could do to that setting that would make your time together more meaningful? Is there a setting where you and your inner child can nurture each other?

• **a base for exploration and stimulation:** Varying amounts of stimulation are necessary for mental health. Adults with positive memories of home often recall rich detailing in floors or furnishings; well-loved views from windows or porches; or places in the attic, basement, under the porch, or in the yard or beyond that could be explored. It may well be the thrill-seeking, heightened awareness of such explorations that helps imprint them in our memories. Stimulation is often also sought via daydreaming, fantasizing, reading, or playing "let's pretend. . . ." A home environment, both social and physical, that supports such activities may well be one remembered with affection in later life. Although it doesn't seem to work if we *provide* an explorable environment for a child or *suggest* a stimulating activity—are there *potential* places, indoors or outdoors, that you can leave alone? Are these places where your child, or inner child, can truly be themselves?

• **a room of one's own:** Many positive memories of childhood include access to a place that is private. This may be a bedroom or bathroom where a child can be alone or unbothered, an activity such as watching TV or staring out of a window that permits psychological withdrawal, or the appropriation of a space where adults aren't around, such as a closet, basement, or hiding place in a tree or under a hedge. Being able to *control* some space and, particularly, who comes into it is an important need which begins in childhood. Can you permit your child a time and place to be alone, without worrying about "what they're up to"? Are you able to let your child daydream or fantasize without suggesting they are wasting time? Is there a place where your inner child can be at peace?

• **changing the environment:** The desire to manipulate the physical environment is another human need that starts in childhood. Whereas most rooms in a home—and adjacent outdoor spaces—are often designed to satisfy adult tastes and needs, children are remarkably resourceful in finding or creating places that *they* can decorate and furnish. These may be "houses" created out of chairs and sheets, beds, and blankets; or they may be a corner of the yard that is symbolically divided into rooms and "furnished" with sticks and stones and piles of leaves. Do you permit your child to move furniture around or drape it with sheets to create a hiding place or "house"? Are there places under the porch, in the basement, or in the yard where a child could move "stuff" around? Do they—or you—have access to a sandbox, Legos, or simple building blocks? Could you bring some empty boxes back from the supermarket?

• **identity and self-esteem:** Few would argue that self-identity has its beginnings in childhood. Although much of this stems from relationships with parents, relatives, siblings, or schoolmates, we should not overlook the role of the physical environment. Children need to have the freedom to express their emerging identities—separate from parents or siblings—through the personalization of space. This might be as simple as letting them pin up favorite pictures and photos or as elaborate as letting them choose the colors of their bedroom walls and drapes. Very often, the most fondly remembered places of childhood expression are not in the dwelling at all, but in some secret den, fort, or clubhouse outdoors. Allowing our children access to environments where they can find or make such homes-away-from-home, and curbing parental fear or desires to "help," may be a greater gift to our children than buying them special furniture or a wide-screen TV. Do your children have access to a place or materials with which they can express their unique identity? Could you leave a half-hidden corner of the yard unmaintained? Could you reserve them a wall in the basement or playroom where they can paint an ongoing mural? Is there a pin-up board in the kitchen or magnets on the refrigerator so they can put up artwork from school? Finally, have you asked your children, however young, what *they* would like in the home, how *they* would like it to be?

Observing your children's expressions of self-identity in the home, reflecting on them with neither judgment nor excessive praise, may open doors for you in connecting with their unique personalities—and perhaps with your own special child-self.

THREE

Growing Up: Self-Expression in the Homes of Adulthood

Are we perhaps on the verge of grasping that the environment is ourselves, for it has given us form, and that creation is nothing but a dialogue between the inside and the outside? Do we not have to exhale and inhale in order to live? . . . Our unconscious self prompts us to act, produce and do. It is through our actions and their products that we reveal ourselves to ourselves.

—OLIVIER MARC, *The Psychology of the House*[1]

It was Carl Jung's account of building his house on Lake Zurich that first alerted me to our complex symbolic relationship with the homes we live in. Jung, perhaps more than any other thinker or writer of this century, fearlessly examined his own psyche and delved into a great range of disciplines which together aided him in his quest to build a theory of the unconscious and the self. He describes how he yearned to put the knowledge of the contents of his unconscious into solid form, rather than just describe them in words. In the building of his house, the tower at Bollingen on Lake Zurich, he was to make a "confession of faith in stone."

"At first I did not plan a proper house, but merely a kind of primitive one-story dwelling. It was to be a round structure with a hearth in the center and bunks along the walls. I more or less had in mind an African hut, but where the fire, ringed with stone, burns in the middle, and the whole life of the family revolves around this center. Primitive huts concretize an idea of wholeness, a familial wholeness in which all sorts of domestic animals likewise participate. But I altered the plan even during the first stages of building, for I felt it was too primitive. I realized it would have to be a regular two-story house, not a mere hut crouched on the ground. So in 1923 the first round house was built, and when it was over I saw that it had become a suitable dwelling tower.

"The feeling of repose and renewal that I had in this tower was intense from the start. It represented for me the maternal hearth."[2]

Four years later, Jung added another building with a towerlike annex. After another interval of four years, he built onto the tower a room for meditation and seclusion, where no one else could enter; it became his retreat for spiritual contemplation. After another four years, he felt the need for another area, open to nature and the sky, and so added a courtyard and an adjoining loggia. The resultant quanternity pleased him, since his own studies in mythology and symbolism had provided much evidence of the completeness and wholeness represented by the figure *4*. Finally, after his wife's death, he felt an inner obligation to "become what I myself am," and recognized that the small central section of the house "which crouched so low and hidden was myself! I could no longer hide behind the 'maternal' and 'spiritual' towers. So in the same year I added an upper story to this section, which represents myself or my ego-personality. Earlier, I would not have been able to do this; I would have regarded it as presumptuous self-emphasis. Now it signified an extension of consciousness achieved in old age. With that the building was complete."[3]

Jung had thus built his house over time as a representation in stone of his own evolving and maturing psyche: It was the place, he said, where "I am in the midst of my true life, I am most deeply myself." This was a place where he could reflect upon—and concretize—who he was and would become. Upon completion and reflecting on how all the parts fit together, he recognized it as a symbol of psychic wholeness.

Though few of us may ever build a house for ourselves, let alone reflect on its symbolic meaning, most of us *do* create some space in the world that is ours and, whether consciously or unconsciously, we shape and decorate it to express our values. The colors we choose, the objects we select, the pictures and posters we put on the walls—all of these have aesthetic or functional meanings of which we are aware. Many of them also are projections, or "messages" from the unconscious, in just the

The evolution of Jung's house at Bollingen on Lake Zurich became a manifestation of the psyche in the material world: The initial tower dwelling representing the maternal hearth was constructed just after his mother's death. (Drawings by Glenn Robert Lym.)

Four years later, in 1927, he added the central structure.

Four years later, a third construction consisted of a tower annex, which became Jung's private place for spiritual contemplation.

Sensing a need for a fourth part of the house open to nature, Jung built a courtyard and loggia by the lake in 1935.

Twenty years later, in 1955, Jung's wife died, and he completed the house with a central tower, representing himself or his ego-personality.

same way that our dreams contain such messages. As with dreams, we can live our lives ignoring them. But if we care about personal and spiritual growth, becoming who we truly are, the messages implicit in the dwelling—its form, location, decoration, and state of order—and our feelings about those messages can be rich sources of insight.

House-Building as Self-Expression: Bill's Constantly Evolving Dwelling

Some people have a hard time expressing themselves in their environment. This may be an avoidance of self-expression, but it may also indicate that their means of expression are via their clothes or their creative work, such as cooking or yard work. Others relish the time spent planning and decorating their home, reorganizing furniture arrangements, or creating endless do-it-yourself home-improvement projects. Bill was someone who clearly used his home environment as his primary means of expression. He designed, built, and remodeled houses all his life; it was his passion.

Bill grew up in a modest house in an Oregon seaport; his father gave him a tool chest for his seventh birthday. He tinkered with wood scraps in the basement. By the age of thirteen, he had built his first house.

"I suppose I was trying to outdo my friends. It was twelve feet wide by twenty feet long, with a porch five feet wide and a little alcove at the back which was six feet square. It was shingled on the outside and had a little stove and doors and windows. We used it for a long time, actually slept in it in summers."

Later, he helped his father remodel the family home, and built, after his return from World War II, a summer cottage in the forest, which is still used by the family. Finally, as a young faculty member at Berkeley, he and his wife bought a small house in the hills. Until the last year of his life, afflicted with cancer, Bill always had some building or remodeling project on the go. Two-thirds of the original house was gutted and rebuilt; he added rooms, installed new heating and lighting systems, replaced windows, and modernized the kitchen, teaching himself new skills as he went along. But this was more than a one-man improvement project, for Bill insisted that the whole family be involved.

"We began by building a complete scale model of what we wanted, with scale furniture and scale people, and we moved them around. The children helped build it, and played with it in its latter stages.

"I'm a person who feels that intimate contact with the real world is a very important part of personality development. People who build their own homes, I think, enjoy a privilege that's quite rare. It's a creative endeavor, one that has cemented our family about a line of action which was important to each of us and developed before our eyes. But most important of all, we learned not to be afraid of a house as being something sacrosanct. With a sledgehammer, my son David destroyed some of the old walls in the house. Not vindictively, as some children destroy houses because they don't like them, but creatively. He was tearing down something which was unsatisfactory.

"All through their growing years, things were happening to the house. There are details that are still unfinished. Maybe they're there because I don't ever want to finish."

When I suggested that the house was his hobby, Bill reacted with feeling. "No, it's not a hobby. The word *hobby* is an annoying word to me. Hobby is something that you do to kill time. This is not a hobby. This is a fundamental part of our existence."

Not only did Bill continue this work all his life, he imbued his children with the same desire to change things. His daughter Gwen and her husband bought a less-than-satisfactory suburban house, tore it to pieces, and rebuilt it to their own needs. He recalled with pleasure how Gwen's construction skills were first put to good use.

"She was employed at Cazadero summer camp as a general helper. It happened that a redwood tree had fallen and smashed the lavatory unit, so a group of boys, under the direction of some of the supervising men, were trying to rebuild this thing. At one point, Gwen saw their concrete work on the new floors and said, 'Where is the steel work in there? Where is the reinforcing?' And none of them had the vaguest idea that that would be a good idea. So she became a kind of technical adviser."

As I do in many of my conversations with people about their homes, I asked Bill if he would speak to the house as if it were animate. He refused to do so, partly, I suspect, because it may have seemed a little silly, but also for a more profound reason.

"I can't do that because the house is me. Because I built it and because it's everything that I wanted it to be; I think of it really as an extension of our family. It is not an object you buy in a showroom, like a car or a piece of furniture. It's us. Its imperfections are as revealing to me as its satisfactions, like a friend or member of the family whose imperfections we can see. They're not serious enough to be bothersome. If we find something isn't working, we change it. I don't think we change our habits to suit the house, which is what most people must do. We change the house to suit us, so it's constantly evolving. We live it, we don't live in it."

Bill clearly exemplified what two social researchers, McClelland and McCarthy, concluded: The greater the control we exercise over an object or an environment, the more closely allied with the self it becomes.

The Emergence of Self-Expression: Angela as an Evolving Woman

For some of us, self-expression in any form may not come easily, and the emergence of a desire to express ourselves in the material world—especially in our home—should be taken very seriously. This is movingly illustrated by the story of how Angela began her journey toward becoming more fully herself. Though she laughingly referred to her story as a "soap opera," Angela's life demonstrated a slow but persistent flowering of self-discovery.

Angela had met a friend of mine, who told her casually of my book. She had just made a life change that had a lot to do with dwelling and self-expression, so

Angela's depiction of her feelings about home at our first meeting.

she called me and asked if we could meet. She lived in a community a hour's drive from San Francisco. It had been a small country town that since the fifties has been engulfed by suburbia. Her house was an older, two-story stucco building set among redwoods and eucalyptus trees. A high fence—unusual in California suburbs—flanked the property on the street. I opened the gate and approached the house through a burned-out summer landscape of yellowing grass, cactus, and lemon trees.

Angela had recently broken up with her lover, Eileen, with whom she had lived for six years. She started by telling me about her lover's ability to create a home, and her own lack of ability—or refusal—to participate in that process.

"Eileen was always very home-oriented and wanted a home very much, while I had always placed myself in dingy kinds of inexpensive places. When we began to live together, she started to organize the apartment and always wanted me to participate, and I would never bring myself to do that. Consequently, all of the furniture belonged to her. I think it was partly because I always knew that some-day I was going to leave. I was just unable to make a commitment, and now I am beginning to understand why. When we met, I was very much a child and I didn't have any sense of myself at all. And she was very much a person of the world, who knew how to take care of herself, knew how to make a home. And she very much took care of me and taught me a lot of things which I resisted. I was always running around in ragtag clothes from the Purple Heart Thrift Store, and she was forever buying me things that were nice, and beautiful things for the house—fresh flowers and all that.

"About the third year of our relationship, we were living in a beautiful flat in San Francisco, when Eileen suddenly got a promotion. We had to move closer to her work, and Eileen said, 'Well, let's think about buying.' And I resisted, saying, 'No, I haven't the money. I can't do it.' Which was really true. And she said, 'That's going to be your excuse for the rest of your life. Let's check it out.' We looked at three houses, and they were all kind of tacky, and neither of us liked them. By then, Eileen had convinced me that I deserved to live in a nice place. Anyway, the realtor said, 'Well, you will have to go higher if you want to have a nicer place.' And he took us here. The house was empty, and I remember walking in here and immediately said, 'This is wonderful!' Eileen wasn't so sure, but she was delighted I was showing any interest at all. We ended up buying the place right away, and I was terrified. In fact, I was in therapy at the time, and we devoted many, many sessions to this idea of ownership and what it meant in terms of commitment and what it meant in terms of 'giving to myself—that I deserve this.' We moved in, and Eileen continued to acquire things. She took a trip to Europe and came back with some beautiful things: the table and these candlesticks. And I still would not buy anything for the house. It bothered her, but I guess she came to accept it. Anyway, we spent some very happy times here for three years; we gave wonderful parties. But the happy times that I remember most are the rainy winter evenings, sitting by the fire and playing chess and having suppers—crackers and cheese with my dog and her cat."

Significantly, the start of the change revolved around a piece of furniture. About a year after the house purchase, Angela decided to build herself a workbench. It turned out so successfully, she decided to make it her study desk and placed it at a window with a beautiful view out to a forested canyon.

"I would rush home from school so that I could sit there for some hours by myself. It was a time when crab were really cheap. I'd buy one and sit eating at my desk with some white wine and my typewriter. That was the beginning—though I didn't realize it then—of my wanting my own home."

At first, Angela could not bring herself to make changes within the house, apart from the desk she made. She started to spend more and more time in the garden. "There were some large succulents in the front garden. I became fixated on getting rid of them, because I wanted to plant vegetables and flowers. I would come home from work, and that's all I could think about—just digging up those giant cacti. It got to a point where I started feeling very possessive about the house. When Eileen came home, I'd be out in the garden, but I'd feel this immense tension in my body—a feeling of possessiveness. I didn't like that feeling and I fought it for a long time."

Eventually, Angela's feelings began to spill over into her relationship with Eileen, and also into some dramatic changes in her own self-concept. Always somewhat self-deprecating, she suddenly let her hair grow and developed an interest in wearing jewelry. This awakening interest in making herself more attractive significantly spilled over into the house.

"One night last May, I had a dream about clothing. I said to Eileen, 'I need to have a chest of drawers,' and she said, 'Oh, well, OK!' Until this point, I had kept my clothes in one of Eileen's file drawers. I knew exactly what the dresser was going to look like. I went to the store—and there it was! I had it delivered, put it in my room, and pulled my clothes out of the file drawer. I washed things that hadn't been washed in years, and threw things out that I didn't look good in. At that point, I knew I couldn't be with Eileen anymore."

After five months of counseling, they decided to split up; it was agreed that Eileen would leave and move to a location closer to her work.

"I remember the day she left. My body at that point was like a board. I sat down on a couch and heard the door close, and I felt all of this tension just draining out of my body. And I immediately began to fix up my room as my own. I bought other pieces of furniture and I shampooed all the rugs. I washed the hearth down and all the floors. I had never been noted for cleaning the place. That was what Eileen did. I spent three days cleaning; I didn't even go to work. It was like a ritual. I felt I was becoming a woman and I was washing away the past."

The chest of drawers that Angela saw in her dream and later purchased.

But a month later, Eileen reversed her decision and demanded to return to the house. Angela moved out and found a place to live which she described as a "hovel." In her own words, she regressed: "I hated being me. I was punishing myself. Again, I felt I didn't deserve to live in a good place. I felt I should be in a dark, dingy hovel, because that's what kind of person I am. I found a place of one and one-half rooms, with scratched-up dark paneling, kitchen linoleum full of stains and dirt. I wouldn't even let them clean it before I moved in. I had to do it myself."

She felt resistant to doing anything to improve "the hovel" except, significantly, she decided to invest a lot of energy in the bathroom. She bought a piece of carpet and took pains fitting it around the feet of the bathtub; she painted the walls and bought a beautiful shower curtain—"which I hardly deserved."

"And then some friends, recognizing what I was going through, bought me some wonderful matching towels. I had never had anything like that before! And I put plants in there—I had never bought a plant before! It was so elegant—I spent most of my time in the bathtub. I even had an open-house party for the bathroom when I completed it. The first thing people said when they came was, 'I want to see the bathroom'!

"That room has done so much for my body image. For the first time in my life, I like my body. I spent a lot of time in there, taking baths and applying lotions. My body has always been a source of discomfort and shame to me, so it was such a surprise to feel this impulse to decorate a bathroom, to make it a sensuous place. Instead of worrying about my sexuality, trying to figure it all out, I've just been sitting in my bath enjoying the pleasure! I've been going through a whole flowering of my sexuality and femininity."

The final turn of events was that Angela offered to buy Eileen's share in the house, Eileen readily agreed, and Angela moved back in. This decision was prefaced, interestingly, by Angela's dog running away from "the hovel," returning to the house and refusing to leave. If, as some veterinarians assert, animals can "act out" unspoken grief or tension in a family, perhaps they can also at times convey unspoken feelings about home and rootedness. I asked Angela what she might want to say to her house if she could imagine it as a person.

"I feel a lot of pride in you. I look at all the houses and I think: None of those houses is as nice as you are. None of them is as bright as you are. And, at the same time, there is a lot of sadness connected with you because of Eileen [fights tears], and I have some fears that [sighing] by buying this house I am somehow sealing myself off. But I thank you for unlocking a lot of things in me that have to do with giving myself pleasures."

When I asked if the house had anything to say in reply, she responded: "I don't think you should feel guilty anymore. I think you have beaten up on yourself for too long. I think you underestimate yourself. When you start putting some energy into me, which you never did really, you are going to see how really beautiful I can be. And you are going to love again, too, because you are a person with deep feelings. And why are you always worrying about the future? You spend too much time trying to control your life and figuring out what's gonna happen. Live for the present and paint me some neat colors. But keep them soft. I know how you like bright colors, but I like softness, and you need some more softness in you."

Angela became quite animated and spontaneously changed places and began to respond to what the house had said. "Well, I can't hear that often enough about worrying about the future. Thanks, you're pretty smart! I'll remember in the future when I am sitting here and I am a little bummed out, that maybe I should talk to you and let you talk to me a little bit. You seem to have some good things to say! You have shown me that it's not a terrible thing to live in a nice place. I deserve to live in a nice place, because [showing a lot of emotion] I'm a fine human being. You are very feminine and you bring out that side of myself that I sometimes repress because it's frightening. I'll always have fresh flowers and soft things, because you are soft and you have helped to bring out that soft side of me. I am learning that vulnerability is necessary in order to feel anything—joy or pain."

Seven years after this conversation, I visited Angela again. She looked older; so did I. The desk was still in the window; the dresser she had first seen in a dream was still in the bedroom. But now the whole house was filled with expressions of her self—soft colors, lacy curtains, comfortable furniture, new carpets, artifacts purchased on a trip to New Mexico, a painting of a woman, naked, brushing her hair in front of a mirror. She had been through an intensive period of Jungian analysis; she seemed much more her own person, at peace with herself.

For Angela, the first insights of a tentatively emerging positive self-image revolved around the making of a workbench which became a desk, and the dream of a chest of drawers which she later purchased. The desk became a place where she could sit, reflect, and write alone; the dresser, a place where she could place her clothes retrieved from a cramped file drawer. Significantly, a person's creative work (writing, in this case) and clothes are both important modes of self-expression. That Angela first selected items of furniture to *support* those modes of expression suggests that some significant objects in our lives do "double duty," both as self-extension in themselves—the desk, the chest of drawers—and as a means to facilitate other modes of exploring and validating self—creative writing and dressing in a more feminine mode.

In one research study carried out to test McClelland and McCarthy's premise that possessions are viewed as parts of the self, E. Prelinger, a psychologist, asked people to sort 160 items on a continuum from "self" to "non-self." Not surprisingly, the body and its parts received the highest "self" score, followed by psychological processes (e.g., conscience, values) and personal identifying attributes (e.g., age, occupation). Next, however, were possessions. As a person's self-image changes, he or she is able to put away or dispose of objects that no longer reflect who they are, and acquire or make others.[4] Thus, where we live becomes a kind of stage set onto which our self-image is projected via moveable (i.e., controllable) objects. The house interior for most people—unlike the structure itself—is rarely wholly fixed or finished. Like the exploration of the self, the arrangement of the domestic interior is often in the process of becoming.

From Institution to Self-Emergence: Joan's First Apartment

*I do not know how much longer I can bear the silence in the next room. It
seems to have spread like an influence, to the whole house, to the furniture
which I love and never thought to speak to, yet now there are moments when
I demand speech from it, not the occasional songs—crack of wood bursting its
bonds of space, easing itself in the hot dry weather . . . but articulate language,
the unique speech of furniture. Lately I have found myself suddenly hammering
with my fist upon the table . . . as if a gesture of violence may help me to break
into the silence of everything around me, to ransack and spill the words which
lie trapped there. Other times I have stroked the furniture, touching it gently as
an archaeologist may caress a newly discovered piece of stone, knowing that in
the end, if it is cared for, it will give up its secret . . .*

—JANET FRAME, *Scented Gardens for the Blind* [5]

Most of us start to express ourselves in our homes or rooms during adolescence,
or when we first leave our parental home. For Joan, who had entered a Roman
Catholic convent at the age of sixteen, this experience was delayed for many years.
When I met with her, I had the extraordinary experience of discussing this process
of transformation as it begins. In her late twenties, while still living at the convent,
Joan began to attend a women's therapy group in Berkeley, and her frustrations
with life in a religious order slowly began to emerge. After much soul-searching,
she decided to leave the order and start a new life "on the outside." Although she
had not been in a closed order, her personal living space had always been spartan.
Encouraged to consider the needs of others before her own, her desire to decorate
the environment had been expended on the communal space of the convent rather
than on her own room. Here is how she described her feelings about a new apartment, her first, six months after she had moved in:

"For the first time, I realized what it was like to have space all my own,
entirely mine; mine because I earned money for it; mine because I chose it entirely
by myself; mine since I could gather and collect whatever items I wanted to put
into it. So I've realized great joy in this apartment. I could fill it with the music
I wanted. I could fill it with the life of plants. For the first time, I really came to
realize that I had a choice.

"The first day I stood in this apartment, all I had was a rocking chair and a desk and a record, the first record that I ever bought. The song was 'I Am a Child of the Universe,' and my eyes filled up with tears because I realized for the first time that I am a child of the universe and I do belong to the universe, not just a narrow segment of it. So this apartment has been a huge support. It's provided time to express my creativity, time for me to do just what I want to do all by myself.

"It's interesting that I put greens and browns and oranges in the apartment, because I myself am reticent to wear those colors. I mostly stick to blue. I like the quiet peacefulness of blue, and yet in my home I just stir up a storm of color. The apartment symbolizes what I am gradually realizing inside myself; I am coming to see my own life, my own aliveness as it unwraps, unfolds with each experience that I have. I know someday when I'm ready, I will move into wearing the warmer colors that this place has allowed me to project. I've surrounded myself with a lot of color and energy. Someday this color and energy is going to be totally inside of me; I will have the warmth of vermilion and gold inside me. What I'd like to happen is for all the aliveness of my apartment to be interiorized, so I walk around with my home inside of me all the time."

In Joan's own words, we see a very specific example of the contents of her unconscious made manifest in her dwelling. Although her conscious self still seeks the "quiet peacefulness of blue" (she always wore blue jeans and white shirts at that time), she is aware of another energetic and assertive side to her nature that is not quite ready for interpersonal expression, but which she is able to project onto her apartment. "What I'm hoping to do is to bring the warmth of the browns and the aliveness of the greens inside of me so that I realize a real balance between aggression and quietness."

It is clear that Joan's move from the convent into her own apartment has allowed her a sense of power and control denied for the past sixteen years. In the convent, decisions were always made for her. If external objects become viewed as extensions of the self when we are able to exercise control over them, it is small wonder that this ordinary apartment with its newly purchased desk and rocking chair have taken on enormous importance to Joan. At this point in her life, manipulation of—and reflection upon—her dwelling environment are very necessary components of the process of creating a new self-image.

A very significant act in this regard was the making of a table from a redwood burl. Joan had always admired such tables and, having purchased a section of rough wood from a lumberyard, she set about sanding and polishing the surface until the beauty of its grain and texture began to be revealed. She talked of this process almost as a meditation and shyly admitted to the analogy she saw in it of herself, as her psyche slowly emerged from that of a cloistered sister to that of a free woman.

First she spoke as if she were the table: "I'm very strong and curved and smooth; I'm very sensual to touch; I have curves and gullies. I am strong, almost impossible to sand; you can sand and sand and sand me before you get to my real smoothness. My outer bark layers are rough and coarse as they should be; they protect my inner heart, my inner softness. I'm a tree, cut and hewn, a container to hold experience, to hold the joy of life. I am a portion of the forest, made serviceable to you. I am a gift, a tree gift to you. I am nature supporting you and holding you and giving you life and strength. I am an opportunity for you to experience an outlet for your frustrations. I've received your conflict and turned it around and given back to you the richness of my being."

I asked Joan to respond to the table: "In the process of knowing you, I came to know myself. I really see all the different shades of your colors in me. We've experienced together the rough coarseness of disappointments and banished dreams. You were ugly at first. As I worked and sanded you inch by inch, I discovered your secret, your softness and your beauty. As I work on myself, I find my own beauty and softness and strength. It's amazing what you hold for me, tree."

Jung proposed that a dream could be a communication from the unconscious about not only past or present circumstances, but also future possibilities. So, I believe, do our dwellings, and the objects within them communicate in the same way—both as mirrors of what is and as suggestions of what might be. It seems very clear that Joan's redwood table has become deeply intertwined with her psyche. It is as if she has chosen this metaphor, knowing that revelation of the inner secrets of the wood will parallel her own inner transformation. It is also significant that she chose wood over any other material, for, as she said: "I've always loved to work with wood. My dad was an architect and contractor, and I'd pick up scraps of wood on his building sites. I learned how to sand from the carpenters, and I always liked the smell of sawdust and the smell of freshly sawed wood. I'd take the blocks home and sand them. I remember the day my dad showed me by oiling them that the natural grain of the wood would stand out and be itself. You didn't have to put varnish or veneer or anything on it to cover it up. I hadn't realized the connection before, but it is part of me. In discovering that redwood table there, as I worked on all its nooks and crannies, I came to see a lot of myself."

In Joan's description of her loving and meditative shaping of a redwood burl into a table, we have a cogent example of the core of a theory developed by George

Joan and the redwood burl table that became a metaphor for her inner transformation.

Herbert Mead in his sociological writings of the 1930s. Mead proposed that physical objects play a central role in the development and maintenance of our self-identity. Indeed our very identity and discrete self is confirmed by the objects we use and with which we surround ourselves. Although speech, body language, and clothing are also significant channels of communicating a sense of self to others and ourselves, they are relatively impermanent and changeable. Therefore, the objects with which we surround ourselves in that most familiar and stable environment—the home—are particularly salient expressions of self. The more we are able to *touch* those objects, the more we gain reassurance of their reality, a reassurance and a level of relating not gained from sight alone.[6]

At some unconscious level, we all know this. We know it when we rearrange and order the objects that surround us. We know it when we seek a release from stress by gardening or pottering with crafts or cleaning house. Joan knew it when she chose to sand and polish a rough piece of wood, and in so doing acknowledged the beauty revealed in the grain as a reflection of her own inner substance slowly emerging into consciousness.

Furniture as Self-Expression: Phyllis' Couch and Table

When a house or possessions are perceived as being inconsistent with our current self-image, we tend to neglect them or willingly dispose of them. When our self-image is confused or going through some kind of transition, we may hold on to the "things" in our lives, being unsure as to which ones truly represent us. As we begin to recover from loss, or establish our first home, or explore a new facet of who we are, physical changes or the purchase of material objects may symbolize and anchor those changes.

I talked with Phyllis in the attractive apartment in the Berkeley hills where she had lived for two years. Reestablishing her life after a divorce, she had returned to graduate school and was delighted with her home in a building complex reminiscent of a French village. In a picture in which she summarized her feelings about her new home, she drew first a red, womblike enclosure flanked by purple curtains. Within the upper part of the circle, she depicted the blue sky and green trees she could see from her windows. In four quadrants of the picture, she drew the four significant rooms of the house. Across the middle of the picture was a black, shaded rectangle; at the bottom, a brown rectangle on which the rest of the composition seemed to be balanced. These two forms represented two items of furniture—a couch and a table—which were extremely important to Phyllis and which seemed to act as anchors, both in her picture and in her life.

"I've never owned a couch before, and it was a big production for me to get one. To me, a couch is *the* big deal of a house, and that's how it is to my family. When my parents came to visit, my father said in a despondent way, 'Boy, I wish Janet (my sister) would get a couch.' Janet lives kind of funky, and I know that they think her priorities are upside down. They would feel as if she's made it if she had a couch. They admired my couch—they used it a lot; they were impressed by it. It's the only big thing in this house, because it's such a tiny house. Something about having a couch means you've made it. When I was married for eleven years, I never bought a couch—we made a couch, but we didn't buy one.

"When I lived with my second husband, we also didn't have a couch; we used a three-quarter bed pushed up against the wall with pillows. When we moved to the country in our last house, in desperation to fill up the gaping emptiness of the room, I went to the house of a lady who was selling her old, crappy furniture and bought a couch and matching chair for seventy-five dollars. So I was forty-two years old before I ever owned a couch! I remember talking about it after I bought it, saying to people, 'Hey, I own a couch,' as if it was a real big thing! I hardly know anybody else who feels that way."

I asked Phyllis what she would say to her apartment if she could imagine it as a person. "Well, I really like coming home to you. I really feel connected to you;

I feel as if you and I are a good couple. You set me off; I set you off. You take care of me; I take care of you. I like to talk to you a lot, and I feel like you're always listening. I run home to you when I'm out; I miss you when I'm gone. I'm really glad I've changed my job so I can spend more time here."

I asked Phyllis to say a little more about the table, which appeared to form a kind of base to her picture. "When I was drawing it, I kept getting flashes of us all sitting around the table at my parents' house when I was twelve. When I was a teenager, we would have supper, and then I would go upstairs to my room and hang out there, and my father would hang out in the living room, and my mother would hang out in the kitchen. And then, somewhere about eleven, we would all drift into the kitchen—sometimes a neighbor would drop in, sometimes a relative—and within half an hour my mother would start making coffee and we'd go raid the refrigerator and we would all sit there and schmooze. And we had a family joke that whenever we got finished with eating and drinking and talking, it was always one o'clock in the morning—which was quite amazing, considering that we all worked or went to school and we got up at six or seven in the morning.

"In my grandmother's house, too, we spent a great deal of time sitting at the table—we were just the kind of people who ate all the time. And there was one other reason: cards. I come from a big card-playing family—whenever they come, even now, we play cards—and that's another reason to sit at the table."

Phyllis' table and couch—each very large, weighty, and expensive—clearly have both a functional usefulness and a significant symbolic meaning. Both were very important in her parental home as well. In this statement of self-expression, she has gone back to both her personal and cultural roots. In looking for a medium of self-expression, Phyllis seemed relatively unconcerned about the form or location of her dwelling and much more concerned about what was inside of it. It seemed probable that this has some connection to her formative childhood homes—apartments in New York City—where the form is taken as a given, but the furnishing of the space was a significant aspect of family life.

Self-Reflection and a State of Order:
Michael's Living in His Rightful Place

In the case of Angela, Joan, and Phyllis—and many other people I spoke with—the house and special objects within it come to be viewed as a profound expression of the inner self. Through touch, care, and manipulation, energy seems to move from the self to the objective symbol of self. But those same objects can also be viewed as a revelation of the inner self; that is, the energy seems to move from objective symbol back to the self, as if to say: Look! This is who you are. You are a person who is soft like your surroundings; or, You are a person who values nature as exemplified by the plants and pictures in your home. It is as though the self/environment continuum could be thought of as simultaneously both the positive and the negative of a film.

One way in which most of us are aware of the almost membranelike connection between self and environment is when things somehow get "out of control" and we feel disordered in ourselves. Who hasn't had the experience of tidying a cluttered desk and subsequently feeling more able to think straight? Or of cleaning out stuff from an attic or storeroom and feeling a great sense of accomplishment, or perhaps a feeling of being more in control?

Michael is an artist who lives in a converted factory in an industrial section of San Francisco. He likes living in unconventional places, spaces that are unusual, adaptable, "magic." Michael grew up in a small Oklahoma town, where his wealthy grandfather had donated a park and a water tower to the community and had built on a prominent hill the largest and most ostentatious house in town. Michael was raised there, absorbing a message from the house and its setting that he and his family were in some way "different." This feeling of being set apart or different has been reenacted in all the homes of his adult life: a barn on a peninsula in Nova Scotia, a loft in Greenwich Village, a villa in Spain, a converted factory in San Francisco. All but the Spanish villa were located high up, with commanding views of the community.

In his current home, Michael converted the upper five floors of a factory into a sequence of beamed rooms with rough brick walls, polished floors, wooden furniture, hanging plants, and sun streaming in through mullioned windows. The effect is spacious, workmanlike, somewhat austere; it is a "no-nonsense" environment. For Michael, a sense of order is essential.

"I am very psychologically affected by what is around me. When I'm in an environment that I feel is constricted, or one that I consider deranged (which are the two ways I describe other people's houses that I do not find comfortable), I am immediately uncomfortable. It's very hard in my own life when I've neglected my home to a point of disorder. When I go into someone's environment and feel that it is indicative of a great deal of care and attention, even if I don't share their taste, I can imagine that that person has a relatively good feeling about themselves, that they actually care. And when I go into an environment that is totally shoddy, that is completely deranged and exhibits a lot of neglect, I do look at that person a little differently.

"I find it upsetting when people accept a kind of average; they absolve their individuality and resourcefulness. It tends to cause a feeling that they somehow have misplaced themselves. And I think your home should help you get in touch with who you are.

"I feel myself here. I think people who feel akin to their environment feel that they're in their 'rightful place.' But that means getting in touch with who you are and being in an environment that enriches the things you need. That's what I mean when I say that one is in one's rightful place."

Clearly, Michael is in his rightful place; he understands himself well and has learned that a nurturing environment and sense of order are essential to his sense of well-being. He articulates more clearly than most of us how he reads another person's inner state from the state of order in their dwelling.

For many people, their home may be the only place where they feel a sense of control. A friend of mine, who works in an office job she does not like, sometimes goes home after a particularly irksome day and rearranges the furniture. It helps her regain a sense of control in that small corner of the world where no one can tell her what to do. Christopher Grampp, one of my students, fascinated

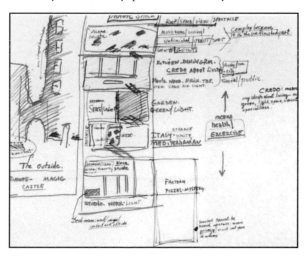

Michael's "rightful place."

by the wide variety of yards he observed in a California city, set about interviewing some of the people who had created them. He found among other things that better-off, highly educated homeowners often had rather wild, "natural," or low-maintenance landscapes around their homes, whereas working-class retired people tended to have yards that were highly controlled—clipped, pruned, raked, ordered. He concluded that those who needed to keep their gardens "in control" seemed to have little control in other arenas of their lives (income, advancement, and so on), whereas those who had more control over their lives—more money, more freedom—could allow their yards to go wild. By pruning the juniper into the shape we want it to be, by moving the living-room furniture around until it's how we want it to be, we reaffirm our own sense of control in the world.

To appropriate space, to order and mold it into a form that pleases us and affirms who we are, is a universal need. Conversely, when an institution such as the military, a corporation, or a religious order wishes to impose its sense of control over its members, one way of doing that is to restrict personal expression in the environment and in clothing. The military and religious uniform, the rules about family photos on the office desk, the regulations about personal items in the barracks—all of these are reminders about not stepping out of line. How we dress in nonworking hours, how we decorate and furnish our private homes, becomes all the more significant for those who may have little control in other areas of their lives.

Living Together Amid Julie's Clutter

Hominess is not neatness. Otherwise everyone would live in replicas of the kinds of sterile and impersonal homes that appear in interior-design and architectural magazines . . . In spite of the artfully placed vases and casually arranged art books, the imprints of their inhabitants is missing. These pristine interiors fascinate and repel me. Can people really live without clutter? How do they stop the Sunday papers from spreading over the living room? . . . Where do they hide the detritus of their everyday lives?

—WITOLD RYBCZYNSKI, *Home: A Short History of an Idea*[7]

Julie welcomed me, smiling at the door of her comfortable urban house in San Francisco with the words: "Welcome to our dysfunctional house! I'll show you around. All this 'stuff' everywhere is like excess fat on someone who is overweight." There *was* a lot of stuff around, though it didn't seem nearly as bad as Julie apparently saw it. There were piles of clothes and household objects on the floor in a few places; junk mail piled beside the kitchen sink; a child's bedroom full of stuffed toys (though the "child" was now aged twenty-four and living in her own apartment).

As we talked, it was clear that Julie felt very bad about her inability to sort out all these objects and put the house in a better state of order. She was very appreciative of the fact that her husband, Sam, did not complain about the mess and in fact viewed it with a loving kind of wry humor. How the house looked did not bother him. It did, however, bother her. They no longer had friends over; her daughter, "a neatnik," gave her a hard time about it when she visited. Julie felt "bogged down" and, despite having time and a nagging desire to sort out her stuff, she just couldn't do it.

After a long conversation, it seemed clear that the state of disorder was for Julie a very meaningful statement—it was not random untidiness. She was in her early fifties, her two children had left home, and she was grieving for the loss of her role as a mother. She had loved having the house full of kids—her own and their friends—and remarked several times how much she enjoyed the "chaos" that kids tend to create. Now she lived alone in the house with Sam, who was very involved in his work and often away from home. Julie was confused about "what I should do next in my life." She had not had a career outside the home; she had done a lot of volunteer work, but no longer wanted to do that, except, significantly, she acted as a "foster mother" to pregnant cats from the Humane Society. When I visited, a large gray cat with six kittens was ensconced in the master bedroom.

The loss of her mothering role, the emptiness of the house, the onset of middle age—each of these would be enough to trigger some kind of psychological response which, in Julie's case, was acted out via her environment. But as she talked of her deceased mother, she admitted to some unresolved anger toward her regarding housework. Her mother had been extremely tidy and house-proud and, on visits to Julie when she was newly married, had expressed her disapproval of her daughter's housekeeping standards with words and withering looks. Julie still felt very bad about this and, we might surmise, was still defying her mother's control over her by leaving "stuff" around the house. Happily for her, the person who shared this environment with her—her husband—was not especially affected by order or chaos. Until they made a decision together to move to a home out of the city—an issue they were considering—he was content for Julie to take her time in coming to terms with the stuff in their house and what it meant symbolically.

Holding on to the stuff that symbolizes children and the mothering years may be a necessary psychological transition for many women before moving on into the flowering of the second half of life. I know that is true for me. My just-grown children are the same age as Julie's, and my house feels empty without them.

The attic which was my daughter's bedroom is still a chaotic storehouse of her stuff, which she occasionally sorts through on school breaks. My son has also left for college and, apart from a few old posters, board games, and one ancient teddy bear, his room has little of him left in it. It now functions as a guest room. I have not left either room as a shrine, but can totally understand women who have to do that, especially if the child memorialized has died, or if the woman—like Julie—does not have a profession or career and after the end of motherhood is faced with the question: Now what?

Dreams as Guides to Future Growth

When we feel stuck in our lives, or in a home that seems to express an outmoded symbol of self, it may help to pay attention to dreams. Our unconscious is often wiser, more all-knowing than our busy, rational, conscious mind.

Ellen was a young artist who at the time of our conversation was growing dissatisfied with her partner, Ray. He did not seem to appreciate her or her effort to make and maintain a home for them. Ellen was starting to think about a separation and returning to her native New Zealand. She passingly referred to a dream, and I asked her to tell me what she remembered.

"I was in a really barren landscape, and there were some people around. Ray and I were there, and then there was this person standing up on a kind of cliff. In the middle, there was this watering hole. I couldn't see to the bottom, but I knew it wasn't very deep. It was filled with water, but the landscape was just brown, barren, bare earth. There was a diving board by the water. We saw that this person was going to dive into the hole: We both knew that this person would get stuck in the mud at the bottom of the hole. So the person dives, and Ray immediately ran around and got into the water to pull the person up. And I did the same thing and then I became the person who did the dive—I'm diving into this hole. But I know that I'm not going to be trapped; there is no fear in the dream at all. Well, here I am diving into New Zealand! The trap for me is to sit down and say 'Why? Why am I going? Why can't I stay here?' I just get really bogged down when I do that."

"Bogged down?!" I laughed.

"Yes, in the hole!"

Ellen did return to New Zealand and started a new life. Her dream gave her some confidence about the outcome of this radical change in her life.

Unlike Freud, Jung also saw dreams as possible prognosticators of the future; for he believed that the unconscious holds not only individual and collective memories but also the seeds of future action. At one period of his life, Jung was searching for some historical basis or precedent for the ideas he was developing about the unconscious. He didn't know where to start the search. At this point, he began to have a series of dreams, all of which dealt with the same theme: "Beside my house stood another, that is to say, another wing or annex, which was strange to me. Each time I would wonder in my dream why I did not know this house, although it had apparently always been there. Finally came a dream in which I reached the other wing. I discovered there a wonderful library, dating largely from the sixteenth and seventeenth centuries. Large, fat folio volumes bound in pigskin stood along the walls. Among them were a number of books embellished with copper engravings of a strange character, and illustrations containing curious symbols such as I had never seen before. At the time I did not know to what they referred; only much later did I recognize them as alchemical symbols. In the dream I was conscious only of the fascination exerted by them and by the entire library. It was a collection of incunabula and sixteenth-century prints.

"The unknown wing of the house was a part of my personality, an aspect of myself; it represented something that belonged to me but of which I was not yet conscious. It, and especially the library, referred to alchemy of which I was ignorant, but which I was soon to study. Some fifteen years later I had assembled a library very like the one in the dream." [8]

Thus Jung sees an unexplored wing of the house as an unknown part of himself and a symbol of an area of study with which he would become very absorbed in the future. In a similar way, attention to our dreams can help us understand not only unconscious issues concerning our current situation, but also clues about some future direction in our lives. At a time when I was feeling very stressed as a full-time academic and single parent of two energetic children, I had the following dream. There was a house—a large, stately English home—open to the public to traipse through. But on this day, it was temporarily closed; visitors were reading the notice and turning away disappointed. I was in the basement of the house, sorting through some oil paintings to see if there was anything there of value. This dream seemed to be telling me it was time to "close up shop," to take a break from all the outside busyness I was experiencing. I needed to spend time sorting through images from my unconscious (the basement) to see what was of value in guiding my future. Several people I interviewed reported having repetitive dreams of their own house with "new" rooms they hadn't seen before. Exploration of these rooms may offer clues to a new direction in life, or nurturing a part of the self that has been overlooked or ignored.

The Objects in Our Lives

In 1890, in an early discussion of the concept of self, William James remarked: "It is clear that between what a man calls *me* and what he simply calls *mine* the line is difficult to draw. We feel and act about certain things that are ours very much as we feel and act about ourselves."[9]

How we act and feel when those "certain things that are ours" are absent is especially telling. A lawyer who lived in Japan for two years remarked, "I was constantly learning that I could (indeed, had to) peel off layers of myself in order to get by in a foreign culture. As the time progressed, I discarded what I habitually ate, wore, read, studied, drank, talked about, thought about, and usually did in almost any given circumstance. Each time one of those layers had to be discarded, there was a tremendous fear of Will I survive this? I was afraid that the central core of my identity would be lost if I let go of this or that layer. Each time it was a surprise to discover that I was still me."[10]

How we feel and act toward *collections* of objects in our homes may be especially telling. When Freud moved from Vienna to England just before World War II, it is said that the transition was made much easier by the safe transfer of his collection of more than two thousand antiquities. Surrounded by his beloved statuettes, he adjusted more easily to living in a foreign land. Freud himself admitted that he had directed his surplus libido onto the inanimate objects and that his collecting activity was an addiction second in intensity only to his nicotine addiction.

Those who have studied avid collectors suggest that some are people whose attachment to possessions symbolizes a detachment from human relations. The children and spouses of such collectors are often reluctant to inherit these collections, which they see as successful rivals for the affection of the collector. A psychiatrist who has treated a number of art collectors reports: "To a man [*sic*] they report that they usually know immediately whether or not a piece really appeals to them and whether they want to possess it. They often compare their feeling of longing for it to sexual desire. This suggests that art objects are confused in the unconscious with ordinary sexual objects . . . many collectors like to fondle or stroke the objects they own or to look at them over and over from every angle."[11]

This quote suggests the extreme degree to which attachment to objects can go. At the other end of the continuum are those who possess very little or whose attachment to those few precious things suggests a healthy nurturing of self-identity. In the movie *Empire of the Sun,* the author Jim Ballard recounts the true story of his boyhood in a Japanese prisoner-of-war camp. Each time he is moved, he pins up a few precious pictures beside his bed, as if to express his appropriation of that meager space as home. In her autobiography, *Blackberry Winter,* Margaret

Mead recounts frequent childhood travels with her parents and how, each night before retiring, she placed a few precious possessions around her bunk in the railroad sleeping compartment to help her feel "at home."

Objects as Connection to Significant People in Our Lives

While the significant people—friends, family, relatives—in our lives are perceived as, in some sense, extensions of self, it should come as no surprise to find that objects associated with those significant others are especially meaningful. Barbara, a graduate student in psychology, had strong feelings about her possessions, particularly those associated with other people in her life:

"That little chest with the missing drawer was in my brother's room. I've had it for twenty-six years. That's a long time for somebody who's only thirty, you know? The piece of material on top is from my mother. That box that says *Rio* on the sides was made for me by my ex-husband, and that's one of his parrots doing a push-up on top of the refrigerator. There's a lot of things that my friends have done for me. Like that painting in the other room. Everything really means something; and at the same time I think it's not such a good thing to be that attached, because they're just material things. What would happen if there was a fire? All this stuff would be gone. I'd have to get over it somehow. I feel like I'm too attached, that I somehow have projected too much of myself onto the house, that I wouldn't be me without it. But part of me feels that when the time comes, I can get unattached. Right now, it feels like this part of my life should be about making a home. I keep thinking of *Harold and Maude.* Did you see that movie? Maude's train car, now that to me is a house! Everything in that place had either been invented by her or given to her by somebody or, you know, really meant something to her. That's what a house should be."

Unless we stop and consciously reflect upon it, most of us are scarcely aware of how much our homes, as well as being functional settings for daily life, are containers for collections of memorabilia. Objects, pictures, furniture, posters, ornaments—all remind us of significant people, places, phases, experiences, and values in our lives. As G. McCracken explains: "Surrounded by our things, we are constantly instructed in who we are and what we aspire to. Surrounded by our things, we are rooted in and visually continuous with our pasts. Surrounded by our things, we are sheltered from the many forces that would deflect us into new concepts, practices, and experiences. Things are our ballast."[12]

The memoirs and journals of contemporary writer May Sarton convey much about the power of home-making to connect us with the past and to bring some balance into a life poised, as hers was, between the old world and the new. Sarton's parents were immigrants—her mother English, her father Belgian. They had lived in the Sarton family home in Belgium—"Wondelgem"—before migrating to Boston. Sarton recalls the magic that that house evoked both for her mother and herself:

"'Wondelgem,' the name itself sounded like magic to me as a child. It was quite literally in another world, since I did not remember it myself . . . a little girl who, in Cambridge, Massachusetts, heard the peculiar tenderness the word evoked in my mother's voice, as if the walls of the tiny apartment where we lived opened out at its sound into a great garden, into a still airy house with roses climbing all over it, and inside, the walls covered with books."[13]

As a seven year old—after the First World War—Sarton visited this magical house of memory with her parents. Here is how she wrote of that visit, many years later: "Like a dream this journey had no beginning. We were there at the gate. . . . At first, my mother and father must have felt their life together violated, trampled down. . . . The dream, so beautiful and mysterious while we stood outside, had turned into a nightmare. . . . But just then my mother cried out, 'Look, George!' She had lifted out of a pile of rubbish a single Venetian glass on a long delicate stem, so dirty it had become opaque, but miraculously intact. How had this single fragile object survived to give us courage? It went back with us to Cambridge and it was always there, wherever we lived. And now it is here, in my own house, a visible proof that it is sometimes the most fragile things that have the power to endure, and become sources of strength, like my mother."[14]

Research on valued possessions indicates that with age, we tend to increasingly value objects that evoke the past; that immigrants tend to value objects that remind them of home; and that women are more likely than men to value objects that symbolize social or emotional connections. The following entry in my own journal, reflecting on significant objects in my house, suggests that I run true to form—as a middle-aged person, an immigrant to the United States, and a woman:

"It all started at the Oakland Museum. The film and exhibit, 'Quilts in Women's Lives,' was so extraordinarily powerful I could barely stay to look at every piece. Wedding quilts, children's quilts, mourning quilts; covers for the bed in which the most significant events of our lives take place: birth, consummation of marriage, conception, illness, death. The bed as an ordering principle in space.

"I returned home, painfully aware that there is nothing I have done to compare with these patient and lovingly wrought creations. Even if I had the skills to make a quilt—where would I find the time to do such work? But as I looked around my house, I realized there are small artifacts of creativity—my own and others'—recording the events and passages of my life.

"Over the front door, a stained-glass window I designed and made to assuage my grief at the end of my marriage. Four trees, two large and two small—Stephen, Clare, Jason, and Lucy. And over all—a bird . . . of hope? Of reconciliation? The dove of peace? We *are* still a family, even though we're not all living together. The window marks a rite of passage, a reconciliation with life as it flows.

"I look around and realize how much my house is decorated with objects bought or found on special trips . . . masks from New Guinea, where Stephen and I had a great adventure and Lucy was conceived. Bird figures bought on the mesa at Acoma, a reclining woman from Malta, an Eskimo figure from Canada.

"Not just the objects of the house, but the very furniture marks passages of moment. Significant events of choice and purchase. The rocking chair we bought at a flea market and Stephen carried home on his head. It was painted red, and as I stripped it to the bare wood, a stream of 'blood' ran down the summer driveway. The sectional sofa first sat upon in Florence's New England mansion, and then selected on the fourth floor of Sloane's with Wendy as chief adviser. The wildflower curtains purchased in London; the cloisonné vase from Beijing; the poster from the British Museum.

"So many memories of England. Could I ever forget? The downstairs bathroom is a veritable feast of memorabilia: the oil painting by my mother of the view over our London garden; the antique print of Liverpool; the poster of wildflowers, so familiar from my chalkland childhood; the poster of British sheep breeds, purchased at a remote agricultural fair on the island of Mull. We impose our values and our memories on our children, not just through what we say and do, but via the objects we place around for them to see. No wonder eventually they have to leave home."

HOME AND SELF-EXPRESSION: EXERCISES YOU CAN DO YOURSELF

What Home Really Means to You

Try this exercise if you'd like to explore what your home really means to you, how it feels to you, or what it might be communicating to you at a deeper level than design, decor, or location.

Sit down at a table where you can work uninterrupted for a while. Have your drawing pad and felt pens or crayons ready. Close your eyes; tense any muscles that feel taut—and then let them fully relax. Take some long, deep breaths.

When you feel centered and relaxed, open your eyes and put down a symbol of what your home means to you. Start with whatever core image comes to mind—it might be a heart, an oasis, or a box. Put this in the center of the page, and then continue with whatever other images, colors, shapes, or words emerge. Don't censor yourself! Be sure to have plenty of colors available; the shades you choose—warm, cool, somber, vibrant—may say as much about your inner feelings as the shapes and words you put down.

Notice if any other homes or dwellings flash through your mind as you do this—a grandparent's house of long ago, a current neighbor's home, a childhood place. Note which room or image or shape or word seemed to trigger that memory.

Be aware of any sensations in your body as you do this. Are you conscious of any feelings of warmth or sadness, any sensation of relaxation or tension? You might try asking your body what it is trying to tell you.

When you have put down on paper all that you feel you want to, prop this picture on a chair or cushion and sit three or four feet away—the distance you would comfortably sit when talking with a friend. Imagining that this picture—this house or apartment—is your good friend, start to tell it how you feel. You might start the dialogue with, "House, the way I feel about you is . . ." and then see what happens.

(You might want to tape-record what you say and listen to it again—later—in a more objective or analytical mood.)

When you feel ready, when you sense that you have said all that comes to mind at this moment, switch places and "become" the house. It helps if you actually get up and sit in the other chair and put the picture to one side. Remembering what you said when talking to the house, what does it have to say back to you? Don't censor anything; you may be surprised what it has to tell you!

If images of other houses or people or objects come to mind, you might try bringing them into the conversation. Perhaps it is a window seat in a friend's house which seems to say: Give yourself a time and place to relax, to observe the world from a safe and comfortable place. Perhaps it is the attic in your own house which seems to say: Come and explore me! I am your creative potential which you have ignored.

You can be sure that any image or salient connection that emerges has surfaced for a reason and, like images in dreams, will yield its message if encouraged to do so. Have a conversation with the attic, or the window seat, or the table: Address it as "you," and let it respond to you in the first person.

Continue these dialogues with house, objects, images, rooms, or people until you feel done. Don't be surprised if you feel tired; meeting ourselves, especially those parts that we have buried, can be draining. It is generally true to say that the unconscious releases into consciousness only what we are able to deal with at the time. As you continue over time to explore all that your home means to you, you might want to repeat this exercise. Don't be surprised if new issues come up; it may be that you are now ready to deal with them. And if some image or emotion repeats itself, it may be your unconscious nudging you—as in a recurring dream—to pay attention to some aspect of your relationship with home which is still unacknowledged or unresolved.

If you feel more comfortable writing than speaking out loud, you might try an uncensored dialogue with your home in your journal or notebook. Starting by addressing your house as "you," ask it the following questions: Who are you? Do you have a name? How do you like being in this particular location? What do you feel about me/us living in you? What is it that you can give to us? Is there something we can do for you? Do you feel loved? Do I feel loved and protected by you? What is it that you communicate about me? What is in store for you in the future?

In recording this dialogue, try to write as fast as you can, not listening to your internal censor, who might want you to say what *it* feels is appropriate. By writing fast and not bothering about punctuation, spelling, and so on, you can hopefully bypass your rational mind and express yourself intuitively. Our intuition is often wiser than our reasoning intellect.

Values Inventory

This exercise was inspired by reading a master's thesis in psychology by Carolyn Verheyen.[15] One way you might "use" your house to understand more deeply what you value, what really matters to you, is to look at all its visible material contents and try to categorize them in terms of what they mean to you. What we place in and around our home are material expressions of our identity, self-disclosure in a safe and private environment. Here are the categories I found when I did the exercise: close relationship with nature (plants, shells, pine cones, and rocks; and watercolors, photos, calendars, and lithographs of trees and landscapes); cultural identity with England (posters, calendars); environmental concerns (books, magazines); appreciation for extended family (photographs); concern for healthy diet (cookbooks, vitamins, vegetable garden, compost heap); spiritual concerns (books, meditation table); writing as prime creative outlet (piles of papers, books in progress, files, stationery); appreciation for informal socializing (eat-in kitchen, small seating cluster around the fireplace, absence of formal dining or living room); enjoyment of outdoors (seating on deck, on front porch, on shaded patio); and appreciation for warmth and coziness expressed through fabrics (drapes, carpets, furniture, cushions, afghans).

In doing this exercise, you may be surprised to find a cluster of objects whose meaning you hadn't been conscious of before; before I did this, I wasn't so aware of how all the art I had purchased, with few exceptions, was of trees or landscapes. Perhaps this relates to my close connectedness to the outdoors in childhood, or my professional role as a teacher in a department of landscape architecture, or my yearning to reconnect with the natural environment as a symbol of interconnectedness with all matter. Perhaps the pictures are related to all three. Whatever the significance, a reflection on specifically how you express your values in your home environment is a worthwhile experience.

FOUR

Always or Never Leaving Home

I got up on my knees on the carriage seat, and leaned far out so that the wind blew the hair from my face. We had always done this in the past when the train took that corner into the valley and we yearned to see again the green arc of the paddocks and the familiar red roads, the roof of our grandmother's house crowned by umbrella trees, and, there on the other hill, Fleetwood's roof, with the bulk of the barn behind it.

"It's still the same," Helen said.

"How can it be so much the same when we are away from it? Doesn't our presence mean anything?"

—JOAN COLEBROOK, *A House of Trees: Memoirs of an Australian Girlhood*[1]

Do you remember the emotions you felt on the day you left home for college, the service, your first job, or a move to another city? Are you someone for whom the thought of leaving home for a vacation or getting rid of possessions arouses feelings akin to panic, or does the very idea of "settling down" fill you with apprehension?

In the previous two chapters, we considered memories from childhood that are echoed in later years and how an emerging sense of self is expressed in homes of adulthood. Here, we will look at several people who have to a greater or lesser extent become "stuck" in terms of their relationship to home.

Though rarely recognized or discussed, our attitudes toward home, dwelling location, interior decor, self-expression in the environment, and so on are frequently closely linked to those of our parents. Either we mirror what we saw and experienced in our childhood home, or we react strongly against it. Our behavior may be as obvious as loving and collecting antiques because our mother did the same, or as subtle as a resistance to sweeping the front porch because it was an obsession of an authoritarian father. Although a critical component of our emotional growth is to separate from our parents and become unique, mature, self-reliant adults, so too is it necessary for us to break away from any patterns of relating to house and home that seem to trap us in childhood, creating serious obstacles to our psychological growth. The stories that follow illustrate some of the dramatic consequences in adult life of always—or never—leaving home.

Possessions as "Family": Claudia's Holding on to "Stuff"

Agoraphobia—literally, "fear of the marketplace"—is a well-documented psychological problem experienced predominantly by women. Discussions of its symptoms and possible treatment tend to revolve around the place feared—supermarket, department store, shopping center—whereas less attention is directed at the place clung to—house, apartment, room. My conversations with people about their homes reveal that some people experience not so much a fear of what is outside the home, but a desperate clinging to what is inside. I have dubbed this phenomenon *domocentrism.* People who are domocentric are so profoundly connected to their house that this relationship has become both a substitute for, and a barrier to, close relationships with other people. In other words, their dwelling and its contents have become such compelling psychological defenses that they appear to interfere with interpersonal relations and with a deeper connection to a person's transpersonal or spiritual self.

Claudia is a middle-aged artist living in a university town. I had noticed her house long before a mutual friend introduced us. There always seemed to be building work going on: At one point, a whole new floor was added, plus a new roof and conspicuous solar panels. It seemed to be bursting at the seams, out of scale with its lot and with the dwellings around it.

That expression seemed particularly apt when I visited Claudia for the first time. Here was an immensely full and cluttered house. Rooms led off rooms with their functions unclear. Each was full of books, with piles of papers, objects, bottles, clothes, bills, records, tapes, and newspapers on every available surface. There were dollhouses and furniture and a collection of old ceramics behind glass. Fishing nets and ferns were draped over windows. Carved wooden mirrors and old photos adorned the walls. There were stuffed animals on the bed, dying flowers in a pewter mug, and the lingering smell of incense. Things were stored in bottles; there were animal collections on shelves, vacuum cleaners, baskets of kitchen utensils.

I had rarely seen a house with so much stuff in it; there was barely room to move. It seemed like the home of a recluse. As it turned out, Claudia was not reclusive, but someone obsessed with holding on to stuff, a hoarder par excellence. Her house was bursting with the possessions of not only her own accumulation of forty years, but also those inherited from her mother and grandmother. She rented rooms to students and built storage compartments in the basement for their "stuff." She hoped that her son would inherit her love of family heirlooms and hold on to them in the same way.

Lest it seem that I am making some kind of judgment about Claudia, let me say that I too am a hoarder: I felt sympathy for her plight of not being able to throw things away, to sort things out, to make decisions about what to keep. But what perhaps made Claudia an extreme case was the degree of clutteredness in which she lived, rendering every room like a storeroom, and—worst of all—leaving her studio so piled up with stuff that she had not been able to paint, her chosen medium, for many years. Ironically, she had named this room "Mendocino," after the picturesque town on the northern California coast where many artists live. Not only did she not live in the actual community of Mendocino, she could not even enter the room in her house that she named after it. Her creative life was at a standstill, her emotional life appeared to be "on hold," her health was not good, and her eyesight was giving her trouble. In short, Claudia seemed to be in a state of material, psychological, and physical paralysis.

Why had Claudia put herself in this position? She spoke of the house itself as "a friend and, better than most friends, always there, always available, nonjudgmental." It was significant that after speaking in this vein, she immediately switched to listing the significant people in her life who were no longer around. "I don't want to leave this house. It's all the security I've got. I mean, my parents are dead, my grandparents are dead, my husband—I wouldn't want him back even if he were available. My brother has gone kind of 'funny' on me. My daughter . . . it's shaky with her too. I could get plenty from my son, but I don't want to overburden him. Except for him, there's no one who really gives the way my house does. I figure to die in this house; you know . . . that's what I have in mind."

When I asked Claudia if she could make a picture of her feelings about her house, she produced a beautiful rendering of the interior of one of her rooms. In vibrant colors, it depicted some of her treasured possessions—stuffed animals, stereo, record collection—and herself, crouching beneath the luscious leaves of a large potted plant. It seemed to depict a person hiding—indeed, I did not even see Claudia in the picture until she pointed herself out!

"Yes, that's me! I'm just sitting there taking in energy from all my things. I'm really very involved with things. I just love them. I don't like to go out and buy them; I like to find them or inherit them. I get a lot of energy from my things when they're not dragging me down by being out of order and cluttering me, which is what they're doing now. After my mother died, the whole downstairs of this house and half the upstairs was piled to the ceiling with cartons—all kinds of nice trash. I've gone through this while dealing with all kinds of financial crises. Actually, I think I've done rather well. There's nobody around tooting my horn for me, so I have to say that myself. But when I just sit and see this last hard-core garbage that won't go away and more of it coming in the mail every day, I get discouraged."

When asked what these things meant to her, Claudia responded: "All these things represent different times. Pictures that belong to different people—my mother, or things belonging to my grandmother. This big blowup of a tintype of

In Claudia's depiction of her home, she crouched behind a large houseplant.

my great grandfather and a daguerreotype of my great, great, great grandfather. These are both black grandfathers, and I am trying to find out more about them and make their pictures a little larger. When I feel spaced out on anything, I've got the family artifacts around to rub and touch and sort of, you know, find out where I am. When I feel these things, there's a feeling that my family, my grandmother, my great grandmother, that the family is still here. My mother had tons and tons of stuff and she had a tiny little apartment. And I feel that it's my place to keep it because my grandmother saved all these things. We have things that go back to the Revolutionary War, because people in my family saved them. I think my son would like to avoid what I've done—letting things engulf him the way they've been engulfing me—he seems to be able to resist better than I can."

This was a woman with many identities—the dutiful child, the protective mother, the artist, the forsaken wife, the landlady—and a host of multifunctional, chaotic rooms that seemed like metaphors for her inner confusion. As she constantly remodeled, furnished, changed, and organized these spaces in her bursting-at-the-seams house, she was clearly also working on problems from the past that were not resolved within her. As she stated, the house and herself were so much intertwined, she often forgot which was which. She had put so much physical and psychic energy into her house that it appeared to have drained her. She hadn't painted for four years; she had little space or energy left for an intimate human relationship.

Perhaps Claudia's need to acquire, store, and care for "stuff" represented a frustrated need to nurture and protect. It also symbolized a profound need to remain physically connected to her family of origin. Touching, even caressing, the objects inherited from her mother enabled her to feel closer to her and left her feeling that her mother would be well pleased. And yet one senses that these same things that gave her a sense of rootedness and connection with the past had also become a trap. They sapped her strength and were constant physical reminders of living in some kind of material and emotional quagmire.

As people approach old age and death, they live increasingly in a world of memory and reminiscence. As physiological deterioration restricts mobility, older people may experience emotional nurturance through surrounding themselves with objects that evoke memories of people and places of the past. But Claudia was not old. At the time of our conversation she was—perhaps—in her midforties. The fact that Claudia cherished—but was also burdened by—so many possessions might be indicative of an inability to acknowledge her own individual separateness—from mother, from husband, from children. The furniture and mementos that were piled in every room were physical metaphors of past relationships that she could not acknowledge as being completed. In her picture, she was an insignificant crouching figure, "gaining energy from my plants," she stated, though it seemed also to be a portrait of someone dwarfed into insignificance by her physical environment. A year after this dialogue, I drove past Claudia's house: A large mural painting had been added to a prominent exterior wall. It was of an apt symbol—a squirrel.

Although Claudia represents a somewhat extreme case, many of us may recognize a glimmer of our own behavior in her relationship to stuff. We each have to find a healthy balance between holding on to or excessively rejecting symbols of our family of origin. Observing Claudia's cluttered home, I found myself slightly uncomfortable. Images of my own stuffed closets, attic, storeroom, and dining room–office flashed through my mind.

I grew up in a time of shortages. In wartime England, many foodstuffs were rationed, as were clothes, coal for the fireplace, gasoline for cars, even feed for domestic chickens and rabbits. During those years, my elder brother and I would venture forth on weekends in the fall and winter to scavenge for firewood. We always found plenty to load onto our wagon, haul home, and stack neatly in the cellar of our house. Though I doubt that I reflected on it much at the time, I think it must have given me great pleasure to contribute, at eight and nine years old, to keeping the family warm. I still continue to scavenge today. Noticing a tree being felled in my neighborhood and hearing the whine of a chain saw, I stop my car to ask if I may take some wood home—much to the embarrassment of my children: "Oh, no, Mom—not again. We've got *so* much firewood." And I am proud of the fact that in the twenty years I've had a house with a fireplace, I have never purchased firewood.

Amassing logs is one thing, but hoarding clothes, boxes, string, plastic bags, wrapping paper, and all kinds of other stuff is another. I try to keep it all stashed away, and my daughter encourages me to dispose of it at her periodic garage sales, but it's difficult for me. Habits die hard. In my childhood we saved, repaired, and reused everything. When self-conscious "recycling" became the thing to do, I couldn't help smiling to myself, thinking of a time when such behavior was so necessary, pervasive, and unquestioned, we didn't even have a name for it. In most nations of the world, outside of the developed, industrial West, such careful use or reuse of materials is still taken for granted. I am a bit of an anomaly in a wealthy nation, but as I talk with people who grew up during the Depression, I find I am by no means alone in my compulsion to keep, store, and reuse things.

While writing this chapter, I passed a neighbor's house. A neat stack of logs on the front lawn had a sign propped against them: "Free firewood." I hurried home and pleaded with my daughter, Lucy, to help me carry the wood to our log-store.

She knew better than to try to dissuade me. But later that week, after a big garage sale in which two-thirds of our stuff failed to move, she stashed it into big plastic bags and called the Salvation Army. Before I had a chance to go through it "just one more time," it was gone. When you're an inveterate pack rat, it's good to have someone like Lucy in your family.

Alone in the Empty Nest: Larry's Bonds to His House

British psychologist Donald Winnicott, having studied patterns of emotional growth in early childhood, found that it is a normal pattern of development to move from an exclusive connection to one's mother to an emotional attachment to a "transitional object," such as a favorite stuffed animal or a well-worn blanket.[2] Gradually, and unconsciously, we move our emotional focus from mother to our toy or blanket, to friends, and, eventually, to a lover, partner, or spouse. However, some people get sidetracked; emotional connections to possessions or home take the place of close relationships to people. Whereas Claudia appears to have replaced her family of origin with inherited objects, Larry has projected his desire for a family connection onto his house itself.

Larry is a lawyer—successful, charming, impeccably dressed. He lives in an elegant stucco house in an upscale district of San Francisco. We met one day, professionally, and he asked me what I was doing. I chatted informally about my book, and he became quite intrigued. "Oh, well, you should certainly interview me," he said, laughing. "I live in a house that is so important to me, I'll never leave it except in a box. My second wife hates it, but I don't care. I can always find another wife; I'll never find another house!" We both laughed. This was someone I wanted to talk with.

A few weeks later, I went to his house. Larry protested that he couldn't draw, but nevertheless put down a fairly accurate picture of the house facade. Then he drew long roots connecting the house to the soil beneath, as if it were a plant. He seemed to free-associate to a lot of words, which he listed beside the house: *roots, prestige, solidarity, permanence.* Finally, beneath it all, he wrote: *Like Dorothy says: "There's no place like HOME."*

Larry's connectedness to his house had long roots into the past and was very tied up with his connection to a much-loved grandfather, now deceased.

Larry was
closely
bonded to
his San
Francisco
home.

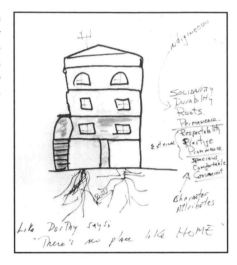

This grandfather had arrived in the United States as a penniless immigrant from central Europe at the turn of the century. Picking up scrap metal in the streets and vacant lots of a major eastern city, he had started his own salvaging business. By the time Larry was a young boy, his grandfather was a wealthy man, a captain of industry, and the owner of a large mansion in the best part of town. It was to this house that Larry and his family went for special meals, religious festivals, weddings, and funerals. Gradually, his grandparent's house came to symbolize stability, rootedness, success, and prestige, and Larry began to identify these as supremely important values.

As a child, Larry moved with his parents a number of times among cities on the East Coast. His father's jobs and absence in the service during World War II caused several more moves among Pittsburgh, New York, and Washington, DC. They always lived in rented apartments. Larry found these moves very painful and determined that his children wouldn't suffer the same experience.

When Larry's grandfather died and left him a considerable sum of money, Larry and his wife—recently moved to California—searched for a house that they both liked. They found a solid stucco house abutting straight onto the sidewalk in the front and overlooking a park at the back. This pleased Larry particularly; the front of the house and its lack of a lawn or garden reminded him of the New York townhouses where wealthier relatives lived; the view from the back reminded him of the grounds around his grandfather's mansion. Here, Larry and his wife raised their three children and held many family events and celebrations. Larry grew very attached to the house. Several times during our conversation he used the word "bonded." He was relieved when, at the time of his divorce, his wife chose to move out and leave him the house.

There were other reasons for Larry's determination to keep the house. At the time of his grandfather's death, the family gave his mansion to a local university as a home for the president. Some years later—to the dismay of the whole family and without informing them—the university sold the property and the house was demolished. Thirty-eight townhouses now stand on the property. Because of this, Larry was even more determined to hold on to his house and leave it and its contents to his children.

Larry remarried, and the house, furnished largely with antiques from Larry's grandfather, soon became an issue between him and his second wife. His wife dubbed it "The Museum" and found it hard to satisfy her own nesting instincts within it. For a period of time, they lived separately for part of each week, he in "The Museum" and she in a country cottage a half hour's drive from the city. Larry occasionally referred to his house, jokingly, as his "mistress." His wife experienced it as a barrier between them.

The first time I talked with Larry was in 1978, during his second marriage. Ten years later, we talked again. He was now living alone in the house; his second wife and he had divorced. His children were urging him to sell the house and move to a smaller place. "I'm rattling around in the empty nest," he joked. "Thirteen rooms is too much space for a single man, but this is where I want to be. I'm bonded to this house." Larry felt it was his only security in a life of many changes. His second drawing of how he felt about the house was remarkably like the first: He drew a sketch of the exterior and wrote the words *Security Blanket, Sea of Changes,* and *Tara—The Old Family Homestead.* He enjoyed entertaining houseguests and putting on large family dinners when his grown children visited. He had a large collection of videos and joked that with food in the freezer, he didn't have to leave the house for days on end. He enjoyed maintaining the house and adding a particular amenity each year. He had just had a satellite dish installed.

Larry hoped to one day marry again, but didn't expect that to be likely: "She'd have to move in here—under my roof, on my terms—and there aren't many women who'd want to do that." Clearly, Larry had chosen the security of a familiar home over a committed relationship. "This house is permanent—forever," he said several times. "Relationships are ephemeral." The evidence of Larry's life and relationships supports that statement; ironically, it is the house itself and his bonding to it that seemed to form the major impediment to a permanent human relationship within the house.

Almost as asides, Larry mentioned two instances in his family when—as he saw it—men had ill-advisedly "caved in" to the wishes of the women in their lives. An uncle (the only son of Larry's much-loved grandfather) had recently remarried and, at the request of his wife, had sold his large, elegant home in a resort to move to a smaller place they could mold together into a home. "I think he was crazy—I would never do that." Larry's own father, now very old, had just agreed to the sale of his home of thirty years to move to an apartment with his second wife. Though they had lived together happily in the house for ten years, it was becoming too much for them to manage. Larry's comment reflected, perhaps, what he felt would happen to him in such a situation: "I think this move will cause my father to die; I don't approve of it at all, but I don't have much to say in the matter. He'll do anything to please his wife; he's very dependent on her. My grandfather—he was different. He had his house built, lived in it for twenty-five years, and his wife went along with anything he wanted."

When I asked Larry about his work, he flashed a wry smile and said he was semiretired. His inherited wealth has allowed him the freedom to dip in and out of his profession and to avoid taking risks in his work life. He apparently felt little satisfaction from his career. Unlike many people who chose their work as a statement of who they are, Larry had chosen his house. Despite the fact that six thousand square feet was far more space than he needed, and that the house has accrued in value from $100,000 in 1964 to $1.4 million in 1989, Larry needed the security of his familiar nest far more than he needed the money that he would receive from its sale.

As I left, Larry remarked that he was now indulging in what fascinated him most—the history of railroad stations. He had written several monographs on the subject and was now working on a book on the conversion of city stations to other uses. It seemed ironic, given his profound attachment to permanence in the form of his home of twenty-five years, that Larry's creative outlet focused on buildings that exemplify the beginnings and ends of a journey.

Excessive Bonding to Home

British psychoanalyst Michael Balint, after considerable clinical work, has proposed that each of us—to a greater or lesser degree—falls into one of two categories with regard to our relationship to the world around us. The first type, for which Balint coined the term *philobat,* is a person who enjoys innovation and ambiguity, who seeks out activities involving a temporary loss of equilibrium (skiing, sailing, climbing, roller-coaster rides), and for whom objects—both human and physical—may sometimes be seen to be getting in the way. The *ocnophil,* on the other hand, clings to familiarity and to secure places and people, shuns unpredictable or thrill-seeking experiences, and cherishes objects, both human and physical.

"Accordingly the ocnophilic world consists of objects, separated by horrid empty spaces," writes Balint. "The ocnophilic individual lives from object to object, cutting his sojourns in the empty spaces as short as possible. Fear is provoked by leaving the objects, and allayed by rejoining them. . . . The ocnophil is confident that his chosen object will 'click in' with him and protect him against the empty, unfamiliar, and possibly dangerous world . . . For the philobat, the whole world is quite different . . . [it] consists of friendly expanses dotted more or less densely with dangerous and unpredictable objects . . . The philobatic world is structured by safe distance and sight. This need to watch is a true counterpart of the ocnophil's compelling need to touch."[3]

Balint suggests that the extreme ocnophil is perhaps replaying an earlier state of primary love: As objects represent the safe, good mother, "empty spaces" represent where mother isn't. This may help to explain Claudia's, Larry's, and many other people's attitudes toward cherished household objects and to the house itself. Ocnophils tend to project themselves onto an object and feel that they themselves are now as safely "held" as they can hold on to the object.

Faced with loss of the primary love object, usually the mother, "the ocnophil deals with the traumatic situation by autoplastic means, i.e., he changes himself; instead of being held, he holds. . . . The major trauma was the painful discovery of the independent existence of important objects. The first reaction is denial, the object is not independent; by clinging the ocnophil can reassure himself that he and his object are still one, inseparable."[4]

From many words and phrases that resounded in my conversations with Claudia and Larry, and others like them, this seemed to be the case. Objects, family heirlooms, furniture, and the house itself are perceived as somehow more reliable than relationships with people. They are always there, dependable. For these people, objects or houses don't let you down.

Domophobia: Always Leaving Home

Whereas becoming excessively bonded to home and possessions represents one end of a continuum, at the other end are people who find it extremely difficult to stay in any one place long enough to feel "at home." For such individuals, having a permanent abode is fraught with too many unresolved emotional issues from childhood. They are, to a greater or lesser degree, domophobic.

For these people, memories of being at home in childhood are largely painful. Home may have been the scene of abuse, or marital tensions, or feeling oppressed by a dominant sibling or parent. In terms of Balint's theory of how people relate to the world around them, these individuals would be termed philobats, those for whom objects—human and physical—are sometimes perceived as impediments. The philobat, in Balint's opinion, may be stuck in an emotional state in which security is not recalled as "mother" (projected onto home, objects, people), but rather is represented by the amniotic fluid in the womb, or even a phylogenetic memory of living in the ocean. The philobat feels secure in "friendly expanses," where objects (home, people) do not get in the way. I have talked with numbers of people who—to varying degrees—are always on the move or fearful of settling down. They experience discomfort or anxiety at the thought of spending time in the home or having a permanent address. The stories of Rosita and Robert represent those people for whom being "at home" is—to say the least—problematic.

I first met Rosita in Scotland, where we were both living in an alternative community near the village of Findhorn. She had heard me speak of my work at an informal evening lecture and approached me shyly a few days later while I worked in the garden. She asked if I could talk with her about the mobile home where she lived with her teenaged son, Sean. She described how on returning to it she would feel good until she opened the door. "Then I feel very bad . . . sort of an empty feeling . . . like I'm an alien. I feel I don't belong in this space; it feels like a motel."

As Rosita put down her feelings about her dwelling in a picture, she depicted her own bedroom and the bathroom as positive spaces of privacy and reflection for herself; likewise, Sean's bedroom and study were similarly private and positive spaces for him. But the spaces that they shared—porch, living room, and kitchen—aroused ambivalent emotions. During a recent illness, Sean had recuperated in the living room and had taken charge of the space; Rosita felt uncomfortable being there. In the kitchen, she was acutely aware that she didn't want to play the traditional role of mother, "making cookies and hot porridge." Interspersed with bouts of crying, she recalled her own childhood and the meaning of home, living room, and kitchen to her mother:

"When I was growing up, my family owned several houses and we moved almost every year. I never felt that I belonged [starts to cry]. When I was at boarding school, I had this feeling that my room was a special place where I could create my own little world, but then the nuns would always come in. They didn't even knock. So I could never really feel safe there. When I married, I dropped out of university and stayed home. I was trying to be a housewife, but I never could cope with the house. I tried to read those women's magazines, but I never seemed able to carry out those things. What I liked best was when, after my divorce, Sean and I were just moving around. We would have the cheapest places we could get; he would have his room and I would have my room. We never needed anything else. Since we moved here, I have just not known how to use the living room. For a long time, it was just unlived in. That was one reason I got a television. I was thinking that maybe he and I would be sitting there together and watch television. When he was sick, that's where he lived, and now it feels like it's his territory, not mine."

When asked about the living rooms of houses she had lived in as a child, Rosita said: "At the house where we lived in England, the living room was full of my mother's antiques. And then at my grandmother's house, there was a very elegant drawing room; we only went in there to have tea. There was another house we had in Australia, where we could go into the living room. In fact, it's the house we had the longest. I have very good memories of that. We had a huge old fireplace, and there was a piano. I was attached to that house, but afterwards I couldn't be attached to anyplace again. The difference was that my mother wasn't there. My parents were both very restless, very unhappy with each other, so they just moved around. They couldn't really separate; they were Catholic.

"I went to so many schools. I spent quite a lot of time on ships too. During all that shuffle in a period around puberty, I got very distressed. What was difficult was always saying good-bye to places and people. It would take me about a year to make a friend, to really get a good friend, and then it would be time to say good-bye. So I learned a lot about detachment. Interestingly enough, I continued the same pattern with Sean. In fact, I accelerated the pattern. We moved frequently. I didn't want to make a home. We lived alone. We lived in group houses. We sort of lived out of cardboard boxes. Sean has happy memories of his childhood, he tells me, when we were on the road; that was probably affected by me, because I was very happy then. It's funny. It goes both ways. The kind of childhood I had was like one adventure after another. It was tremendously exciting to wake up onboard a ship. I was always special at boarding school; my mother would ring up and say, 'I want you to leave this weekend.' Everybody else would have to stay at school. We would pack our bag and we would get on a train. . . . We weren't like ordinary people! Even now, my mother is continually on the move. She has a house in London where she sort of pops in. She can stand about a week before she takes off again.

"She's got friends all over the world, and she will go from one to another. It is a neurotic pattern. She has been speeding it up. She has been going to a lot more places a lot faster, and I feel she is really afraid that she will get some health problem that will make her stay in one place. Her current house—she feels it's too much for her, and that she can't clean it all and control it. I feel that too. Gosh, I never realized that we were so similar. Amazing! Ugh! I mean, there I was with Sean, roaming around, determined I wasn't going to be like my mother, without realizing I was just repeating it all!"

I directed Rosita's attention back to the picture and pointed out that in the space labeled *kitchen,* she had written the words *distress, ice cubes,* and *feel some anxiety about being in this room.* Rosita gave a long sigh and then continued:

"I just have flashes of this kitchen at our home in Australia. It was very pretty [crying]. My mother was an interior decorator, and her houses always looked beautiful. There would be this lovely coloring in the kitchen. Very bright, unusual, visionary, kind of exciting, and yet it was just an awful place to be [laughs sadly]. It's all to do with how she felt about the kitchen. She absolutely hated the realm of cooking and dispensing food. At the same time, she felt that was her role, and she is an excellent cook. She kind of enjoys it and resents it at the same time. So there is all this ambivalence. She would wake us up at night to come and wash the dishes. There was a lot of neurotic behavior to do with the kitchen. I have my own brand of neurotic behavior; it's not the same as hers—I just hate anything to do with the kitchen. Why I really like living here in an alternative community is having somebody else cooking for me! A lot of my difficulties in the kitchen are over my role as a woman; Sean feels I'm not being a mother to him. He wants what we all want in a mother—a very nurturing sort of mother who will have steaming bowls of hot porridge ready, cookies coming out of the oven, and all that. I don't think I have ever made cookies in my life. And he resents this. Every so often I feel guilty about it."

I asked Rosita what she would name this home. Significantly, she couldn't settle on one name, but gave it two: her own bedroom she termed *"le nid"* (the nest); the remainder of the shared spaces she called "the motel," and added, "I'd like to take a big ax and chop this part off the house."

Rosita has, in some ways, lived a privileged life: She traveled, went to good schools, and came from a moderately wealthy family. Yet she has also inherited considerable emotional scars. In psychological terms, she may be acting out an intense need to bond with her distant, always-on-the-move mother by repeating her actions and, in particular, her attitudes toward rootedness and settling down. As often happens in such situations, unless we make a conscious effort to break the pattern, we, in turn, pass on the same messages to our children.

Many people experience tension in the home with their teenaged children. In Rosita's case, perhaps this difficulty was exacerbated by Sean's emerging masculinity, played out through territorial claims in the house. Rosita tried to fend off her son's territorial claims, assertive behavior, and loud music; while he, in turn, resented her need for quiet, private reflection. The physical places where they met—kitchen and living room—had become spaces of alienation and conflict. At the time of this conversation, it seemed that Rosita and her son had each overdeveloped one side of their personality—his, the assertive, macho male; hers, the shy, retiring female—at the expense of the other. The need to create more of a balance was initially brought home (no pun intended) to both mother and son by their incessant conflict over shared space.

Not long after this conversation, Rosita sold her mobile home. Her son moved into a small apartment of his own, and Rosita happily moved into a house with two other women and a small child. She rid herself of the burden of ownership, separated from her son who was now an adult, and found a soft retreat for herself in a warm and affectionate household where she had no responsibilities to organize, decorate, or maintain the dwelling. For the time being, she had settled down.

The conflicts personified in Rosita's relationship to her house were complex and intergenerational. If our personalities are in large measure shaped during childhood, it is not surprising to find that so too are our attitudes toward home. Rosita's mother was emotionally unable to settle down in one place and was deeply ambivalent about her role as the parent who prepared food. These same attitudes were being replayed by her daughter. Would Rosita ever "settle down"?

Three years later, I met her again. She was sharing a house in London with four other people and working as a freelance editor. The house was a very cheap rental because it was due to be demolished for a road-widening project within a year. Rosita had found yet another temporary home.

Always Leaving Home: Robert's Seeking Privacy Elsewhere

Robert was a young interior decorator living in a modest rustic house in an older suburb near San Francisco. He heard me speak about my work at the C. G. Jung Institute in San Francisco and phoned the next day to ask if he could talk with me. He had recently married for the second time. The house he and his wife lived in pleased neither of them.

Expressing his feelings about the house in a picture, Robert put down a large red circle with arrows going out of it in all directions. "This house is a center that things reach out from. I need it to be inwardly containing, and I have to struggle to achieve that because everything wants to reach out and be constantly moving, including us; we get carried with it. I can't quite understand it. It's not that we can't see outside. In fact, we have wonderful views of light and foliage, and that seems to draw our attention outside. I've never thought of it before, but the effect of the house on our lives is constantly having us go places—hiking, or bike riding, or just going somewhere. I feel the need to have more of a home, to have this house nurture a sense of home. We come home and it's not warm and receptive and enclosing. We don't feel like we want to be here for a long time; so we go back out again."

Robert's house was a dwelling where life seemed to be draining out at the edges. It had one of the most curious floor plans I had ever encountered. Approaching the wood-shingled, one-story house via steps and a front porch, I entered directly into a large, square, central room. It felt like a large foyer or entry hall of the house; no less than seven doors opened off it, leading to all the other rooms—kitchen, bedrooms, office, storeroom, and bathroom. While it was the primary circulation space of the house, it was also the living room! At several points in our conversation, Robert agonized over its lack of coziness and warmth and his inability to make it into the heart of the house. As the largest room in the house, it was the obvious choice for a living room, yet however skillfully arranged, it always felt like a space you pass through on the way to somewhere else, a room you leave to get to your destination. What is curious is that Robert, with training in architecture and interior design, had chosen a house with such serious problems of livability.

As we continued to talk, it became apparent that Robert's behavior regarding his current house was a replay of his relationship to his parental home. Growing up in a southwestern university town, where his father was a professor, he had quite a pressured childhood. He described his mother as "very domineering." He shared a room with an older brother and had to go elsewhere to seek privacy. At school, there were a lot of ethnic tensions in the schoolyard. It's perhaps not surprising that Robert remembered much of his childhood as "leaving the house."

"Yeah, we lived in a house that was a lot like this, actually. I hadn't thought of that before. My way to get away was to leave the house and go out to the woods. I created these forts that were houses, that I didn't tell anyone else about. Finally, I did a very interesting thing: I asked my dad to come and help me camouflage my fort, and he did. Making contact with him to ask him to camouflage it was an excuse, because I had done a really good job of hiding it anyway; I always had. Every couple of weeks, I needed to go out and cut some pine boughs and put them down as a floor, as nice carpeting—which is about what I'm ready to do to this whole house right now—carpet all these wood floors. Wow, that's really a trip!"

Many of us underestimate children's need for privacy. We fear, perhaps, that they will become loners, daydream too much, or develop

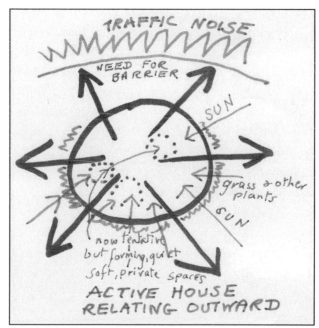

Robert did not feel at home in his house and was always leaving to go "someplace else."

poor study habits. But clearly, persistent intrusions on privacy can have long-term effects. Robert drew the rooms in his current house with dotted, penetrable, tentative boundaries. He recalled with a wry smile that that was just how he felt about the rooms in his childhood home. "There was never anyplace that was private that I could have as my own. I always felt that my mother was looking over my shoulder and directing my activities. If I was in the middle of some kind of play, she would come and tell me to do something else. She wouldn't say, 'Would you wind up in five or ten minutes?' but rather, 'Move from here to there.' I didn't like it. I needed to get away and have my own space that I created and that wouldn't be molested."

It is important to remember that many of the problems we inherit from our childhood may also have a positive side: the lonely, only child who develops a rich fantasy life expressed as poetry in adulthood; the eldest child burdened with watching siblings who develops a capacity for nurturance. In Robert's case, his mother's intrusions on his activities within the house were complemented by an extraordinary degree of freedom outside the house. "I'm amazed that my mother would let me go into these vast, endless woods, because they went forever. I would usually take my dog, an Irish setter; we'd run across bears and mountain lions and deer and other things. I usually carried weapons with me, a bow and arrow, which I was pretty good at, or a hunting knife."

Recalling his pleasure at creating those secret forts and homes-away-from-home, Robert decided to become an architect. Halfway through his training, he became disenchanted; he felt he was learning how to create large, imposing structures but not how to make pleasing, warm interiors—his initial aim. So he switched to interior design. He wanted to create nurturing home environments as he had done for himself as a boy. However, he found he often got caught in the midst of marital problems when consulting with couples on residential design. He eventually opted out of residential work and began to specialize almost exclusively in the interior design of medical and dental offices and hospitals. However, the creation of a warm, pleasing center to his own home remained tantalizingly just beyond his reach, a reflection perhaps of his unwillingness to come to terms with the family dynamics of his childhood now replicated in his adult home.

From Childhood Frustration to Adult Affirmation

The following letter to "Dear Abby" recently caught my eye:

Our thirty-year-old daughter lives with us in our modest home. She has her own room, pays her way and is a rather private person. She has a very good job and leaves home looking as if she has just stepped out of a fashion magazine. So what is the problem? The condition of her room is disgusting! Everything (including cobwebs) is covered with a layer of dust and body powder so thick the furniture looks white. There are heaps of clothing on the floors along with newspapers, magazines, shoes, cans, bottles . . . I could go on and on!

If she lived in her own home, her sloppiness would be none of my business, but since she lives in my home I feel it is very much my business. She flatly refuses to allow me in her room to clean it up. (I have seen the mess through the open door.) I don't want to make an enemy of her as she is my only daughter and life is too short. To add insult to injury, the one-woman office she runs is spotless! How can I get her to clean up her room?

LONG-SUFFERING MOTHER

Dear MOM: *Since apparently you never bothered to insist that she clean her room—and keep it clean—she probably assumed you didn't notice, or didn't care. Nothing will change unless you demand it. Tell her that enough is enough, and you can no longer tolerate her making a pigpen out of a room in your home. (Cans? Bottles? Do you have cockroaches and mice yet?)*

My immediate reaction was that this is a woman who—for some reason—cannot leave home. Like so many people younger than her, she has chosen to distance herself from her mother by deliberately creating a state of disorder in the room she still occupies in her mother's house. Clearly, she is able to create an ordered environment, as she has done so at her office. Perhaps for her, like for many people, it is less threatening to challenge the other person's values or control over her life nonverbally than by direct confrontation. Thus, the chaos in this woman's room cogently communicates to her mother: I may still be under your roof, but I'll do just what I please in my space. In fact, I'll live in a way that will really get under your skin—that will cause you to write a letter to the newspaper. Her "rebellion" via the medium of the environment may reflect the anger she feels at her inability to leave home.

Since it was generally our mothers who nagged us to clean up our room, whose decorating style made its mark on our surroundings, it is not surprising that many people who *have* made a healthy separation from mother also choose to symbolize this via the interior design of home.

Katy's mother was an interior decorator. In the house of her childhood, her mother controlled everything about the environment: She designed and oversaw the rehabilitation of the house and the landscaping of the garden; she chose and arranged the furniture; she selected and bought her children's and her husband's clothes. Although Katy kept reiterating how she admired her mother's taste and design abilities, she clearly also felt a powerful need to assert her own taste in her present dwelling.

"I never was allowed to like anything that my mother didn't like. I can remember when I went through a phase of mint green, and she hated it. I felt guilty for liking it. And when we did my room over, it was pretty much the colors she wanted. I hate gold, and, by God, if my room isn't done in gold grasscloth. That just isn't me. And when she comes here, she talks about how terrific I am and how well I do everything. But she can make some comment about the color of a chair and make me feel terrible for having put it there—when I know I like it! I really respect her taste, but it's hard for me to have my own taste around her because she's such a strong person."

Nancy, a university professor, recalls a similar situation: "The house where I grew up felt like all of it was my mother's, including my room, because she had totally decorated it and wouldn't let me do anything in it. It was annoying, as if I couldn't ever really feel at home in any part of it, even the part that was mine. And yet it was the only place where I could be by myself. And I would do that a lot when I was a kid. It was decorated with these heavy French fabrics that were much too hot for the Texas climate. There was a bedroom set, so all the furniture matched, and I always thought it was very ugly. And it had this wallpaper that was just terrible: roses all over everywhere, twining roses on the walls and on the ceiling. I'd lie down and go to bed and I'd see these flowers all over. I used to have nightmares about Briar Rose being stuck among all the roses, unable to get out. It was claustrophobic; I felt that I couldn't break away from it and didn't for a long time.

"My mother and I have different tastes. If she saw this place, she would give me something to try to make it better. I'll usually keep the things she has given me for a while out of some kind of guilt, and then with great relief give them away. There was a print that she once gave me, and I had it up on the wall. I remember one day, I just went and took it down and put it in the closet, facedown. I just felt it was watching me all the time, saying, 'You can't even decorate your own room.' I wasn't going to have it because I knew the place was just fine."

For Anita, growing up in a housing project, her memories from childhood are of a functional, sterile environment. "I grew up in a couple of houses. The first was in Buffalo, New York; it was a government housing project for low-income families. I lived there until I was thirteen. It was terribly utilitarian and kind of cold. My memories of my family aren't cold—just the house itself. It was like living in a box. We had very little money, so the furnishings were very plain. I think they were hand-me-downs from my mother's brother. I don't remember any kind of personal touches or the feeling that it was beautiful, even my own room, which I longed to have beautiful. I had asthma when I grew up, and my mother had a thing about dust. There were no little things that would gather dust. There were no curtains, no rugs, no spreads. Then we moved to Denver, and it was only slightly better there. It still wasn't aesthetically beautiful. There weren't any pictures that I remember; there weren't beautiful carpets; there were no plants.

"I got married when I was twenty-one. As soon as I had my own home, I became interested in making my environment more beautiful. The first home we bought was absolutely exquisite. Just a little tiny box of a house, and I decorated it and started moving into blue colors. The decor has changed over the years, but the kinds of basics that make me feel good

Anita has expended a lot of energy in making her house beautiful as a reaction to the drabness she remembers from the homes of her childhood.

haven't. I like having things around me that make me feel good. I've got stuff all over my house that I just take such pleasure in looking at and being with."

For Anita, now in her midforties, making a house beautiful is a major focus of her life. She earns a good living as a psychotherapist, and a considerable proportion of her earnings are spent, not on entertaining, eating out, extravagant clothes, or travel, but on making her interior environment "exquisite." Every piece of furniture, many of them oriental antiques, has clearly been selected with loving care; the whole ensemble is a work of art. This has clearly been done to nurture her own aesthetic needs—not for status. She rarely entertains and, by her own admission, is something of a social recluse. Anita recognizes that this focus of both financial and psychic energy is in part a reaction to the lack of beauty she experienced as a child.

Always or Never Leaving Home: Recognizing the Pattern

For the first time in my life, I have an inkling that the world holds other places . . . to be, and I yearn to be there. You can leave home without either running away or getting lost. Entering new space, you can open yourself and let it enter you, pour in, mingle, incorporate itself into the new person you are once you've been there. I'll still hate leaving home. I'll always believe myself in danger of dissolution. But gradually I'll learn to light out anyway for the delayed satisfaction of having gone.

—NANCY MAIRS, *Remembering the Bone House*[5]

The conflicts aroused by the need to leave our parental home and all that it symbolizes may stay with us throughout our lives. It may be expressed by a compelling need to be on the move and not settle down, or by the contrasting behavior of holding on to home and possessions as tightly as mother and childhood home once held on to us. Although these might represent the extreme ends of a continuum of always/never leaving home, many of us display behaviors somewhat in between. How many people do you know who nurture objects and furniture inherited from much-loved parents or grand-parents? How long did you leave some of your stuff (books, sports equipment, school mementos) at your parents' house as a kind of foot in the door? Do you know people who, having experienced early abuse or neglect, have blotted from memory the details of their childhood home, or who have chosen an adult home as different as possible in style or location or decor? If you find it hard to pay as much attention to your home as you would like, might this be "retaliation" toward a parent who could not pay attention to you?

Because home is frequently associated with mother, this ambivalence toward home often echoes an equal ambivalence to mother or the mother figure. Until very recently, homemaking in this culture was almost exclusively the role of women. When we recall homes from childhood—their decor, furnishings, atmo-sphere—it is probable that the responsibility for that lay with a woman. It was the house of our mother, grandmother, aunt, or best-friend's mother. A generation or two ago, fewer women than today had the freedom to express themselves in a job or career. Home was often the one place where they could convey who they felt themselves to be, as mother, spouse, or person in their own right. Hence, many of the stories recounted here relate back to the mother's relationship with home. If this book were about work and breadwinning rather than homes, no doubt there would be more stories about fathers as positive or negative models.

Our childhood home remains with us—in a shadow form—throughout our lives, sometimes reproduced symbolically in colors, furnishings, or layout, sometimes prompting us to create a home in complete contrast to what we remember.

Whether the pattern is one of holding on to possessions or of avoiding staying long in any one place, *recognition* of the pattern is a critical first step. Whatever the issue is that seems to block us from a full and satisfying life, identifying and verbalizing that obstacle is essential. For as long as it remains unconscious, it has far more control over us. When we do recognize how we trip ourselves up, it is important that we not constantly chastise ourselves for this behavior. As long as the issue keeps arising, it serves us to acknowledge it, embrace it as who we are at present, and then let it go. Ironically, it seems, the more we acknowledge and embrace who we are—"warts and all"—the more likely we are to grow and eventually move beyond those blocks that impede us.

ALWAYS OR NEVER LEAVING HOME: EXERCISES YOU CAN DO YOURSELF

A Problematic Relationship with Home

Reflect on where you now live. Let your mind wander over anything about this home that comes up for you. Does it feel like a home to you? If so, what is it about its form or location or furnishings or ambience that enhances that feeling?

If it doesn't feel like home, is that okay with you? Perhaps you are in a period of transition in your life, and a feeling of home is not of paramount importance. If it doesn't feel like home and that bothers you, what is it about this place that is un-homelike? Don't censor yourself! It may be as small—but fundamental—an issue as the lack of comfortable chairs to relax in and read. It may be a more profound issue, such as the wrong location, or a dwelling that is too big or too small, or too dark or too noisy.

Are there some ways in which you relate to this dwelling that are puzzling or irritating to you? Do you, perhaps, have too much clutter around, yet never have the energy or time to deal with it? Do rooms feel spare, empty, or undecorated—despite the fact that you can afford to make them more comfortable? Is there a yard that you feel unable to keep in control? Perhaps you have no outdoor space and feel frustrated because you can't plant a garden.

The point of this exercise is to focus on the frustrating aspects of your relationship to the place where you live, issues that are especially bothersome because there appears to be nothing, rationally, that is preventing you from fixing them. Focus particularly on repetitive patterns, for it is often in these that the core problem resides: Do you keep choosing the "wrong" house, or holding on to one that doesn't suit you, or ignoring certain rooms, or resisting "putting down roots"? When some repeated pattern reveals itself, consider your parents' attitudes toward your childhood home or homes. Is there some echo in your own behavior or feelings? Are you rebelling against some feeling or situation from the past?

If your parents are still alive, is this something you could talk with them about? They too were children once, and their attitudes toward home that you see yourself repeating may be better understood if they could talk about their childhood and *their* parents' feelings about home. If you have children, notice whether they are repeating the pattern or have chosen to do the complete opposite as a way of declaring their independence, or something in between.

There are no quick fixes to a problematic issue around home that seems rooted in childhood. Talk with a friend or partner; let the issue settle into your consciousness; pay attention to your dreams, or sudden, seemingly irrational flashes of intuition. Write in your journal. If the problem you see repeated seems intractable, seek professional help. A good place to start is with a drawing of your childhood home or homes, where it all began. If you see this as a pattern that has been repeated for several generations, you need to be the one to break the pattern. It may be difficult or painful but, ultimately, it could be the greatest gift you give to yourself—or to your children.

Relating to the Clutter in Your Life

If you, like many of us, hold on to so much stuff that you find it irritating, you might try the following exercise.

Take a pad of drawing paper, or just a plain 8½-by-11 sheet, and draw a rough sketch of the floor plan of the house. Don't worry about details, such as where doors are located and the like—just show where the rooms of your house are located. Now, take a colored pencil or pen and scribble everywhere in the house where there is stuff that you'd like to sort or get rid of but don't seem able to. When you've finished that, see if a name for your house comes to mind. I don't mean a name like "Fred," but rather a descriptive name like "The messy house I love" or "Home is where the clutter is." Be imaginative! Print the name of your house at the bottom of the page, prop the paper on a chair about four feet away, and address this house and its contents as if it were animate: "Hello, Bursting-at-the-Seams House, here is what I feel about you . . . ," and see what happens. When you feel drawn to do so, change places with the house and let the house tell *you* how *it* feels: "Well, you know, Tom, all this clutter in the basement is making me feel constipated; I don't feel good about it . . ." And so on. You may well be surprised at what transpires.

When you've finished your dialogue, ask yourself the key question: How does this stuff and clutter serve me? You may already have a sense of the answer, but ask the question anyway. For most people, a bad habit they'd like to stop or "cure" is often, unconsciously, serving them in some way. For example, the person who eats excessively and is overweight may unconsciously be doing this to keep people at bay, to assure himself that he is "not attractive." A person who constantly leaves large piles of stuff around her home although she has the time and physical ability to deal with it, may unconsciously be venting her anger at a parent who was always on her back to tidy her room, even though that parent may long since be deceased. People who find themselves unwilling to clear up stuff that is annoying someone else in the family may want to look more closely at that relationship. A parent who avoids changing the room of a child who has left home for college needs to recognize this as an expression, perhaps, of grief or confusion at the loss or change in the role as parent.

Knowing why we do something—unfortunately—does not guarantee we'll stop it. However, understanding our hidden motivations is a good start. If your problem is clutter and you now understand what it means but you still can't clear it up, it might be worthwhile to call in a professional organizer, a person whose job it is to help people de-clutter their office, home, or closets. My office at the university was once so full of piles of paper, books, reports, boxes of slides, and so on, that I was too ashamed to let my students see it and instead held my office hours at a nearby cafe. Eventually, with the assistance of a wonderful woman who specializes in office organization, I got out from under the mess and started using a logical filing system she devised for me. My office still gets cluttered every semester, but at least now I can tackle the job myself and know where to place (and find) things. Incidentally, this same woman remembers "tidying her room" as a fun activity her mother did with her. Now she does the same for other people. We pack rats of the world should all be so lucky as to encounter such a person.

Memories of Feeling at Home

If you are one of those people who finds it hard to settle in one place, or who yearns for a feeling of being "at home" in the dwelling you reside in, the following exercise may be helpful.

Think back to anyplace in your childhood where you did feel at home. David Seamon, who has written on the phenomenology of home, suggests that a feeling of at-homeness for most of us seems to combine the qualities of rootedness, security, a sense of "ownership," restoration, feeling at ease, and warmth.[6] It may not have been your house in totality where you felt at home; it might have been a place in it—the kitchen, a hidey-hole. One woman I spoke with recalled that lying on her bed was the only support she felt in childhood and that, as an adult, when she feels stress, her first instinct is to lie down. Maybe for you, at-homeness is associated with a particular event in your home—Christmas, Thanksgiving, your birthday. Or it may have been a special hiding place, den, clubhouse, or favorite play spot that you found or made away from home. Whatever the place, recalling its qualities of at-homeness may assist you in reconnecting with the feelings it evoked—security, rootedness, at-easeness, warmth. What can you do with such memories? It seems to me that there are at least two ways to use them. One, when feeling particularly stressed or insecure, try closing your eyes, breathing deeply, and returning in your imagination to that place; absorb its positive feelings, experience them in your body, and bring them back to this time and place. If your mind frequently slips back to that fondly remembered home-place, it may be a clue that there is something there for you, something of value that you need to explore.

A second direction might be that some of the qualities of at-homeness of that place might actually be incorporated into your present dwelling-place or places you now frequent. Perhaps positive memories of a tree house might be telling you of a need for a room to call your own, of more privacy or time alone. Fond memories of a cozy chair may be reminding you of how much you liked to curl up and read and how you give yourself neither the time nor the place to do that as an adult. Perhaps warm memories of Grandma's kitchen might be evoked for you by chintz curtains, a round wooden table, or lingering over meals—despite contemporary pressures to not waste time and to decorate in the latest white-on-white theme. If your house could grace the pages of *Architectural Digest* but you don't feel "at home" in it, what have you gained?

FIVE

Becoming More Fully Ourselves: Evolving Self-Image as Reflected in Our Homes

*What a tight wadding I have wound about my Edward in order to protect him
(and me), in my mind at least, from the stain and mildew fertilized and set in
growth by this perpetual downpour of time. I keep forgetting that time leaks
through . . . He and I shall never again be lovers. This town is my lover, this house,
this land; these provide an area, an accommodation of love which human beings
have never been able to give me or which, lacking the constructive ability, I have
never been able to build for myself from cut and measured blocks of flesh and blood.*
—JANET FRAME, *Scented Gardens for the Blind* [1]

It is a fact of being alive that nothing ever stays the same. Just when a job, a
relationship, a direction in our life, a home starts to feel settled and comfortable,
something emerges that starts us on another path. It may be as dramatic a change as
losing one's job or losing a home to fire, or as subtle a nudge as persistent dreams
or a nagging sense of something "not quite right." A dramatic loss can—once we
have fully acknowledged and experienced the grief—be perceived as an opportunity for growth. Although none of us would consciously wish upon ourselves such
pain, once it has happened, we can use the emotional opening up as a trigger.

In this chapter, we will look at dramatic life-changes experienced by two women—Jean and Marilyn—and see how they were able to transform a crisis into an opportunity for change. Then, in order to understand how to recognize and learn from those more subtle but persistent nudges, or indications of restlessness, we will return to the stories of Joan, before she decided to leave her life in the convent, and Barbara, whose satisfaction with her "Japanese teahouse" is ever-so-slightly undermined by her intrigue with her neighbor's more "chaotic" home. Finally, in the account of one man's deep satisfaction with a single basement room and another's with a sparse mountain hut, we see how the simplest of living arrangements can, for some people at particular moments in their lives, be perfect.

Jean's Search for the Jewel Box

I met Jean one weekend at the house of a mutual friend. When she heard about my work, she grew very excited and asked me to come talk with her about her desire to leave her unsatisfactory apartment.

Jean lived in a 1950s Marin County suburb north of San Francisco. I approached her house down a wide street, with views of the dry yellow hills on either side. It was a hot afternoon in late July. Small stucco and wood houses were set back behind conservative suburban lawns. I walked down a side driveway to reach her apartment—neighbor dogs barking wildly—and climbed the exterior stairs at the back of a modest stucco house. The apartment was essentially one large room, relatively sparsely furnished. An attractive oriental rug covered most of the dark linoleum floor, but the few items of furniture were pushed back against the walls, leaving the room with a slightly empty look. A desk with shelves above was situated against one wall; against the other walls were a stereo and speakers, a bookcase, a rocking chair, a narrow single bed, and a lamp. Apart from the rocking chair and bed, there was nowhere else to sit. It didn't seem as though Jean often—or ever—had visitors. On her bedside table were candles, tissues, and a few books—*Realms of the Human Unconscious, The Healing Journey,* and *Existential Sexuality.*

Apart from two tiny pictures and some dried flowers, there were few decorations: no pictures, photographs, or posters, no plants or ornaments. The apartment didn't feel lived in or cozy. There were boxes around, as though she was packing to leave—or had not yet unpacked to stay.

I asked Jean to put down her feelings about this apartment in some kind of picture. She drew a broomstick figure lying on a bed, surrounded by a swirling, thick brown enclosure. Beyond the brown enclosure was a black one, but, significantly, there was an orange path that led out of it. Beyond the house, she drew the trees and dry yellow hills around her; the hills and ocean not far to the west were depicted in green and blue. A striking diagonal feature cutting across the center of the picture was the freeway, outlined in black, leading from her Marin County apartment to friends and activities in San Francisco. At the bottom of her picture, she depicted people and cars on the Golden Gate Bridge, over which she must travel to get from her suburban apartment to the city.

The strong and dark tones in which Jean portrayed her disliked apartment were contrasted with the brighter colors (orange, yellow, blue) and lighter strokes (colored pencils instead of markers) with which she sketched the city, where she spent most of her time. She began to talk about—and to—her current apartment:

"I'm in a place that is not my home. There are feelings of sadness that I've put myself in this position; surely no one did it to me. I don't know why I moved here. I was afraid I wouldn't find anything else. Lately, I've avoided being here; I've stayed down in the city most of the time. [She started to address the house directly.] You're bare and plain; you aren't soft. You don't give me a place to display myself. I feel annoyed with you. I feel sorry for you. You could be very nice if someone bothered to fix you up. Why didn't I fix this place up? In the past couple of years, I haven't fixed places up because I haven't been so certain that I deserved to live anyplace."

As Jean discussed other places she had lived, she began to describe becoming so attached to a

Jean's depiction of her current disliked suburban apartment and her route to visit friends in the city.

place that she felt almost embedded within her dwelling. She described a flat in Berkeley where she had lived for ten years and which she still remembered with bittersweet nostalgia.

"I felt so at home there. It was so beautiful; I loved the way it looked, the way the light came in [starts to cry]. I really loved you. You cooperated with me; you didn't resist me. You really gave me a home. I used to say that if anything happened to that place, I wouldn't be able to survive. I was devastated when the owner died and I had to move. But it was a boon in some respects. I had become very crystallized there. I used to think of myself as a prehistoric ant embedded in amber. It was just as well I had to leave; it was the start of my breaking my attachment to things. I feared that if I didn't have that particular car, or the particular job that I had then, I would be totally helpless. I would be in the middle of the Atlantic in a bathtub—not even a rowboat! But the actual leaving wasn't easy. I found a place in the same neighborhood. The room was just like the one I was leaving. I spent a day taking boxes over, but I kept hearing this voice from somewhere, saying, 'No.' I went back to my old apartment, lay down, and started screaming to God to get me out of my body. I was amazed! You know, I don't ordinarily do things like that. So I listened to the 'No' and moved all my things back again. Then I found a place to house-sit. I did finally move, and I didn't die or disappear or disintegrate."

Shortly after this traumatic move, Jean took a three-month trip and visited all the homes she'd lived in while growing up. As she recalled the first home she could remember, she started to describe a situation very much like the one in Berkeley—a much-loved home, a forced move, an emotional outburst, and an eventual leave-taking.

"I was born in Miami. My father built us a house, and it was beautiful. It had an enormous living room, white and tropical. The backyard was full of citrus trees. My godmother, whom I was named after, gave me fern plants, and we planted them in the yard. It was my house—my parents were stuck in their own problems, and no one supervised me. I had a bike and went everywhere by myself. I went to the movies; I'd stay overnight at friends' houses. Then my parents got divorced. I got very upset; my father was going to sell the house and we all had to leave. The night before we were supposed to leave, my brother and I were furious that it had been sold, that someone else was going to live there. So we took all the pillows in the house and cut them open and streamed the whole house with feathers, and then wetted them down. I guess I was about six or seven.

"We moved to a small rented house. The rooms were small, dark, dingy; it felt confined. We had a landlady who told me I couldn't keep my cat. She hauled my cat off to the Humane Society and made me ride along in the car to hold the cat."

In the period shortly following this move, Jean recounts that her mother was "crazy . . . less and less in control." And that her brother, Tommy, got more and more upset and violent until he was finally sent to an institution. It is small wonder that Jean has an emotional reaction to moving.

In her high-school years, Jean lived with a grandmother in Cincinnati. It was in an old but elegant apartment house. She found an unused storeroom at the top of the building and made it into her own room. "I carved out a little space and kept everything at bay." Thus, like her current suburban home, Jean created a space that protected her but which in time also became a trap.

"Like that apartment in Berkeley, I got myself into a situation I could not move out of gracefully, so I had to create a deterioration. I took an overdose of sleeping pills to get myself moved out. I slept for six or seven days and woke up in the hospital. I sure was 'safe and sound'! There was no way in; there was no way out. Then they moved me to a clinic in New York; for the first time, I had a home and a family. Well, that's overstating it, but I felt very much at home there; I very much felt in a family. I was living in an institution, but it looked like a home, like a city apartment building. It was a very exclusive clinic. We were a very sophisticated bunch of nuts! Richard Rogers and Marilyn Monroe were there while I was there."

After nine months in the clinic, Jean returned to her family in Cincinnati and shortly thereafter ran away and started her adult life in California. It seemed that Jean's life had been a series of happy places she'd been forced to leave and unhappy places where she felt trapped. Guiding her back to the present, I asked her to draw a picture of her ideal home, the kind of place where she would really like to live. Without hesitation, she took a bunch of brightly colored pencils and began creating a shadowy "frame" around the

Jean's image of an ideal home environment.

sheet of paper. It was the start of a picture of her ideal apartment, the place she hoped to find in the Marina District of San Francisco. As in her first picture, she began with a boundary. But this time the boundary formed the frame of the picture and was wispy and multicolored. She described it as a nimbus cloud. Strands of color—orange, blue, purple—extended into the apartment interior, almost like smoke. It seemed less like a barrier, more like a halo. She drew a plant, musical notes, a bottle of wine, books, a lighted candle, herself lying on a bed or couch, and two people sharing a candlelit meal at a round table. In the center of the picture was a window with a view out to a park, where a person was walking a dog, and to the bay, with sun shining on a sailboat. Under the window and presumably inside the apartment, she wrote the words *safe & sound.*

There could hardly be a greater contrast between Jean's two pictures. In the first, she apparently was either confined within the thick barriers of a small and unadorned apartment or escaping via the freeway to friends in San Francisco. In the second, her home had expanded, as it were, to fill the whole picture, and contained color, music, plants, books, and companions. She felt "safe and sound" within this cloud-enfolded nest, yet had a view out to the world beyond. She was in the city, yet her view was of water, grass, animals, boats, and the sun. In the first picture, she appeared claustrophobically confined with nature around but with a need to escape to the city. In the second, she was in the heart of the city, seemingly gently enclosed in a colorful nest, yet with visual access to the world of nature. There seemed little doubt that in the second home, she was prepared to express herself; in the first she could—or would—not. She remarked about the boundary in her second picture:

"It looks like a soft enclosure rather than a barrier. I'm inside it because I'm choosing to be nestled safe and sound, rather than trapped. The image of a jewel box keeps coming back to me. I am a jewel box. I contain all kinds of treasures—rubies, diamonds, mushrooms, toads . . . I want to keep looking at all those nice things. This time, I'll keep the lid open."

If the dwelling truly is an expression of the self, Jean's choice of her present apartment and her unwillingness to express herself within it are strong messages of her feelings of isolation and undeservedness. As a single woman, she has chosen an apartment in a neighborhood largely comprising young families, with her friends and interests far away in San Francisco.

As Jean described earlier dwellings, she recounts a life of alternating security and anguished involuntary moves. At the time of our conversation, she was on the verge of a more mature and settled relationship with home. Unlike earlier situations, when Jean created such a profound bond of dependency with her home that moving away triggered extreme panic, or when she forced a move upon herself by attempting suicide, she had this time chosen a setting with which she felt little connection. She had resisted personalizing her apartment and she had left many of her belongings in boxes. Her fantasy of where she would *like* to live was easy for her to express. Significantly, she envisaged it as "a jewel box." Clearly, this jewel box is also a metaphor of the self or of the transpersonal dimension of the psyche. Jean is ready to look at the treasures within and to do so partially via the environment she plans to create for herself.

Six months after this conversation, Jean wrote to me that she had moved to an apartment in San Francisco's Marina District, very much like the one in her picture. She was much happier, and life had taken a positive turn. But before she could make this positive step and move on to the next phase in her life, she first had to acknowledge her own "stuckness," even embrace and laugh at it as being "just the way things are."

The first necessary step for any move or change in our lives that we yearn for is total awareness: being with who we are, how we are, where we are *at this moment*. The natural human tendency of denying or burying present pain just keeps us stuck in the suffering. For Jean, the honest acknowledgment of her sad stuckness—and its repeated pattern in her life—was the start of a healthy move toward change. Allowing herself to draw and describe where she would really like to live permitted some psychic energy to move in that direction. She was making a positive affirmation of need, and, within a short time, the kind of place she wanted as a home had manifested in her life.

Stuck in Ambivalence: Marilyn's Refuge and Prison

Ironically, for some people at particular stages of psychological growth, the attainment of a seeming ideal may ultimately prove confining. There ensues an almost agonizing conflict between security and movement, between feelings of comfort and the yearning need for expansion and change. The dwelling may be safe, but it may also be constricting. I met Marilyn—an English woman in her early forties—while we were both living at the Findhorn community in northern Scotland.

Marilyn had enthusiastically invested a great deal of energy in renovating and modernizing the cottage where she had lived for four years. At the time of our meeting, she felt strangely disaffected by her home; it felt like a burden, something holding her back from social contacts, from expanding into a more fulfilling sense of herself.

Marilyn's cottage was a long, low, two-story structure built of stone and roofed with slate, comparable to many similar rural cottages in the northeastern Scottish county of Morayshire. Its location, however, was not typical. Originally built as the gatekeeper's cottage at the bottom of an uphill drive to a large Victorian hotel, a later road had squeezed the cottage and its small, elongated garden into the position of a "traffic island." A minor road passed both in front and at the back of the house; the cottage sat isolated, its nearest neighbor a small garage where buses and trucks were repaired.

When I asked Marilyn to put down her feelings about her cottage, she immediately went to work with crayons and markers. Within a short time, she had produced a striking depiction of her cottage, surrounded by a high black fence. Inside the fence, on the front door of the cottage, she wrote the word *Help*. Outside the fence, a crowd of people were looking in. I asked her to describe what she had drawn:

"When you asked me to do a drawing, the first thing I thought of was a prison. The bars of this prison stretched high up into the sky, and I felt troubled when I was drawing them. I felt a lot of isolation and loneliness and a sense of being locked away. I am inside this circular prison. All the bars are around me.

Marilyn's depiction of her cottage home: the "refuge" and the "prison."

The next thing I saw was the sun, just outside the bars. The sun is on the other side of the bars, and the sun is crying. I got tears. Then I saw birds in the sky, and felt that outside this prison there is a lot of joy, a lot of happiness. The birds are singing, the sun is shining, and everything is nice out there, but I can't experience it directly because of my imprisonment. I drew the cottage looking very small and confined, and the garden, wild and overgrown, out of my control. I have always been deeply ashamed of this garden because I can't come to grips with it. It always gets on top of me. As I was drawing the front door, I wrote *'Help'* as if I am locked in there, in the cottage, which is very beautiful—and feels like a prison to me. Then I drew the people around the wall, looking over the wall into the cottage. They're all friendly and nice, they want to rescue me, but they can't reach me because I am behind the bars. Whilst I was drawing, I kept thinking: I don't know what I'm doing in this cottage. I have never liked it. I never wanted to live here.

"And now I feel trapped, because I am terrified of selling it. I am really scared of being homeless, and I don't know where to go. I want to move. It feels very sterile in this cottage . . . very lifeless. It is my everything. It is my home, my safety. Nobody can get me. Nobody can hurt me in here. It's like a refuge and a prison. I can't seem to have one without the other."

A refuge and a prison are two powerful images that appear to be opposites: a refuge, a place to which one retreats for safety from some kind of hostile outside force, and a prison, a place in which one is involuntarily confined, from which one would like to escape. I sensed, from her use of these words and from the emotion that was apparent in her drawing, her tone of voice, and her body gestures, that it might be revealing for Marilyn to continue the dialogue with her house. I asked her to imagine speaking to it as if it were a person:

"Well, cotty, it's like this: I feel a love/hate relationship with you. On the one hand, I really love you, because you are safe and cozy, and I have managed to make you into what I want. Everything in you I have made with my own hands. I've stripped all the nasty paint off your wood, and I have decorated all your walls, and I have painted your ceilings. I've put so much energy into you and I feel drained. But when I think of selling you, I feel frightened. I mean, where would I live if I didn't have you? So . . . I love you and I hate you. I feel like you're an unwanted child. I never wanted to live here. Even after four years, I still don't want to live here. It feels all wrong. I just don't want to be here." She then burst into tears.

When Marilyn recovered, I asked her to change positions, to try to imagine what the house might have to say: "I feel kind of sad that you never wanted me. I feel like an unwanted child. Uhm . . . [thinks for a long time] . . . I mean I'm a nice little house! Why don't you want me? [Laughter] Aren't I cozy and warm in the winter? I want you to go on living here forever. I mean, isn't it nice to open my front door and to walk into me? You can't possibly sell me! I won't let you [loud laughter]!"

At this point, Marilyn shifted her position. "It really frightens me. You are a seductive little house. You are cozy. You are nice to come home to. I mean, if I could lift you, take you somewhere else, I would. You just sit here in the middle of nowhere! With no neighbors. You remind me of myself. You know—you're a cute little house, but you are all alone. Just like me!"

After a while, Marilyn began to speak again as the house, to take its part: "I don't want you to sell me, Marilyn. I want you to go on being my owner, because you look after me. Nobody will give me the love and care and attention that you give me, and I don't think you can sell me, even if you want to, because I don't think that anybody would buy me. I mean, only an idiot like you would live in me. You have created me. I am your child."

I found myself drawn into the dialogue and, addressing the house, I said: "Would you let Marilyn take away that part of herself that she has put into you?" The house (alias Marilyn) replied promptly and in a forceful tone of voice: "No! I want her to go on looking after me. I mean, she still has lots of work to do. She hasn't oiled my doors and she promised that she would. And she has to wash my windows and wash the curtains. She knows all of this. Everything needs doing. The carpet needs shampooing. She hasn't got any time for anything else. I am the thing she should be looking after."

I commented, "Hmm, you are a very demanding house. Do you think you should come first in Marilyn's life?"

Marilyn responded, "Absolutely! She needs to replace my wash basin. It's cracked [laughing]. And then she needs to take care of my roof. I want a nice little wall around me. I want her to spend all her money on me. I don't want her to spend any money on going to America. I want her to stay here. I am afraid, if she goes to America, she will come back and sell me. You really need me. [With a smirk] I need you and you need me [laughing]. What would you do if you didn't have me? You'd be lost."

Marilyn continued, "I know there is something unhealthy about this house, and it has to do with . . . with keeping up a certain standard—always having it clean and tidy and neat—always feeling under incredible pressure to keep it clean. I am just exhausted from this house. I just want out. [Laughter] I just want to break the dependency, because I am dependent upon it, and it is dependent upon me. It reminds me a bit of my mother."

Childhood toys in Marilyn's bedroom, a clue to her ambivalence toward her early life.

Despite all her ambivalence and anguish over owning and caring for a very demanding house, the house clearly also gave something to Marilyn. I asked her if she could talk about the positive aspects of her relationship with her cottage; it seemed that there must be some or she would have left long ago.

"It's mine! [Almost hysterical laughter] It's mine. Nobody can take it from me. Nobody is going to say, 'You've got to get out!' Nobody is going to evict me. It feels like it's really . . . uhm . . . repeating a pattern I have. The pattern is that I am not safe in the world, and the people are out to get me. I think this goes back to my childhood, when we constantly had problems. We always lived in awful, awful apartments, where we were always having problems with the landlord or with neighbors, and we were being told to get out or . . . My mother always paid rent, always had to make ends meet, never had enough money. Just incredible insecurity. My mother constantly saying to me, 'You need to own your own house. People who own their own houses are really lucky.' And I guess that's what I was heading for most of my life."

I asked Marilyn to do a second picture depicting—as best she could—the other important dwellings of her life. Significantly, in a picture of the first home she could remember—a flat in central London where her father had died—she also depicted prison bars and wrote the word *"Help!"* She was completely surprised when I pointed out the similarities with the picture of her current home.

After her father's death, she and her mother moved many times, from one depressing flat to another, until, at the age of twenty, Marilyn moved away, first to a girls' hostel in Brussels; then to several shared flats in London while going to a teachers' training college. Finally, after she began work as a grade-school teacher, Marilyn bought herself a small house in a London suburb.

"I just loved that house. I was very happy there. It gave me a lot of comfort. It was like the perfect mate. I had visualized it. Two years before I bought it, I drew the picture of my dreams, the position of the kitchen and the lounge and the color of the carpet and the color of the walls and the color of the outside—mustard yellow—and the bay window and the bottle glass and the garden and everything. I spent a good eighteen months searching for this house and eventually I found it. When my friends saw it, they were absolutely dumbfounded. When I saw it, I knew immediately. It was a rainy Sunday afternoon. I looked into the estate agent's window, and there was this little house, number 37 Arlington Road, and I said to my mother, 'That is the house.' I didn't even have to walk inside. It had everything: the mustard carpet, the white walls, the big back garden, sun on the garden, bay window . . . everything!"

After living in this "dream house" for four years, Marilyn learned of Findhorn, an alternative community in the north of Scotland, whose spiritual philosophy she felt especially drawn to. After several visits and without knowing exactly why, she felt compelled to sell her London house and buy the cottage we were currently discussing. She did not feel ready to commit herself to becoming a full community member, so she selected a dwelling that allowed her to make a small living serving bed-and-breakfast guests and began to work part-time, running a small bookstore for the community. At the time of our conversation, she had lived in this cottage for four years. I asked her who were the people peering through the fence that she had drawn around the cottage.

"I would say they are Findhorn members. They're the people in the community whom I miss out on. I'm down here, missing all these people, missing my relationship with them. Here I am decorating, painting, gardening. My world is very limited by those bars. My world revolves around my cottage."

The last remaining image in her first picture that she had not referred to was the sun, shining sadly beyond the fence. I asked her to speak as if she were this sun: "I am expansion. I am growth. I am openness. I am your potential. I am your shining higher self. I am out there and I want you to come and claim me. I want you to come and be the sun, and I want you to get out of this prison. All your feelings about needing to get out of this cottage are very right. In a year's time, you will be selling this house, and during this next year, you're to go through a lot of growth. You are to follow your heart. I think you know what you must do next. It doesn't matter where you go. Now is the time to open up and come out of your shell. You are coming to the point where you'll be able to exist without this kind of security." There was a long pause, Marilyn whimpering as though not wanting to face it. "You need to heal yourself, Marilyn. You can do that in a number of ways, but you won't do it living in this cottage."

What was so striking and moving to me as I listened to this long dialogue were the changes in Marilyn's tone of voice. When she spoke as the house, her voice was demanding, petulant, even cocky, like a child who knows she has her parents just where she wants them. "You dare defy me!" the house seemed to be saying. When she spoke as Marilyn, she was at first sad, hesitant, unsure—her voice low. It was as though she didn't know how to deal with this demanding child. Finally, when speaking as the sun, she sounded very sure, very clear and balanced. The sun represented her inner wisdom which, through all the petulant arguments, knew calmly and honestly what to say and what should be her next step.

Why did Marilyn choose her house as a metaphor of her feelings of entrapment? Some people feel stuck in a job that no longer satisfies, others in a relationship that has become barren. From Marilyn's account of her early life, it seems clear that the lack of a secure home was a recurring painful experience for her mother and herself. The ambivalence of her feelings toward this refuge/prison probably mirrored her ambivalent feelings toward her mother—the sole source of physical and emotional nurturance after her father's early death.

The clue to this mother/house connection came in an offhanded remark when Marilyn said, "I am exhausted from this house . . . I just want to break the dependency, because I am dependent upon it, and it is dependent upon me. It reminds me a bit of my mother."

Marilyn's mother was still alive at the time of our conversation, living in a housing scheme for the elderly in southern England. Although geographically distant, she continued to make strong emotional demands on her daughter via phone calls, letters, and requests that she visit. At some level, Marilyn had never completely detached herself from the mother who had urged her throughout an unhappy childhood, "You need to own your own house." Mother and house had become emotionally intertwined: The cottage provided Marilyn with security, shelter, and comfort, but its constant demands kept her separated from social contact. Marilyn was at a crucial point in her life when the need for balance between security and adventure, between home and away, between mother and friends had to be addressed. For some people, this urgent demand for psychological growth may be experienced via intuitive flashes or recurring dreams; for Marilyn, it was experienced in the very environment she had created for herself. The conflicting emotions engendered by "refuge" and "prison" could no longer be ignored.

In Jungian terms, Marilyn was in a temporary state of alienation—necessary before a reconnection with the higher or transpersonal Self. According to Jungian theory, the cyclic process of psychological growth tends to proceed through alternating experiences of what is known as *inflation,* or too close an identification with the self, and *alienation,* or a rupture in the ego-self connection. Thus, in a moderately healthy state, the needs of our personal ego-self and of a transpersonal higher, or spiritual, Self are in reasonable balance. At this point in her life, Marilyn was out of balance—her ego-self was prevented from the growth her higher Self demanded. Jung wrote that in looking for the "right path" in one's continuing psychological development, one should pay special attention to that which attracts and repels at the same time. For Marilyn, this was clearly leaving the cottage—something longed for and equally feared. And in turning to the Self, which—even in a state of alienation—is waiting to be called upon, she received guidance as to her next step in life.

About nine months after this conversation, as Marilyn's higher Self predicted, she did sell her house. With the proceeds, she moved to California to start the next step in her life: studying for a professional degree in psychology. She had broken through the bars and followed the advice of her higher Self. The feeling of entrapment in her cottage had seemingly been a necessary step on the way; without the anguish, without the tension between refuge and prison, it is doubtful whether Marilyn would have been motivated enough to move on to this next stage of her life.

The Intruder Escapes: Joan Finds Comfort in the Basement

Jean and Marilyn both managed, after quite a struggle, to move from an environment that had taken on the characteristics of a trap to one that permitted them to flower. Experiencing a similar situation, how would we know which way to turn? Returning to the story of Joan, the Catholic nun who left her convent, we find a clue. After joining a women's group, Joan slowly began to articulate her growing feeling of being trapped, both within the order and in the house she shared with twelve other sisters in a poor neighborhood of Oakland. The house itself began to take on the tone of a prison. She felt like an intruder, as if she no longer belonged. Six months after she left, I asked her to recall her feelings about that house and to imagine what she might have said to it. This was her response:

Joan's image of the convent, where she felt at home only in the basement.

"House, you're very tall, straight, and cold-looking. You had much potential, and your potential is all painted over. I feel very cold as I walk up your steps. I feel your doorknobs that might fall off, making it almost impossible to get into some of your rooms. I feel very blocked off and unwanted. There's only one area in all of you that I really felt at home in, and that was the basement. You had a musty and a clean smell at one and the same time. I loved your low ceiling. Even though your brick walls were worn with water seepage, there was a warmth about you. The rest of you is really sterile and cold, and I don't want any part of you. I didn't really feel alone when I was down in the basement. It's strange, I felt much more alone upstairs, sitting in the midst of people. I felt a lack of belonging, like a foreigner and an intruder.

"Oh, house, I'm so glad to get out of you. Your sterile walls and your high ceilings and our cramped quarters sapped my life. I really know now with certainty that saying good-bye to you was absolutely right, that I was really and truly nurturing myself to allow myself the freedom to be who I am as a person and not confined by your sterility and cleanliness, your high walls, and the antiquity of your customs."

Reviewing Joan's account in terms of her path toward a fuller flowering of who she truly is, it seems clear that the convent came to represent for her a place of alienation. While living there, she felt "blocked, unwanted, alone, like a foreigner, an intruder, closed off, confused." Certainly, the environment didn't *do* this to her; other people in the same house had positive feelings about it. Joan was at a stage in her own inner growth when she needed to move from a state of alienation from her inner self to a state of realignment. She projected onto the physical fabric of the convent building her own feelings of being confined and closed off. In it, she found just one place—the low-ceilinged, warm, and musty basement—where she felt at home.

It is a remarkable fact of human growth that when the time is right to move from alienation to reconnection with the self, a place will often emerge that embodies and generates a feeling opposite from alienation—a feeling of warmth, connection, wholeness, wisdom. It may be a fantasy; it may be a real place. You might see yourself tending a garden or building a beautiful stone wall. You might inexplicably find yourself noticing birds in flight or be attracted to the sound and sight of moving water. Or, like Joan, you may find yourself drawn to a musty basement. For Joan, the basement was a symbol of earthiness, spontaneity, growth, emerging sexuality. It was a place to which she could escape, as she did eventually on a grander scale—by leaving the convent. Whatever the image, if acknowledged and attended to, it can provide a beacon of hope in the journey toward the balanced state between ego and higher Self.

Two Visions of Self: Barbara Lets Down Her Guard

In her introspective autobiography, written in the form of a diary, Anaïs Nin saw quite clearly both the security and sustenance that can ensue from living in a house that reflects one's own self-image, and the phenomenon of projecting onto the home one's inner fears and anxieties.

"When I look at the large green iron gate from my window, it takes on an air of a prison gate. An unjust feeling, since I know I can leave the place whenever I want to, and since I know that human beings place upon an object, or a person, this responsibility of being the obstacle when the obstacle lies always within one's self.

"In spite of this knowledge, I often stand at the window staring at the large closed iron gate, as if hoping to obtain from this contemplation a reflection of my inner obstacles to a full, open life."[2]

For some people, a valuable insight into an undeveloped aspect of themselves is triggered by observation of another person's home. Such was the case with

Barbara, a graduate student in psychology living in a simple wooden house in San Francisco. The interior was a striking, warm, woodsy living space with views over backyards, rooftops, and the San Francisco Bay. Light streamed in, and there were patches of color, flowers on the table, plants in the kitchen, a red-and-blue oriental rug, prints, a bright calendar, and a stunning Tiffany lamp of orange flowers and green-swathed leaves. The feeling was of peace, calm, solidity; pride in a beautiful, self-made environment; things chosen with care; colors, textures, styles blending together.

When I asked Barbara to put down her feelings about her house, she did so in a somber brown picture—some steps leading up to a doorway. It was simple, quiet, ordered. As she started to describe her house, she several times made references to it as a "Japanese teahouse." This was her ideal, what she had been striving for. It meant for her order, simplicity, peace, and the minimum of possessions, each symbolizing much more than its material form. She started to describe her picture of her house:

"It has a very holy kind of doorway. You can't just walk in with your everyday street personality; you have to enter slowly and with reverence. It's hard to speak of the essence of this house; it's not verbal. It's much more atmosphere, harmony, color. But that doesn't mean I don't have emotions about it—very strong emotions—peace, solitude, gentleness. That's the inside of the house; but it's also me, what I see when I look inside. I rent this house from a friend, who rebuilt it. Gradually, it's becoming less of him and more me. We're in the process of merging with one another—the house and I. My intent is to create a place where you don't even notice there's a difference between inside and outside; you're never bombarded by anything. The more I discover about the house, the more I discover about the world and myself. It's a kind of harmony I'm trying to capture, like the rhythm in nature."

Barbara's words, her tone of voice, her house, her manner were all of a piece. So it came as a surprise to me when she admitted that she also liked people's houses that were quite unlike her own. In particular, she liked the house next door, where her friend Jane lived. As she started to describe it, it seemed the very antithesis of her own ordered dwelling: "I have always loved houses that were like little hippy-houses, where everything was all made out of wood, and they cooked dinner and left the kitchen dirty, and there were thousands of old tin cans full of stuff—weeds and things brought in from outside. I've loved being in that kind of disorder. It's sort of a natural kind of disorder that I like about the outdoors. There's no yard I like better than the one next door, that's so incredibly overgrown. My yard outside, my plants, I mean they look like they were part of the Prussian army, all growing like soldiers in little rows. Jane's house next door is very small. There's a mattress on the floor in the bedroom, covered with an old Indian print bedspread. There's a tiny white stove in the kitchen and a bunch of old orange crates with jars of bulgar and brown rice, and chamomile teas. Everything's sort of dirty; tidy but dirty, old, and sort of moth-eaten. It's really comfortable when I go over there—I never have to think about cleaning up. I don't have to be neat and clean; I can really let down my guard and be disorderly."

This, then, was a person with two visions of self as expressed in the environment. Barbara seemed quite clear that the harmonious teahouse was her preferred expression of self, yet she had a sneaking admiration for the more chaotic, lived-in feeling of her neighbor's house. At one point, she started to describe Jane's house as "more emotional," and then stopped. Perhaps the key was in a later description of her mother, whom she described as "the strongest woman in the world." She was of Greek descent—"very sensuous, very tactile—yet not quite approving of it." Barbara's house seemed to be an expression of her self, but one that mother would approve of. Her neighbor's house expressed that unacknowledged part of Barbara's character—her shadow in Jungian terms: spontaneous, emotional, unplanned—that she secretly wished to experience more. Barbara's house was seemingly a perfect expression of who she was right then, but not an expression of what she might fully become.

The Log Cabin in the City: Olaf's Move to a Simple Dwelling

In creating a home, we each have different needs for privacy, for order, for enclosure. As our lives progress, what we expect and need from our home may likewise change. The following two stories are of men who sought to simplify their lives via a move to a very basic form of dwelling. Both had lived previously in more affluent settings; both, in their middle years, voluntarily turned their backs on their former lives. The move to a simple dwelling—in the one case, a hut, in the other, a simple room—is both a symbolic gesture of renouncing the distractions of the world and a reflection in the material world of a kind of mental and spiritual cleansing. The need for some people to do this is both universal and timeless: The first story dates from twentieth-century California, the second from thirteenth-century Japan.

Olaf was a single man in his forties. He lived alone in a basement room under a modest, single-family house on the corner of two quiet streets in the flatlands of Berkeley. Through work exchange (painting, maintenance, and the like) with the owners, he lived in the house for free. He was writing a book on community; he earned his living by working on construction jobs.

When asked to put down his feelings about his room in a visual image, Olaf—without much hesitation—drew a log cabin in the woods, with smoke coming out of the chimney. Despite its urban setting, this was the image that Olaf felt best expressed his contentment with his room. "I feel warm and cozy here—like a log cabin in the woods. I feel good about the neighborhood, the park nearby, the sounds of birds. I put a moon in my picture because I do most of my writing from 2:30 to 8:00 A.M. Then I leave at 8:00 for my construction job. This room has all I need—a bed, a desk, bookshelves. Out in the basement, I have a shower and toilet, a fridge and hot plate. I've decorated the walls of the room with pictures and images—each carefully selected as a reminder of what I value."

The room and Olaf seemed to be in a state of warm, mutual accord; this was indeed a room-as-haven. It was small, personal, cozy, neat—with all that Olaf needed for his "monklike" existence. He had not always lived this way. He came from a moderately wealthy family with whom he had a close relationship. His fondest memories are of ranchland near Santa Barbara that his parents purchased in 1949. There, living in tents during ten years of family vacations, they slowly built a series of houses.

"It was a wonderful experience! That's where I got my building skills—

Olaf at home in his basement room.

working with my dad and mother and sisters. My two sisters each have a house there, and we have a 'group' house where we meet for family reunions at least once a year. I might live there myself one day, but it's too removed from city amenities. My ideal would be to live in a community in a city apartment building—with periods, too, in some kind of country community, perhaps in a yurt in the woods. I do enjoy the country, but I love the city too."

Olaf grew up in the suburbs of Cleveland and Los Angeles; he took a degree in biology, worked as a researcher for some years, then entered theology school and became a minister. After several years as the pastor of a church, he became a marriage counselor. At the time I talked with him, his desire to write a book on community had caused him to retreat to a simple room, work as a carpenter, and live on very little money. He did not own a car and he rarely ate out or entertained. He was a member of what has been termed the "voluntary poor."

Olaf's room seemed a perfect setting for his current style of life. In speaking to the room as if it were animate, he said: "I really appreciate how you've helped me stay focused on what I'm trying to do. The smallness keeps me living simple and light—I can't keep too much! I don't want rooms which pull me into different moods; I even blocked my one window with a bookshelf so that I wouldn't be 'pulled' out. Since I work here at night, the light is not an issue. The smallness keeps me focused on what is in front of me—and I don't have to bother with heating. Sometimes there are slug trails on the floor—I love being close to nature here!"

When I asked Olaf to free-associate to the word *home,* he quickly said: "Cozy, lights on, good people, happy noises, interesting nooks and crannies." When I asked if this place—his room—was "home," he gave a long sigh and paused a while: "That's an interesting question. It is, but some voice inside says 'No!' I feel at home in so many places. Home is where people are that I love! I've lived in too many places, and each one has been a gift, has brought out different parts of me."

Certainly his current room and lifestyle, though far from elegant, totally suited his current concerns. It was ironic that in working for many years on a book about community, Olaf had cut himself off from all but a few friends and lived—as he described it—"the life of a monk." With his book published, he hoped to conduct workshops and move back into a real community.

Though this form of home may not be everyone's choice, what this room provided for Olaf was the essence of house-as-haven. It was a place to sleep in comfort, to keep his belongings, to eat and bathe, to engage in creative work, and to decorate with images that reflect who he is and what and whom he cares about. It provided shelter, warmth, privacy; it was a container of memories. He was very happy there. When I asked him to give this dwelling a name, he called it simply "The Log Cabin."

Retreat to a Simple Hut: Kamo No Chomei—A Final Resting Place

On the other side of the Pacific Ocean, eight hundred years before, another man withdrew to a simple dwelling and wrote about it in "Record of a Ten-Foot-Square Hut." Kamo no Chomei lived in Japan between 1153 and 1216, in a period of considerable social and political upheaval. After witnessing a number of natural disasters (fires, whirlwind, famine, earthquake) and ruing the "undependability of our dwellings," he withdrew from the world, became a Buddhist monk, and built himself a tiny hut on the slopes of Mount Hino. In a moving account he wrote a few years before his death, he records the essence of dwelling—at its most simple and at its most profound.

"Now that I have reached the age of sixty, when my life fades as quickly as dew, I've put together a lodging for my final days. I'm like a traveler who prepares shelter for one night, or an aging silkworm spinning its cocoon. . . . It measures only ten feet square and less than seven feet in height. . . .

"On the east side of my hut I have extended the eaves out three feet so as to provide a place for firewood and cooking. On the south I constructed a bamboo verandah, with a shelf for vases and other Buddhist articles. . . . Along the east edge of the room I've spread soft fern fronds to make a place to sleep at night. In the southwest corner I put up a hanging shelf of bamboo with three leather-covered boxes on it . . .

"As to my surroundings, south of my hut I have rigged a bamboo pipe that feeds water into a rocky basin I have fashioned. Since there are plenty of forest trees close by, I have no trouble gathering whatever brushwood I need.

"This part of the mountain is called Toyama or Outer Hill. The trails are buried in creepers, the valleys dense with vegetation. But I have a clear view to the west, which is some aid to my meditations . . .

"When I tire of intoning the *nembutsu* or am not in the mood to recite sutras, I simply give myself a rest and neglect my devotions. There's no one to stop me and no one to feel ashamed on my account . . .

"If I am still in the mood for music, I often play 'The Melody of the Autumn Wind,' blending it with the sighing of the pines, or perform the piece entitled 'The Flowering Fountain' to accompany the rippling of the water.

"Sometimes I dig cogon grass sprouts, pick rock-pear berries, or gather basketsful of cress or tubers of wild taro. Other times I go to the rice fields along the border of the mountain, gathering up fallen ears of rice and weaving them into ornamental wreaths. Or if the weather is fair, I clamber up to the peak and gaze far off in the direction of my old home . . .

"When I first came here to live, I in fact expected to stay only a short while, yet now five years have passed. My 'temporary dwelling' has become an old home of sorts, the area under the eaves heaped with decaying leaves, the foundation overgrown with moss . . .

"Small as it is, it provides room enough to sleep at night and to sit in the daytime, all that is needed to accommodate one person. The hermit crab prefers a little shell because he knows the dimensions of his own body . . . And I am the same. Knowing my own size and knowing the ways of the world, I crave nothing, chase after nothing. I desire only a peaceful spot, and delight in being free from care."[3]

For this Buddhist monk, the hut became his final resting place, meeting his simple needs for a place to sleep, to shelter a few belongings, to venture out from to take a walk, to gaze at the riverboats, to pick flowering reeds, and to return to for a quiet nap. In the face of natural disasters and the uncertainties of aging, the hut became a place of stability, for living in the moment. At this stage in his life, it was all Kamo no Chomei needed. His hut and its setting reflected perfectly who he was, and thus he was deeply content. As Thomas Moore has written in *Care of the Soul,* "The flowering of life depends upon finding a reflection of oneself in the world . . . We will never achieve the flowering of our own natures until we find that piece of ourselves, that lovable twin, which lives in the world and *as* the world."[4]

EVOLVING SELF-IMAGE:
EXERCISES YOU CAN DO YOURSELF

Discovering a Neglected Part of Yourself

How can you begin to identify and understand a changing image of yourself through your relationship with the environment? There are a number of cues to look for. One would be a subtle or perhaps nagging dissatisfaction with your current dwelling-place. You may find yourself reluctant to spend time there or to invite friends over. One woman I worked with, for example, after a divorce and the departure of her children for college, found herself increasingly alienated from the master bedroom. When she finally converted it into a study and created a new bedroom in a smaller former guest room, her life as a woman in her own right—neither wife nor mother—took a positive and creative turn.

Another cue would be an unwillingness to personalize, decorate, or put any "mark" on your home. You may leave walls bare though you have plenty of pictures or photos you could put up. You may, like Jean, leave belongings in boxes, unwilling perhaps to admit you are here to stay. You may feel that this house or apartment at some time expressed who you were, but it now feels out of sync in some way. You may even feel—as did Marilyn—that your home has some kind of uncomfortable hold over you, that it is making what feels like unreasonable demands.

If any of these cues resonate for you, it would be worthwhile having a heart-to-heart conversation with your house, as described in the exercises in chapter 3.

It would be revealing, too, to focus on one feature in your drawing, or in your house, that *doesn't* have the same alienating or discomforting feeling. In Marilyn's case, it was the sun outside the prison bars that seemed to enclose her cottage. It may be a feature in your drawing that you're surprised to find there—a flower, perhaps, or a bird, a cloud, a soft cushion, or a landscape. Try to speak as that feature: "I am a bird flying free above the house" or, "I am a soft place where you can relax and be yourself." Just see what happens! Don't censor yourself. Perhaps tape-record what you say, because in listening and listening again to your own words, you may have important insights as to the half-hidden part of yourself that seeks expression.

Another approach is to focus on where in your home you feel most comfortable, or which rooms or spaces feel particularly alienating. These can be significant clues as to what path you need to explore in discovering hidden aspects of self. In the case of Rosita, living in the mobile home with her son, she was well aware that the kitchen felt uncomfortable to her. In exploring this, she recognized her discomfort with traditional "motherly" tasks like cooking. In the case of Joan, who left the convent after sixteen years, her first clues about her need to change came in her feelings of alienation in the convent, her experience of comfort in just one place—the basement. For Barbara, struggling to free herself from the very strong influence of her mother, it was the slightly unkempt but "more emotional" house of her neighbor that offered a clue to her own need to expand. In my own case, it was my garden/inner child/intuitive woman that nagged at me for attention.

If there is a place or an image like this—real or not—that resonates for you, which "pops up" into consciousness, perhaps when you least expect it, this is the place you need to explore. Your unconscious is wise beyond your knowing! A dialogue or conversation with this place may provide important guidance. Imagine it as your teacher; ask what it has to tell you. You may be very surprised at the outcome.

Re-creating Home to Accommodate a Lost Part of the Self

If you sense that part of you is not receiving attention, or is being overshadowed by a more dominant facet of the psyche, you might try this exercise. Sit in a comfortable chair, on your bed, or somewhere where you can close your eyes and not be disturbed for an hour. Take several deep breaths and let yourself relax. Try tensing each muscle in turn—from your feet to your scalp—and then let it go.

Now imagine yourself walking along a trail through a beautiful meadow or forest. The sun is shining, birds are singing, and you feel happy and relaxed. After a while, you see another person walking toward you. You are intrigued—Who is this person? You are eager to meet him or her.

As the stranger approaches, you realize it is a part of yourself, a part you have lost touch with. The two of you sit down and start to converse. You get to know each other again.

When you feel that you know what this person represents, imagine a perfect environment in which the two of you could live comfortably together. Don't worry about what is possible, what you can afford—just let your imagination create this place for you.

When you feel that you've explored it sufficiently in your mind, bring yourself slowly back to the present and record what you imagined, either by writing in your journal or by drawing a picture or symbol. Finally, consider how—in reality—you might create such a place, by modifying or rearranging your present home or by moving. Talk it over with a friend or counselor; their questions may help you further ground this image.

SIX

Becoming Partners:
Power Struggles in Making
a Home Together

When my father left in the morning to work on the fences, or one of the three
boxes that watered the sheep and cattle, my mother heard no human voice
save the two children. There was no contact with another human being and
the silence was so profound it pressed upon the eardrums. My father, being a
westerner, born into that profound peace and silence, felt the need for it like an
addiction to a powerful drug . . . To those who know it, the annihilation of the
self, subsumed into the vast emptiness of nature, is akin to a religious experi-
ence . . . For my mother, the emptiness was disorienting, and the loneliness and
silence a daily torment of existential dread.

—JILL KER CONWAY, *The Road from Coorain*[1]

Creating a home together may be one of the most taxing negotiations any
couple has to make. Each person brings to the situation a history of environmental experiences, dating back to his or her first awareness of home in infancy
and childhood. Each has—largely unconsciously—created a set of spatial and aesthetic preferences that will influence feelings about a range of issues about home,
including location, size, form, style, decoration, furnishings, privacy, territory,
and use. Where one of them is an architect or designer or otherwise has a strong
visual sense, further complications may arise. If one or both have previously been

married or lived with a partner, there may be decisions about space or decorating made in an earlier relationship that now have to be renegotiated.

Sharing a room or apartment may place strains on a relationship as each person tries to find enough personal space in a setting that may be only marginally large enough for two. A rental apartment, for example, makes few demands on the renter as to long-term upkeep but offers few creative rewards in terms of altering space or putting in a garden. On the other hand, moving into an owner-occupied house has its own set of rewards and difficulties. Although the amount of space may not be an issue, the use of "extra" rooms, the carving out of private territories, and decisions related to furniture and interior design may become points of tension and argument. Ironically, few of us receive any life-training in these significant decisions! As children, our home—its location, form, decor, state of maintenance—is a given. Rarely before adolescence (and sometimes not then) do parents consult their children about environmental changes. Upon becoming a couple, we are suddenly thrust into unfamiliar territory, sometimes resulting in a severe strain on the relationship.

As a couple starts to make decisions together about the house, one usually takes the lead in making suggestions, which the other agrees with, modifies, or vetoes. If one has a more visual sense, is more of a homebody, or has training in design, that person takes the lead. In heterosexual couples, it is not necessarily the woman who does so, although women's traditional role has been homemaking. With some couples, the major issue is one of territory—who will have control over which rooms. With others, it is a matter of design style—avant-garde versus traditional, contemporary versus country, Victorian versus hippy-funk. Or it may be that one person is comfortable working for a salary inside the home whereas the other is not. Whatever the issue, hopefully it is slowly worked out in a process of give-and-take, just as other relationship issues are negotiated. If the dwelling is indeed a material expression of individual values—an expression of the ego-self—it is small wonder that coming to terms with the sharing of space is one of the most delicate components of living together.

Finally, no one self or pair of selves is a static entity. Not only do two selves cohabiting need to understand their own and each other's spatial needs, they also have to adjust to individual changes in the need for space over time. When the differences between two or more people sharing space become so acute that separation is the only solution, those differences sometimes first become manifest in clashes over the use and meaning of domestic space or in increasing demands for time and space alone.

Working Out Differences: Paul and Helen

Paul and Helen are a couple who have successfully worked out their differences with regard to the creation of a home. They are both in their late thirties and have been together for eleven years. They met in graduate school and for much of the past decade they have been investing their energies in a planning-consulting business. They ran it first from their apartment and now from commercial office space; they have more than twenty employees and are very successful in their field.

While the firm grew, Paul and Helen remained in a very small one-bedroom apartment. They spent relatively little time there, because the business absorbed all of their energies. Ten months prior to our conversation, they had moved into their first house. They had searched for it for more than a year and looked at about seventy properties—"quiet" was number one for both of them, since their work lives were so active and people-filled.

The house they finally bought was in the Berkeley hills on a steep, wooded lot. It dated from around the 1940s and had a large picture window looking west toward San Francisco Bay, visible through the trees. When they first saw it, it was decorated and furnished in a style totally opposite to their tastes, but they felt it had great potential. They knocked out several walls, put in skylights, added two windows, ripped off paneling, and retiled two bathrooms. From the moment they moved in, they entertained a lot, despite its unfinished state. When I talked with them, they were both excited about future plans in and for the house.

I asked them separately to put down their feelings about the house in visual form. The pictures they composed had many similarities—a good indication that there was basic agreement between them. Paul drew a group of people sitting at a round table, with arrows reaching out to the view; Helen drew a rectangle to symbolize the house, held up by dollar signs (their investment) with clusters of people, and arrows to represent spaciousness and view. Though they had sought out quiet surroundings, they reveled in having enough space for people to visit, stay, and share meals with them.

As is the case with many couples, Paul and Helen had different ways of "meeting" the world around them. Paul is more auditory than visual; he likes to have music on all the time and has set up a room in the house with a music system and synthesizer. At their business, he is the one who runs public meetings and has good listening skills. Helen, on the other hand, is more visual; her first degree was in interior design, and she recalled how—with her first paychecks—she bought prints and blown glass and sat in an almost bare apartment, enjoying them. In their decisions about the house, it was often Helen who took the lead or had the strongest opinions.

In the business that Paul and Helen have created—among other things—they train individuals and groups to listen to each other, to argue things out, and to reach a consensus. They laughingly talked about how this had put them in a good position to listen to each other and reach compromises. Helen liked an avant-garde decor; Paul was more conservative. Helen wanted a "poufy" sofa; Paul wanted something more "tailored." They searched until they found something that satisfied them both. Helen wanted granite countertops in the kitchen with rough edges; Paul could accept the granite but wanted the edges smooth. Helen wanted stark white kitchen cabinets; Paul wanted wood. Sometimes, they admitted, they have a "big argument," but they see this as just a stage in the process and not as some terrible breakdown in their relationship.

Considering the intensity of both of their work lives, with frequent meetings, conventions, public lectures, and plane trips, the relative isolation and complete privacy of their house was very pleasing to them both. For couples in which one is employed outside the home and the other works at home (as a homemaker or for a salary), the issue of privacy may not be so easy to agree on. Typically, the one who goes out to work seeks a more private home location than the one who stays at home, for whom privacy may be experienced as isolation and loneliness.

Their first owned home has given Paul and Helen more than privacy and an investment. As one of them remarked: "It has given us weekends! At our tiny apartment, there was nothing creative to do there except cook. We tended to go back to the office. There were *always* deadlines. Now we leave the office on Friday and actually spend the weekend doing something *other* than work. We work on the house or go out looking for wood or fabric samples. It's so much *fun!*"

As is the case with many people, Paul and Helen could relate some aspects of the choice of this house to values carried from childhood. Paul recalled growing up in quite a cramped house in a working-class neighborhood in Cleveland. Not far away, there was a house on a hill with large picture windows taking in the view. "I used to point it out to my parents as we went by and say, '*That's* the kind of house I want to live in!' Now I'm just thrilled to be in *this* house!"

Helen had grown up in a typical suburban house in North Carolina. "It was all these separate rooms—doors closed. I always wanted a house which would be *open,* where you could see from space to space, and where only the bedroom and bathroom would have doors. I guess that's *just* what we're doing here."

In all respects, Paul and Helen seem to have found their "right place." Its privacy and quiet provide a contrast to their hectic work life. The physical work on the house balances out the verbal focus of their professional lives. They have the skills to meld their different tastes into a decor that both can feel is comfortable and nurturing. And—though unconscious of the fact when they bought the house—each has found a place with echoes of a childhood dream. Their success in making a home together was not because they had identical tastes, or because one person made all the decisions and the other happily agreed, but because they had certain shared needs (for a private location, for space to entertain) and because on areas of aesthetic differences, they really *listened* to each other and worked out a compromise.

Couple in Conflict:
Pat and Tom's Contrasting Images of Home

Not all couples are able to resolve aesthetic or style differences as smoothly as Paul and Helen. In the case of Pat and Tom, conflicts over style became the focal point in a troubled relationship. Pat is a friend of mine from graduate school. When this dialogue took place, she had just separated, very painfully, from her husband. Because a great deal of their conflict was apparently over a house, she was eager to talk about it with me.

Pat and Tom had been together for several years; it was a second marriage for both. Since the children of both previous marriages were away at college, they decided to live out a lifelong dream—to move to the country. Tom gave up his job in an architectural office, and they bought a run-down but fixable house near the coast in southern Oregon. Tom had skills as a carpenter and a passionate interest in building and design; he set about transforming the house. And that was when problems began to emerge: The more he got into the work of changing the house, the more it became apparent that his and Pat's views on what makes a desirable home were radically different. As Pat started to talk to me, she could barely contain her anger. I asked her to speak to the house directly, as if it were animate.

"You piss me off, house. I think you have some cute little numbers going but basically they don't disguise the fact that you're ugly. We tried to make a silk purse out of a sow's ear, and it's still a sow's ear. You're not craftsmanlike. You don't embody the things that I think are important. You're not cozy. You're a product of a lot of insincere stuff. You're supposed to represent agreement and you don't. You represent a one-man dream, not a two-person dream. There are some features that I asked for, but you're not mine. You're *not* mine! You and I have rather a distance between us. I never appreciated you. I still don't!"

I asked Pat if she'd be willing to respond as the house. Without hesitation, she quickly changed positions.

"Well, you know, I don't really like you either! You never got into the spirit of me—you never really wanted me and so of course I'm not responsive to you. I'm doing my best with not a whole lot of help. Given all that I *didn't* have, I'm not doing so bad. It's true that I'm crude and I'm rough, and I'm not very warm, and I'm kind of a hodgepodge of styles. But you have to admit I'm a big improvement over what I was."

At this point, Pat impulsively changes places again. "Well, yeah, you're a big improvement over what you were, but you just don't make it! You're cavernous, you're very hard to heat, you don't have good proportions, you don't have any nooks and crannies where people can hide, you are just not together. You don't represent a haven, you represent a chore."

I asked Pat if she'd be willing to take Tom's part, to say what *he* might say about the house if he were present:

"Oh, you are so beautiful, you are so great! You are my creation, you are perfect! I mean, look at all the work that went into you—look at all the genius that it took to redesign you. You were nothing when I started with you, just nothing. And I made you into this great thing. I completely ripped you open. I took out all your insides and just re-created you from scratch. Pat has no capacity for appreciating it. It was my idea to pull out the original ceiling and make that great big pointed ceiling. I mean that's the most gorgeous feature of the house. I like two-story spaces. I mean that's really what counts in architecture. You just can't do *little rooms*. You have to do *BIG SPACES,* so when people come in, they say 'Ahhhh.' Right? I would put a cupola up there and people will come from miles around to see my house!"

Tom—at least in Pat's eyes—clearly had very strong ideas about design and interior spaces. I asked Pat to switch, become herself and talk about what *she* liked.

"Coziness—which means a space that I can see and feel and kind of pull in around me. When I lived in a Victorian house, it was like living in a flower. That was after my first marriage and before I met Tom. I painted the two front rooms pink with a rose ceiling and apricot with an orange ceiling. It was just like a rose. It was very warm; you could feel it coming around you and holding you on the inside, like in its heart. Wherever you sat in that house, it felt good. It was like an enclosure. It was welcoming and warm. I would sometimes sit with Tom when he was designing houses for other people. And he would design very austere kinds of spaces, very four-cornered spaces, very quadrilateral. And I'd always say, 'Let's put bumps in! Let's put in an alcove out here and a bay window that juts out here.' My Victorian house had a round bay and bumps everywhere. To me, that makes something out of a room. It gives it some feeling, some uniqueness that you can anchor yourself to. Tom's stuff all the time had to be very 'moderne.' His stuff always rose high up—so many of his designs were two stories high. Sometimes, it featured a four-storied space! My preference is for individual rooms that are self-contained and each has its own style and its own quality, that you can close the door to."

Of all the people I have talked with, none have had such radically opposed environmental values as Pat and Tom, values that came into the open only when the issue of remodeling a house together was faced. These contrasting values about the dwelling were similarly expressed in quite opposite views about the landscape. Tom had been attracted to the wild, rugged setting of their house—steep hillsides of rough grazing punctuated by exposed rock and massive pine trees. There was little in the landscape that was tamed or cultivated; it reminded Tom of the moorland in his native Scotland, a landscape he had stomped across during the stormy moods of adolescence.

Pat's preferred landscape was radically different. She had grown up in a city and in adult life had come to love the quiet, ordered, cultivated environment of orchards and farmland. "I like places where people have planted things. I just am not a wild, rugged person. I love the way men have transformed the land. I just love a well-taken-care-of piece of land. It makes my heart rise up. And this wild, rugged stuff just makes me want to go and dig a hole, hide, and call help! Beyond this glowering cloud mass and these blowing away fields is the ocean. HUGE! Full of magnetism and wild, rugged stuff and, while I love to relate to that on a vacation, I couldn't stand living next to it. It's too much. I want something calmer. I'll tell you where I used to go. There is this wonderful brook, a beautiful, little, very fast-flowing stream. It is so lovely and tiny and I can watch it trickling among all the rocks. It has all these lovely little sounds—it didn't *crash* and *roar*. There's a little trickle over here and trickle over there, and if I listen real clearly I can hear this one and then that one and then all together like a little concert. It was music. Beautiful little ballads, little flowers growing, little pebbles showing."

At the root of this stormy disagreement over environments was the fact that for years Pat had been a traditional wife, allowing Tom to make the major decisions about where and how they lived. This was how *her* parents' marriage had worked; this was what she thought being a good wife was all about. But now, in the 1980s, after raising children and returning to college to develop her own interests, she wanted a more egalitarian marriage. So did Tom, apparently, but when it came to locating and creating a new home, his old need to be boss could not be suppressed. Pat recalled that before the purchase of their country house, they had rented a cottage for some months, and it was here that things had started to go wrong. She had wanted a room of her own, where she could close the door and go to draw or think. Tom promised to build it but kept procrastinating, and in the end, never did so.

If we consider the many ways in which Pat and Tom's values are in opposition—in the rented cabin, the landscape, the remodeled house—there seems to be a basic dialectic between *openness* (of dwelling spaces, landscapes) and *enclosure* (of rooms, dwellings, fields). It is possible that this contrast is also one between predominantly masculine and feminine viewpoints. In studies of where children play, boys are observed much more frequently in wide-open spaces, girls on the edges of spaces or in semienclosures. In a master's thesis in landscape architecture, Berkeley student Louise Mozingo discovered that men in urban plazas tend to sit in exposed, up-front locations whereas women more frequently sit at the back or in more secluded places.[2] Another Berkeley student study by Tony Chiao found that, of two frequently used teen hangouts in that city, one that was on an exposed street corner was most frequently used by males; the other, in a secluded courtyard, was used mostly by females.[3]

Throughout much of the history of the human species, man has been the hunter, the one who had to peruse distant vistas for prey and approaching enemies. Women stayed in the encampment/village/home and were responsible for children and domestic animals, whose wanderings are best limited by enclosed spaces. Thus, women may have been culturally conditioned to favor enclosed places; men, to favor wide-open spaces. If, indeed, there are gender-specific spatial proclivities—as my interviews and some research studies suggest—it is small wonder that there are sometimes conflicts between couples over the creation of homes and the selection of a setting for that home.

A Home Divided in Two: Nancy and Lewis

Although masculine and feminine are gender-associated principles, they are also aspects of each person's internal makeup. For each of us, our growth toward emotional maturity requires that we come to terms with the two aspects of our psyche that often seem to be struggling for supremacy: the soft, nurturing, sensual side, traditionally perceived as feminine; and the more assertive, intellectual, out-in-the-world side, traditionally labeled as masculine. Each of us incorporates both these elements, and if one is overemphasized, the other will struggle for recognition. Thus, for the stay-at-home wife and mother, the issue may eventually arise of how to express a more assertive, action-oriented component of the psyche, frustrated in a life devoted to caregiving; whereas a woman immersed in the cut-and-thrust of the business world may conversely yearn for homebound motherhood. Similarly, men in a society that encourages and rewards aggressive competition may experience a nagging desire to express a more passive or accepting aspect of their nature. Those men who are by nature more gentle and nurturing may find themselves struggling with issues of assertiveness, boundaries, and control. It is the rare person who comes to some sense of balance without the experience of pain.

This balancing issue arose in a number of my interviews. In the case of Joan, the strict schedules, uniform, and austere style of convent life had come (albeit unconsciously) to symbolize the powerful masculinity of the established church. In leaving her religious order and creating her own environment, Joan was reestablishing a more comfortable balance between her own assertiveness and her newly emerging femininity. In the case of Nancy—an attractive, successful academic in her early

thirties—I was lucky enough to hear her describe a fantasy of how she would like to live, and then, five years later, to talk with her about the place she had created. There were some remarkable similarities between the two. Both had to do with this same issue of internal balance.

When Nancy was a graduate student in her midtwenties, she was one of a small group of women students whom I led in a guided fantasy about an "ideal environment." I asked them to imagine they were walking on a beach; they felt warm, relaxed, happy. Then they were to meet another person, who represented a part of themselves they had lost touch with. Finally the "two" were to imagine an environment in which they could live comfortably together. Nancy saw a house on a cliff with two distinct parts: a softer, more colorful half that contained a bedroom and a library; and a more straight-edged, "cooler" half that was the living room. The two halves of Nancy's house were connected by a bridgelike kitchen. (The fact that her image was of a house on a cliff did not, I think, have some deep symbolic meaning; the fact that I had located the fantasy on a beach apparently influenced a number of people to create their ideal beside the ocean. I later changed the wording to "You are walking through a meadow.")

Nancy commented on her image: "The part I feel I have lost is the soft part, which is represented by the bedroom and the library. I really feel as if these two are connected; the library is soft even though it is wooden. It is a very old and medieval library, with stained-glass windows like a church, and is full of beautiful, musty, leather-bound books. It contains a lot of loving and caring; working there is almost sensual, very soft and very creative. It feels very romantic, and has a strong connection with my grandfather. He was an editor and had all these books, and some of them were old children's books. Beautiful old leather-bound books. And when I was a baby, he used to sit and read to me, and everybody would say, 'Oh, she can't understand anything you say.' But here was one person who was saying, 'I know you have a mind. I know you enjoy these things. I want to talk with you. I want to tell you what I'm thinking.' I was aged one to two and a half.

I think my memory of this place is very romanticized; I remember him having this long white beard, which he didn't have. He had a very short one. He wasn't as soft as I remember him. But I imagined somehow the ease of working there, that somehow there was this right situation and you would sit down at your desk and it would just come; you would have all the books around you, and they would just be absorbed."

In her "ideal," Nancy equated the soft or feminine image with the bedroom and with a sensual medieval library, the image of which is clearly tempered by memories of a loving grandfather who used to read to her in such a space. She described the more geometric masculine half as the living room of her rather stylish upper-middle-class parental home. It was a space she remembered as being dominated by formality, "good behavior," and rules of etiquette. It is interesting that the bridge she chose to connect these two was a kitchen, where she perceived the preparation and eating of food as both a neutral and a connecting reality.

Five years later, Nancy was living in a rented urban apartment with Lewis. Their space had, like her fantasy, two halves and a connecting link. But, interestingly, the activities that took place in the "hard" and "soft" sides of the home had shifted compared with her fantasy of five years earlier.

The living space that Nancy and Lewis shared was, in fact, two adjacent apartments; the two halves were quite distinct, with a front door to each which could be shut. The connection was a short section of semipublic hallway. On what Nancy identified as the "soft" side (intuitive, emotional, sensual) were the bedroom Nancy shared with Lewis, the kitchen where they enjoyed preparing food together, and a living room where entertaining was considerably less formal and more personal than in her childhood home or her fantasy dwelling. Since both Nancy and her lover were academics needing study space at home, and one small apartment could not provide living and study space for two, they decided to rent the adjacent apartment when it became vacant. This then became the more "hard" (rational, functional, intellectual) half of the dwelling.

Nancy's depiction of the home she shared with Lewis. Like her "ideal" drawn five years earlier, it had two halves and a connecting link.

Unlike the fantasy, where Nancy had imagined an almost sensual study where creativity "just flowed," she now had a more realistic view of writing, which entailed a lot of hard work, struggle, and "grind." To top off this intriguing and highly functional living arrangement, the more hard-edged, pragmatic work space happened to look out over a city intersection with cars, buses, and people passing by; the more soft and sensual living and sleeping areas overlooked a huge tree, which attracted birds and virtually blotted out any view of houses or city life.

For reasons I don't remember, I interviewed only Nancy. Here is how she described these two halves: "It's a place in which two halves and two people have come together, have been able to find enough room to balance and to merge. There is the side that has all the books and is simple and sparse and made up of planes and straight lines and looks out over the city. The other side is soft and low and round and looks out over trees. It's a side for bringing in friends, and it's a side for dancing, and it's a side for eating food and making food and for making love and for being close, for taking baths. It's a side for water and sunlight and bodies. The thing that works is that neither one of the two sides has to be given up. They are balanced. When it is necessary, I can close one part of myself up: I can be totally on the side that is intellectual and scholarly and reserved, or I can be totally on the side that is sensual and soft and open."

I then asked Nancy to speak to this house (or rather pair of apartments) as if it were animate: "I really love you. You have made it easier for what was a major step in my life, of beginning to live with someone whom I really love and could let love me. You made it easier by being very simple and by having the possibility of those two sides of my life that I've been thinking about for years. It was as if you were a very good friend who was helping these two people to be together, and yet giving them room to be apart. It's a most wonderful experience, doing work and just throwing yourself into it, and then making this gesture about leaving it behind; actually having to pull the door hard to slam it to get it to lock. It really lets me be able to go to the other side and relax. Also, I think it lets me feel that I can enjoy things like cooking because I'm not looking at my work all the time. When I start taking books over to the "soft" side, that's a sign that I'm worrying. It never feels good. And it suits Lewis well, too, because when he works, he works hard; when he stops, he doesn't want to carry it over too much. One person said it was the utmost mind/body split, which is really one way of looking at it, and yet what is so nice is that there is never any tension about it."

For professional women of a certain age, myself included, the potential role conflicts between work and home are compounded by the cultural baggage we carry about men "going out to work" and women "staying at home." In the workplace, both are expected to be efficient, professional, asexual, and emotionally guarded; at home, both are expected to be more casual, relaxed, and nurturing—especially the woman. This has been her traditional role at home—as wife, mother, daughter, lover. When one or both members of a couple work and live in the same space, role problems are likely to arise; the need to find an appropriate balance between work life and domestic life, the rational and the emotional, becomes essential.

In a very concrete way, Nancy and Lewis solved their need to find a balance between the intellectual and the sensual. However, not everyone needs, or wants, to express the contrast or the balance in this way. For some, the expression may be in quite another medium than the physical environment. Or the exploration of balance may be dealt with quite internally, via dreams. But for Nancy—trained as an architect and at the time of our conversation engaged in writing her dissertation on architectural history—that balance had to be expressed via the physical environment.

Order versus Chaos: Nicki and Martin's Conflict over Tidiness

The more I have talked to people about their houses, the more anguished stories I hear about conflicts between husbands and wives, parents and children, roommates and lovers, not only over style, but also over the way in which the dwelling interior is organized. This is not a question of decorating styles or design, but a very fundamental conflict between order and chaos: "He is always dropping things on the floor; I'm always picking up after him." "I like the room ordered and neat; she just doesn't care." The issue doesn't seem to be so much one of cleanliness as the need of some people for visual order and harmony, and for others, complete obliviousness to this issue. By some twist of fate, such people often end up sharing houses with each other!

Such was the case of Nicki and Martin, a young couple who had been living together in Nicki's San Francisco apartment for two years. Just prior to my conversation with Nicki, Martin had moved out. His room was still as he had left it, and it was this room that Nicki largely chose to focus on in our conversation.

"All the beauty and life of the room is hidden by the nonstop clutter—almost every inch of every horizontal surface is covered in junk. I'm really upset right in my solar plexus when I think about that confusion and chaos. I find it so upsetting, I hate to come into this room; as a result, I'm losing several beautiful plants. I won't come in here to water them; I've asked Martin to do it, but he won't. I used to live this way myself—in crazy disorder. I was depressed and started feeling suicidal. Eventually, I got some help and started coming out of it. Then I wanted order and more order. It means more to me all the time."

I asked Nicki if she could imagine Martin being with us and I asked her to tell him what it was about this room that upset her so much: "I resent you, Martin; I resent your craziness, I resent this disorder. I resent the fact that every item you touch you do not put back in its original place. I resent you because you come home to a good home and a good woman and a good relationship, and you don't partake of any responsibility in that relationship. This disorder is just a manifestation of your lack of responsibility. I feel very infringed upon; I feel like this is my home, too, and I don't want that craziness."

Then I asked Nicki to imagine what Martin might say in response. "I open the door and just walk over all the clutter. It just doesn't bother me. I do appreciate the colors in the room and the old furniture, but none of it means much to me. The clutter doesn't matter. I'm comfortable. Order doesn't do anything for me."

Clearly, order does do something for Nicki. At the end of our conversation, she remarked, "With my next lover, I want to go out and create a home together. We didn't do that, Martin and I, and, because of that, I feel we suffered."

Order and chaos—a fundamental dialectic out of which, many cultures believe, the world was created. All creation myths have at their root a fundamental need to place the apparent chaos of the world into some kind of structure or order. The scientific revolution in the West had at its base the search for fundamental rules or order in the complexities of nature. Now, with chaos theory, the basic attempt to find order is being questioned. Small wonder that the issues of chaos and order in the dwelling—our own small corner of the universe—raise such profound emotions. We hold strong views yet barely understand their meaning. A husband or lover may create a chaotic environment or procrastinate on home-maintenance projects in order to communicate nonverbally (and perhaps unconsciously) anger at the spouse. Sometimes—and for some people—the expression of anger via the relatively neutral medium of the physical environment is preferable to expressing it in words and exploring what the anger is really about.

For Nicki, Martin's chaotic room was unacceptable and was clearly a major irritant in their relationship. I did not speak with Martin, so I have no idea what this disorder expressed for him. We can assume it may have been a means of communicating something to himself, or to Nicki, or someone else significant in his past.

House as Home, House as Status: Alan and Marion's Conflict over Location

For some couples who build or buy a house together, an issue of contention between them may not be one of aesthetic style or state of orderliness but rather what the house *means* to each of them as a social symbol. If for one of them it is primarily a symbol of social identity and for the other it is a statement about family and nurturance, there may eventually be some kind of clash over these differing goals. This was apparently the case with Marion and Alan, living in a large, imposing, architect-designed house an hour's drive from San Francisco in an upscale rural enclave. Alan was a medical specialist who had been very successful in his career, working long hours and earning a high income. Ten years previously, he and his wife, Marion, had commissioned an architect to design them a house on a hilly site with a spectacular view of wild landscape and a glimpse of the Pacific Ocean. The house was built, and the couple and their two daughters moved in. The interior was subsequently featured in design magazines and Sunday supplements—the American Dream come true.

As time passed, however, the dream started to unravel. Gradually, Marion became more and more disaffected from the house. Poor construction meant that she, as a stay-at-home wife, was often supervising repair and maintenance projects. The steep hillside site proved to be excessively windy, often fog-bound, and although affording a spectacular view, was not conducive to outside play for the children. But most problematic of all, for Marion, was its location, far from the cafes and bookshops and potential work opportunities she wanted to explore. When I talked with her, she was feeling so frustrated and upset, she often felt sick

Marion's depiction of the house she now disliked, symbolically engulfing her creative needs and spiritual growth.

to her stomach as she drove home: "Some days, I feel so bad about living here, I just want to turn the car around and drive away. I feel I'd rather live anywhere but here—even in a tent."

As Marion described the process of creating their home, it became clear that her husband had made all the pivotal decisions—house location, choice of architect, design features, and so on. She had willingly acquiesced at the time, not feeling able to make her needs heard. Now, a decade later, approaching middle age, and with child-rearing largely accomplished, Marion was becoming more her own person—and was sick at heart about her home. For Alan, the house was a status symbol; he loved the attention from the magazines and relished entertaining professional colleagues who gasped at the breathtaking living room and panoramic view. For Marion, the house was a home for the family, but increasingly also a base of operation from which she wished to explore the world, creative work, and friendships, and thus discover more fully who she was. The remote location of the house and its frequent need for maintenance attention were constant barriers to her exploring the world and her self. Her husband did not share—or sympathize with—these concerns. He liked the privacy and quiet of the location in contrast to the stress and constant human-contact demands of his job. He loved the house as an imposing symbol of his wealth and success, and felt that his wife ought to be grateful for how well he had provided for the family.

The couple eventually divorced and sold the house. Marion moved to a city apartment, enrolled in art classes, and started on a long-delayed career. She did not blame Alan for the problems that revolved around their house, but rather blamed herself for being too "weak and submissive" at the time they moved there, not feeling she had the right or strength to have equal voice in the decisions that her husband took upon himself. Alan grieved as much for the loss of house as status symbol as he did for loss of family.

This story reaffirms the necessity for couples to talk honestly about what house and home mean to them and to discuss the pros and cons for each of them of particular locations (suburban, urban, ex-urban, small town). A research study conducted in New York that followed couples who did—and did not—move from a middle-income city apartment complex to the suburbs found that men were more likely to be happy in a suburb, women in the city. For men, the status, privacy, and quiet of owning a home in the suburbs more than made up for the stress of commuting. For many women, in contrast, the suburban "dream" did not make up for their distance from work opportunities, friends, easy access to child care, and cultural stimulation.[4] As more and more married women and mothers enter the work force, the demand for family-oriented housing in cities and older inner suburbs is likely to increase. Like Marion, fewer and fewer women are going to buy into the suburban or ex-urban dream, however much it may fulfill their, or their spouses', need for a symbol of status.

Moving Unravels a Marriage: Louise and George

In the early years of their marriage, Louise and George bought a modest suburban ranch house and enjoyed fixing it up as a home for their expected family. When their children were high-school age, Louise was anxious to return to graduate schoo,l and, somewhat reluctantly, George agreed to move to a house in the hills above the Berkeley campus. George was nervous about moving to the "radical" environment of Berkeley after the more predictable social setting of the suburbs. In order to compromise on this issue since the move was primarily her wish, Louise agreed to the purchase of an imposing, austere house that was definitely not her style. As she described her childhood home, which she saw as her "ideal," she spoke of a house with homey nooks and crannies, enclosed rooms, and "surprises." Her father had cut holes in the walls of both the attic and the basement, just so the children could crawl through and explore. "You could get all the way around until you were under the front porch. It was creepy and scary; we sort of dared each other to go in there . . . Once we were going to repaper a wall, and my father put out lots of crayons and let us draw all over the wall; everybody who visited drew characters and all sorts of things. It stayed that way for a long time; it was so much *fun!* People really loved to come because it felt so uninhibited and kind of crazy, and they didn't know anyone else who lived like that. George could never have lived like that."

Shortly thereafter, after each had compromised, their marriage started to come apart. Although I'm not suggesting that the move to Berkeley caused the breakdown of this marriage, the difference in values that this move made more explicit was one of a range of issues around which Louise, in particular, was no longer willing to compromise.

It is important to reiterate that when a couple find they have different aesthetic tastes, or differences in what a house means, this does not indicate some kind of irreparable gulf. Life would be dull indeed if a partner were our mirror image! We are all extraordinarily complex creatures, each on a path of personal development, each with different familial and environmental roots. The environment of home and neighborhood is just one arena in which differing values may become manifest. These differences can be seen as a lens through which to explore other, less visible issues—the fear of change, the desire for change, the threat to a man of a woman's career, a woman's anger at the time and energy her husband invests in work. It may be easier for both to start with the conflicts manifest in the environment, but unless they go beyond these to what they symbolize, they have sidestepped an important avenue of growth. Couples today have access to professional counseling and to myriad books and magazine articles—all of which can help them analyze and translate into understandable terms human behaviors of control, resentment, and anger. A generation or two ago, this was not the case, as exemplified by the story of Michael's mother and her house.

Grand Hotel in Oklahoma: Creating a Fantasy Dwelling

In the course of a conversation with Michael, a San Francisco artist living in a converted factory, he started to talk about his parents. What he recounted was a poignant story of husband-and-wife conflicts acted out via their dwelling:

"What the house meant to my mother was very much tied up with social status. Decorating the house every year and the furniture she chose gave her sense of who she was. There was a bedroom that was my mother's kind of 'ode to being.' I remember how strange it was because it was a small bedroom with imitation Louis XV furniture. It was all gold satin: The bedspread and the curtains and the chairs were all gold satin, and the room itself was in the most pretentious and absolutely out-of-place style that you could imagine, some kind of very thwarted idea of Versailles. And this was so strange since we were in Oklahoma, in an oil town, and there was nothing my mother had ever seen like that.

"Many years later, I saw a film called *Grand Hotel* and I realized that this was a replica of Greta Garbo's bedroom in the Grand Hotel. For my mother, it symbolized a certain kind of world she could never belong to or ever have. The bedroom took on a symbolic ritual of a place in which she could live out all her fantasies in some kind of dream world. It always amazed me that no one else seemed to be aware of what was going on symbolically. It wasn't until I was grown and I saw that movie that I realized it was something that had influenced her very, very strongly.

"It had a great deal to do also with my mother's family. They all lived in very, very poor small houses in which people were very unaware of their style of living. My mother obviously wanted to separate herself as much as possible from that, which is probably why the house became such a vivid symbol. It had very much to do with the fact that she felt that she should have been married to a millionaire or somebody who was enormously wealthy. Her disappointment in not being able to fulfill that somehow came out in the house. . . .

"For my father, a house was somewhere you slept in, left, and came back to. It did not have any other than a practical function. But he could be alienated by other people's lifestyles; if people used candlelight to eat by, he would promptly complain that he could not see the food. He insisted that we have neon lights in our kitchen, which of course practically killed my mother. He didn't want my mother totally in control of the environment, so he would insist on the things that he knew would make her feel awful to show his dominance and control over the situation."

Again, we see here an acting out on the environment as a substitute for direct verbal communication: Many people find it easier to leave a room in disarray, or procrastinate in building a promised studio, or insist on neon lights in the kitchen than to confront the dissatisfaction with the relationship in a conscious way.

It may be that what a home symbolizes for each person is more critical than almost any other issue. In all the conversations I had with couples who were comfortably making and sharing a home together, they all seemed to be in accord over the basic function and meaning of home. Concerns over privacy, territory, and personal space can usually be negotiated or made to work via house-remodeling or a move. But if one perceives the home principally as a symbol of status, the other as a nurturing vessel for family life, or if one cares deeply about homemaking while the other seems to just use the place as somewhere to sleep without appreciation for the partner's efforts, it may be more difficult to avoid resentment and conflict.

Beliefs about gender roles are often at the root of these problems. If a man sees the house as principally a place to recharge his batteries and then go back out into the world, he may just be replaying what he saw his father do, and turning his wife into the all-giving, always-available "mother." Some women are content to replay their mother's role and see this arrangement as appropriate. But many women may feel emerging resentment. Developing herself as a full human being may not include being an undemanding wife or partner. For Marion, her desire to explore a career was stronger than a conflicting desire to stay with her husband. For Michael's mother, the need or opportunity to leave was not an issue, so she instead withdrew into the fantasy world of the Grand Hotel.

Despite societal and media pressure toward more egalitarian gender roles, it is hard for many people to let go of what have been the traditional roles of men and women in a marriage. Even though both may work and have careers, the man may feel it is demeaning to take care of the laundry, and the woman may feel it is not her job to take out the garbage. In a study of professional dual-career families in Chicago in the late 1980s, it was found that 80 percent of domestic work was still done by the woman.[5] Those jobs that men did undertake largely comprised outdoor chores like yard work, exterior repairs, emptying the garbage, and taking the automobile to be serviced.

A return to city living, or to older, mixed-use neighborhoods, or to "empty nest" communities serves the needs, particularly of women, where smaller, more efficient dwellings free up their time for personal growth, careers, and other pursuits. The burgeoning interest in this country in co-housing (long established in Denmark, Sweden, Norway, and the Netherlands) suggests that it is women's demands for the opportunity to share traditionally female work (cooking, child care) that is beginning to make changes in how housing is built and organized. It is often the woman who is first attracted to the idea of co-housing, because shared meals several evenings a week in a common house, plus on-site child care, are likely to ease her domestic burdens as well as offer the potential for a more neighborly lifestyle. The man may at first be more reluctant, be more concerned about the potential loss of privacy, just as men in the more traditional move to suburbia are seeking privacy while many women are fearful of potential isolation. As the next generation of young men and women emerge into adulthood, it seems likely that more social experiments like co-housing will be discussed and embraced, enabling a greater balance of what have traditionally been perceived as men's and women's attitudes toward home.

Home Is Where the Self Is

In every relationship, couples express their conflicting or similar needs and values through the medium of the home environment. The personal need for self-expression in the environment is present to a greater or lesser degree in everyone; but since we are each unique beings on a particular path of psychological growth, it is not surprising that couples sometimes find themselves in different places or diverging directions as time passes. Those differences, as we have seen, can become concretized in conflicting attitudes toward the environment—the need for wide-open versus enclosed spaces, orderliness versus chaos, dignified versus informal decor, rural versus city living. Those differences in environmental values are not the core of the conflict but rather clues in the material world about something partially hidden in the individual psyche. They are, in some ways, akin to a dream that relays a message or clue from the unconscious about an issue that needs to be acknowledged, a path that needs to be explored.

At their most basic level, these conflicts relate to the fact that people use the domestic environment symbolically in different ways. For Michael's mother, the house was a status object, a need that her husband despised and tried to thwart. For some people, like the designer Tom, the house is an expression of aesthetic taste, a place that may bring professional praise and ego support; Tom's wife, however, yearned for just a cozy refuge. For Nicki, home is a place for the expression of order and beauty; for her partner, it has no such meaning—the primary mode of self-expression being elsewhere, at work, for example, or in studies or clothes.

When one person in the family—mother, wife, husband—molds a place in terms of their own environmental needs and biases, others—children, spouse, lover—may find this place not at all supportive of *their* self-identity. Initial discomfort may lead to open conflict and then eventual separation so

Home-as-haven may become home-as-trap as a person's self-image changes but the dwelling remains the same.

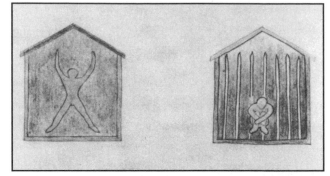

the self who feels unexpressed can find and mold a setting on their own terms. The stories recounted in this chapter do not depict selfish, unyielding, or neurotic personalities, but simply instances of the normal human condition of growth and change. Most of the people I have talked with about house problems are very much "in the world." They are lawyers, social workers, economists, teachers, architects, planners, artists, and—yes—therapists. Struggling as individuals to maintain some kind of emotional balance between work and family life, between the outer world and the inner, couples often find themselves out of sync. It has happened to most of us or to someone we know. The secret to riding out these difficult times is communication and compromise. Self-identity is not an immutable, stable structure, but is in a state of flux throughout life and is particularly liable to reassessment at specific stages of the life cycle (puberty, young adulthood, midlife, retirement, old age) and at times of critical change (death in the family, house purchase, birth of first child, divorce). When the place where one is living—that very sacred central reference point of human existence—no longer reflects and embodies the self that you believe yourself to be, there are two possible choices for correcting this self/place imbalance: stay and negotiate with family and partner for a change in the environment, or move and express a new sense of self in a new place. If a physical move away from an environment at odds with one's self-identity is not possible, a person may resort to withdrawal or fantasy or the creation of other settings, imagined or real—successful defense mechanisms that aid in protecting a threatened self-identity. When the possibility of moving is present, the final decision to do so may be prefaced by considerable anxiety, emotions, dreams, and conflict, reflecting the fear of living alone and, most important, the fear of exploring and making manifest a new, emergent sense of self.

 BECOMING PARTNERS:
EXERCISES YOU CAN DO YOURSELF

Making a Home Together

Falling in love and deciding to live together are happy but serious occurrences. When the honeymoon is over, differences may surface regarding issues of privacy and boundaries. It is wise to explore these issues before the Big Move.

One way to start is for each of you privately to write or draw what *home* means to you. For one, a place to have a garden may be essential; for the other, a private space in which to tinker may be really important. This is one level of negotiation that is essential to discuss before looking for a house or apartment or engaging an architect.

In order to bring to the forefront other issues regarding the location, form, style, and spatial division of a place you'll call home, it is a good idea for each of you to do a drawing or sketch of the dwelling in your past that most felt like home. Perhaps it was your grandmother's house, visited on special vacations; or a summer cottage you went to with your family; or the home of your best friend, where you spent time after school. Or it might be your own childhood home. Whatever the place, try to remember what it was about its physical arrangement that seemed to convey that feeling of home. You can't build-in the aroma of Grandmother's apple cake, but perhaps there is some quality of light, or warm texture of carpeting, or special area in the garden that you can try to reproduce.

Meanwhile, your partner may have different, even conflicting images of fondly remembered homes. Before you move in together, it would be good to discuss these and try to work out a compromise. When my husband and I first lived together, we had some painful disagreements over interior decor. He was a student, and we had little money; we bought most of our first pieces of furniture at garage sales. He disparagingly referred to my preferred style as "Scandinavian moderne"—I had been strongly influenced by a year of living in Sweden with a boyfriend. I referred to his sixties, quasi-hippy style as "Victorian funk." Then, in the third year of our relationship, we moved into a wonderful, big apartment that had two living rooms, and we each furnished one according to our preference. Lo and behold, we started spending time in the other's room, proof that there are ways to work out differences about interior styles, even if what results will never make the pages of *Architectural Digest*.

Working out Differences

If you are already living with someone and some issue in the home environment is becoming an irritant, a good place to start is for each of you to take a sheet of drawing paper (or just an 8½-by-11 page) and, using colored pencils or markers, put down in pictures, diagrams, or words what *this* home means to you. You might try using different colors or symbols for those parts of the house where you feel comfortable, those parts that bother or irritate you, and those that are neutral. It might be good for the two of you to do this while sitting in different rooms and then, after an agreed-upon period of time, to come together and share what you have recorded. This is a good time to practice loving listening. Try to listen with complete openness, not commenting, denying, protesting, or disagreeing with anything your partner has to say. When he or she has finished, you will have your turn.

The exercise sets a baseline, so to speak. When you both fully hear what the home means to the other, areas of disagreement or discomfort can be explored. For example, let's suppose your partner is really bothered by the state of disorder

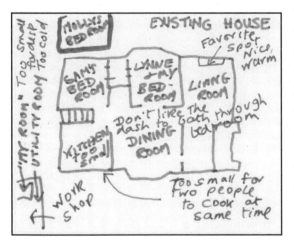

of your desk; perhaps you can move its location so that you can shut a door, and your partner doesn't have to see it—and you can go on being as disordered as you like. Or, let us suppose you are upset by a picture in your living room painted by your spouse's first wife. Perhaps you have never fully realized how much of an intrusion this feels like; or perhaps you knew

One partner's views of the pros and cons of a home shared with the family.

it, but never felt comfortable expressing it. How you deal with this issue is up to you as a couple (hang it in "his" space? put it in storage? leave it where it is?), but the first step is to become aware of your feelings, express them, and have them acknowledged.

A lot of issues about sharing space have to do with control. Most of us are fearful at some level about boundary intrusions; we express our apprehension via body language, patterns of speech, behavior toward others, and, in some cases, via our "marks" on the environment. If the disordered office or the first wife's painting turn out to be issues of maintaining a sense of control, perhaps you can work out other ways to feel secure within your boundaries without upsetting your partner. Again, the particular solution is up to you, and it may need to be negotiated over time. Territory and control issues, like other relationship concerns, may need time to work out and may need to be renegotiated again and again.

It is a good idea to repeat this exercise on what your current home means to you at perhaps yearly intervals. As people age and develop, or change roles (from career woman to mother, for example), the demands they place on the home and on their partner via the home will inevitably change.

This is scary stuff! Wouldn't it be better to let sleeping dogs lie—to tolerate the disorder or the decor issue? That may be—it is up to you. Only you as an individual or a couple can tell if the irritant is a superficial blip in your relationship or a projection onto the physical environment of some potentially deeper conflict.

SEVEN

Living and Working: Territory, Control, and Privacy at Home

The resources of the English language would be much put to the stretch . . .
before a woman could say what happens when she goes into a room. The rooms
differ so completely; they are calm or thunderous; open on to the sea . . . or give
on to a prison yard; are hung with washing; or alive with opals and silks . . .
How should it be otherwise? For women have sat indoors for all these millions
of years, so that by this time the very walls are permeated by their creative force,
which has, indeed, so overcharged the capacity of bricks and mortar that it
must needs harness itself to pens and brushes and business and politics.
> —VIRGINIA WOOLF, *A Room of One's Own*[1]

There should be at least one room, or some corner, where no one will find you
and disturb you or notice you. You should be able to untether yourself from the
world and set yourself free, loosing all the fine strings and strands of tension
that bind you, by sight, by sound, by thought, to the presence of other men.
> —THOMAS MERTON, *New Seeds of Contemplation*[2]

Questions of who has access to or control over which rooms in a home is critical in any arrangement where people live together. A great deal of our social training has to do with respecting other people's needs for privacy and territory. We bring up our children to respect each other's personal space in a shared bedroom; we teach them "not to bother Mom when she's in her studio," or "not to talk to Dad while he's reading." We learn that the Robinson's front lawn, despite its lack of a fence, is private property and not a place to ride our bikes across. We learn to knock at the door of our counselor's office in high school, and not to enter until we are invited to do so. The rules and norms of behavior are culture-specific, hence our sometimes puzzling or embarrassing experiences in foreign lands when we don't know the meaning of a half-open door or when we don't understand how close it is appropriate to stand when conducting a conversation with a stranger.

Having some space of one's own in the home is fundamental to balanced relations within a couple or a family. A person's own bedroom or study or workplace permits him to seek privacy, to make it clear to others that he needs time alone. Such a space is also critical in that it allows a person to express her own identity through what she puts into the space, how she decorates the walls or what she puts on display.

Amazingly, very little research has been conducted on this fundamental aspect of living together. Though the most relevant study is not American, it is worth mentioning for the light it sheds upon space in the home. A psychologist in Italy questioned thirty-six young adults who still lived with their parents and forty-seven who were married and living in their own homes. All were working and were in their midtwenties to midthirties. The first fundamental difference found was that those who still lived with their parents perceived the home as a whole as being under the control of a parent (usually the mother), but saw at least one room in it (usually their bedroom) as being under their own control. Conversely, married couples saw their home as belonging equally to both, but most saw no particular room or space within it as being exclusively his or her own.

The people who still lived in parental homes were more likely to see their friends outside the home and less likely to assist in housework or home maintenance. The home as a whole was not a place where they could express themselves; indeed, for some, it was a place where they felt their identity had to be repressed. More than a third of those living with their parents felt there was nowhere in the home that was an expression of their self; among married couples, nearly two-thirds felt that the entire home was an expression of self, even though it was shared. Hence, as discussed in earlier chapters, leaving your parental home is a critical life-transition in terms of expressing who you are via the form, location, decoration, and state of order of the place where you live.

In a book entitled *A Psychology of Building,* architect Glenn Lym describes a number of cases of student couples sharing space. Relating the story of one

Harvard couple, he described how the husband spent much of his time in his study but took frequent breaks to walk in and out of the living/dining/bedroom portion of the apartment, where his wife spent much of her time: "He paced back and forth between his realms to assure himself of his commitment to both. Yet he wanted the separation between the realms to assure himself that neither would contaminate the other."[3]

In the case of another such couple, the wife, Joan, felt that the apartment she shared with her student-husband was too segregated into two realms—the husband spent much of his time in a study, the wife in the rest of the apartment. Joan wanted the apartment to feel whole by minimizing the separation between those spaces. At first, her husband's study door remained open, and she felt the space to be reasonably integrated. Then, having purchased an oriental rug which their cat started to pull at, he moved the rug to his study and kept the door closed. Joan felt excluded from his world and in time developed a door-opening ritual. She confided: "When my husband is not home, I open the study door, even though I know the cat will go in and pull on the rug. I just leave it open and that way the study becomes a part of the apartment."[4]

In neither of these examples did Lym describe the reactions or feelings of the other partner. But later in the same book, he describes in some detail the process of understanding and responding to the different and sometimes conflicting spatial desires of couples who have hired him as an architect. In the case of a couple he called Laura and Phil, he was hired to design an inexpensive house for them on a very constricted lot (twelve by ninety feet). They had evolved a life in which activities revolved around a living room, and both expressed a preference for the spatial feeling of a barn. But as Lym presented preliminary ideas to them, he began to discern quite different ways in which they defined the places that constituted home: "Laura had explicit expectations about the boundary conditions of each home place. . . . Phil, on the other hand, did not care one way or the other for explicitly defined, focused, or bounded places. . . . Laura stressed a home with explicit places; Phil delighted in place-to-place transitions. . . . Phil had a spatial order of home as a set of fluid and evolving social situations. Flow, change and escape were just as real to him as participation in any given situation. Laura, on the other hand, had a spatial order of home as a set of explicitly structured situations."[5]

Lym, as the mediating architect, solved these seemingly conflicting viewpoints by designing the house as a series of spaces delimited by open doorway portals that could be read both as connections between spaces for Phil and as the boundaries for each room for Laura.

Many architects report the need for extreme tact and sensitivity in dealing with client couples; the very act of deciding to have a house designed for them can often bring into the foreground differing environmental values that sometimes reflect fundamental opposites in how each views the world. I have met several designers who have gone so far as to give up working with couples altogether because they found the delicate balancing act of architect-marriage counselor too stressful a role.

Relinquishing Control over Space: Teresa and David's Home

When Teresa and David got married, they had to resolve a number of knotty issues over territory. The house belonged to David, who had lived there for sixteen years with his first wife. Over time, David was able to relinquish control over this space to Teresa. They found a reasonably comfortable balance between space that was "his," "hers," and "shared in common," but only after some difficult struggles. For example, the sharing of a study came about only after some tense discussions and a "big argument." Teresa had wanted to convert the small room off the living room into a quiet sitting room; David wanted it as an office-study. There was something of a standoff; David started to construct a large table to claim the space as a study. The completion of this table, together, cemented the perception of this room as *shared* space. Each had half of the table and the shelves on either side of the room. Teresa remarked: "David was ready to do something with the room, so he took the lead. I wasn't ready—I resented it at first, but it's okay now."

The sharing of this relatively small room might have been more problematic but for the fact that their fairly spacious house allowed them other, more private, work spaces. Teresa, an architect, claimed as her space a former dressing room next to their bedroom, where she had her drafting table. David claimed as his space a workshop on the first floor of the house, where he had benches and tools and formerly conducted a business of repairing musical instruments. In the backyard, a freestanding studio was being adapted into a shared work space. "I think of it more as mine," David remarked. "I worked on it before I met Teresa, and I'm doing more of the work on it now—but I'm in the process of giving up space."

Perhaps not surprisingly, the one who claims a particular space tends to either spend more time in it than the partner or to have done more work on it, or both. Teresa felt that the garden was largely hers because she cared about it more and spent more time in it. "The garden was part of the reason I moved in! First I took care of the parts closest to the house, and then I just expanded. We made 'big' decisions together, like where to put a new path or bed, and David may do more of the occasional heavy work—but basically I tend the garden. I feel more attached to it than to the house because I helped create it. For a period of my childhood, I lived in Mendocino with my brother and had my own garden there when I was ten; before architecture, I did a bachelor's degree in botany."

David had a passionate interest in bamboo. He had ten varieties (all noninvasive) growing in different locations in the front, back, and side yards. During his childhood, his family had a bamboo grove on a lake in Wisconsin: "I remember lying on my back, looking up, the canes clicking above me." As with so many of the people I talked with, David had re-created a fondly remembered element of his childhood environment in his home of adulthood. Although such a need might bring about some tension in a couple relationship, in this case it did not, as Teresa remarked, "I garden around his bamboo."

Teresa and David's negotiations regarding territory were complicated by the fact that they rented space in the house to two students. The spaces they shared with their tenants were generally clear and unproblematic—the front steps and porch, the kitchen, pantry, and back bedroom. The only room where tension over territory was apparent was the living room. It was a large, high-ceilinged room, decorated with kites, flags, fabrics, masks, and gilt-framed photographs. It was furnished with over-stuffed chairs, a bamboo-framed couch, and a rocking chair; a beige carpet covered part of the floor. At the time of my visit, there were half-burned candles on the mantelpiece and a globe

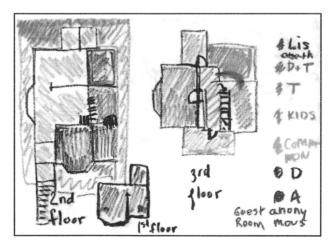

David's depiction of territorial "ownership" of rooms in the house he shared with his wife, Teresa, and two student tenants.

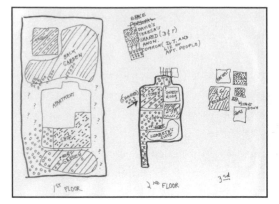

on a table piled with newspapers. It felt like a house of students—slightly funky, made up of bits and pieces. As they talked about this room, David and Teresa conceded that although nominally it was space "in common" with their tenants, it was, in fact, their space. This had come about in a number of ways: the objects that decorated and furnished the room belonged to David and Teresa (in fact, almost exclusively, they were David's); the room had to be traversed to reach the third floor (exclusively David and Teresa's part of the house) and their shared study off the living room. They used the space more, both to be in it and to pass through it. Thus, they had, unconsciously, appropriated the room as "theirs."

In shared or communal households where the dwelling is rented, the living room tends to become neutral or unclaimed space, as residents concentrate on personalizing their private rooms. In communal households where the dwelling is owned by one of the residents—as was the case with David and Teresa—the living room almost inevitably becomes the space of the owner, creating tensions unless the owner's "claim" to this room is made very clear from the start.

Neither David nor Teresa saw this as their ideal home but liked the idea of improving it over time. David clearly felt more attached to the house than Teresa, not surprisingly, considering his long residence: "In some ways, this house is a pile of junk—cheap and thrown together. The structure isn't too good, but it suffices as a framework. I feel like I've reconstructed every bit of this house—I'm not neutral about it! I feel very attached to it; if I left, I'd want to take a lot of it away with me. I've built myself into a corner!"

When I asked if this was his "ideal," David responded: "A house is a lot like a relationship—you make it as ideal as you can." As an outside observer, this house "felt" more like David's than Teresa's—maybe because I knew of his long residence in it, the extent of the work he had done, and the memories of child rearing and family life I sensed it must hold for him. David and Teresa were newly married when I spoke with them. Time will tell whether the house becomes more of Teresa's domain.

Territory in the Home

Two Israeli psychologists—Arza Churchman and Rachel Sebba—have carried out an interesting study of territoriality within the home among middle-class families living in a cluster of owner-occupied, high-rise apartments in Haifa. Each family member was asked to classify each room and piece of furniture in terms of who it belonged to. The apartments were found to be divided, in people's minds, into three kinds of areas: those that belonged to the whole family—the living room and bathroom; those that belonged to a subgroup in the family—parents' bedroom, siblings' shared bedroom; and those that belonged to individuals. In this latter category were an individual's own bedroom and the kitchen. These were relatively modest apartments; there was no separate dining or family room, so the kitchen was the place where the family gathered for meals. Interestingly, only one-third saw this room as belonging to the whole family, though each family member had a permanent chair at the table; more than half said this room belonged to the mother.[6]

Although no strictly comparable study has been conducted in the United States, common sense suggests that such a study of family territories would result in somewhat similar findings. Although the designation of the kitchen as largely "mother's space" may well (hopefully!) be changing as father and children take on more domestic responsibilities, the perception of the bedroom as the exclusive space of an individual or couple no doubt repeats itself in this culture.

When a couple decide to live together and each has previously lived alone for some time, sensitive negotiations over space, territory, privacy, and control are essential. Judi and Gregor were one such couple; my conversation with them was punctuated with comments, one to the other, about privacy, control of space, and territorial intrusions—"petty imperialism," as they liked to call it.

Gregor and Judi's House "That Love Inspired, True Grit Built, and Creativity Made Insane"

Before the disastrous fire that destroyed it and three thousand other homes in October 1991, the house of Gregor and Judi was situated on a steep lot on a winding, hilly road in the Oakland hills. It was set among similar, architect-designed spacious houses amid a landscape of eucalyptus and live oak trees. A long set of wooden steps led up to the front door, and, once inside, another set of steps led up to the main living area of the house. A wood-beamed kitchen-eating area with leaded-glass windows looked out on the hillside; through two arched porticoes, one moved into a large space where Gregor had a desk and a computer and many boxes of firewood to feed the Swedish stove. At the other end of this large room, a double bed was set up on a carpeted platform with fabric draped above it from the ceiling. An area for hanging clothes covered the end wall of the room, and one moved on into a beautiful bathroom—with hand-carved wooden fixtures, a sauna bathtub, and an outdoor shower.

At the time of our discussion, a large addition to the house was being built by Gregor for Judi with plans they had worked out together. This addition would include a living room, bedroom, bathroom, and studio. The addition would be accessed from one interior door linking it to the original house and by a front door and interior stairs opening off the front porch of the house. Thus, the two parts of the house could—conceivably—at some time, become two separate living spaces or apartments.

At the time I spoke with them, Judi and Gregor had been living together for eighteen months; prior to this, they had dated for seven years. Both had been extremely cautious about the decision to live together. Gregor had never shared a dwelling with anyone since he left his family home; he was now in his early forties. For the past twenty years, he had been slowly constructing this house when time permitted from his job as a truck driver. Judi had lived in a number of shared apartments with women friends, but for the previous three or more years had lived alone. "During that time," said Judi, "I viewed this house—Gregor's house—as a pretty magical place, a refuge, a place of peace and wonder—discovering all the incredible details. And I still find things I haven't seen before."

When Gregor and Judi debated the decision to live together, Gregor was concerned about an invasion of his space, while Judi insisted that she have space separate but adjacent to Gregor. At first, they had discussed building a second house on the lot, for Judi. Later, these plans changed to the idea of a second house attached to the first. Finally, they agreed to a set of rooms for Judi, accessible from Gregor's house yet capable of feeling quite separate. Gregor drew up plans for these rooms in three alternate locations—beside, in front of, and above his original house. They decided on the latter location, and started to build during the weekends. Gregor had a huge workshop under the house with lathes, power saws, and the like, and he was a very skilled carpenter, builder, wood-carver, and designer.

For a year and a half after this decision, Judi continued to live alone in her apartment and to work on the addition with Gregor on the weekends. Finally, this arrangement became too expensive, and Judi moved in. As we talked, the addition was perhaps two-thirds completed, but not yet livable space. The space they shared together—the kitchen/eating area, Gregor's living room/office/bedroom space, and a bathroom—seemed immensely cluttered. Judi's furniture from her apartment filled much of the kitchen area; the remainder was stored under the house, in Gregor's workshop. The living-room space, created by Gregor for himself, was also cluttered with furniture, as well as the boxes of firewood. If Gregor feared that Judi would "invade" his space, that did, indeed, appear to have happened, though nothing in our conversation indicated that he resented the intrusion. Rather, it now seemed that it was more Judi's wish to have separate but adjacent space—and she was getting impatient at the time it was taking to complete it.

I asked them if they could put down their feelings about this evolving house in some kind of graphic depiction. Gregor drew a diagrammatic outline of a house in green with clusters of "action and interaction" in orange inside it. Blue lines on two sides of the house represented the sky and coolness. On another side, he indicated the garden and trees that bounded the house on the uphill side. On the fourth side were "waves" of orange, yellow, and red energy "impacting" the house from the outside world/road side of the lot. I asked him to give the house a name—he called it, straightforwardly, "The McGinnis/Kaye House."

I asked Gregor if he could speak *as* the house, what might the house want to say? He responded: "It's nice that you have a companion to share me with now, and that you're adding to me to make room for that

Gregor's image of the house he shared with Judi.

Judi's image of the house she shared with Gregor.

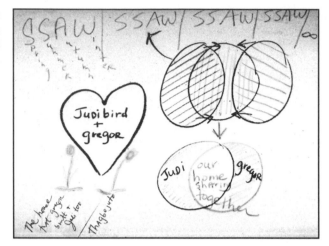

companion. I know it's tough on the both of us right now—demanding on you to add this new space, and pretty tough on me as I was getting pretty comfortable the way I was. But I'm getting used to the idea of being bigger and happy that you're carrying on the same aesthetic qualities in the addition. It will be nice for you to be done so that you can get on with your life and not have to toil, after a forty-hour week, on evenings and weekends."

Judi's picture of the house had many references to time and her relationship with Gregor in it. She called the house "The house that Gregor built & Judi too." She drew three overlapping circles: one represented Judi's space, one Gregor's, and one the space that they shared. In a second diagram below the first, she redrew the three circles with the shared space somewhat larger; in it she wrote the words: *Our home sharing together.* Across the top of the picture, Judi wrote the letters *SSAW* (spring, summer, autumn, winter) again and again; these referred to the years that were stretching out between their decision to live together and the completion of her space. Not infrequently, she remarked, she would wake up in a panic and plead with Gregor to finish her part of the house. Judi spoke about the house and her relationship:

"It's hard to separate this house from Gregor's and my relationship. The house is a natural progression of our relationship; as we poured concrete—I kept on putting little hearts with Judibird (my nickname) and Gregor in the cement. It's a statement of Gregor and Judi building our life together. I've never lived with anyone before; I've never built a house before—so there was fear moving in."

I asked Judi if she could have a "dialogue" with the house; she agreed readily and began by speaking to the house: "I'm really ready to have you be finished! I had no idea what I was getting into—and I'm overwhelmed with how much Gregor must fully love me because he *did* know what he was getting into, how much energy it was going to take! You're going to be beautiful, exciting, a place of joy and creativity, a statement of aesthetic pride as well as of Gregor's and my commitment to each other. You're very important to us."

She switched roles and became the house speaking back to Judi: "It's all your fault that I'm not finished! Gregor and I were quite content together in our own little world, and while the end result of your work together is going to be wonderful, I was very content and happy before, and the work has made me very dusty and cluttered. And yet, I think you bring a wonderful completeness to Gregor's and my life—you certainly make us a lot more twentieth century. I'm still trying to deal with the fact that you brought in all these high-tech things like microwaves and dishwashers. We were living a very simple life! But I think Gregor and I are enriched by your being here."

As she finished speaking as the house, Gregor commented, "A+!"—and they both laughed.

As Judi talked, it seemed as though she was gradually softening to the issue of her and Gregor sharing space. "It's funny, but originally I wanted this door, between the two spaces, to have double locks, like a connecting door between two hotel rooms, so that we would both have to make a conscious decision to unlock it and be together."

"She'd invite me in when she felt like it," Gregor retorted, laughing, and Judi agreed that that seemed unnecessary now. Judi continued, "The living room in my part of the house started as my living room, but now I see it as part of our shared space. We both had different ideas about the flooring—I wanted an oak floor and Gregor wanted Spanish tile. So eventually, we decided to do both, and Gregor drew up a beautiful curvilinear plan of how they could both be part of the same room. And after seven months of looking, we just found some tile that we can both agree on.

"We are learning when to compromise and when to not. We both have the power to veto. I didn't like Gregor's design for stained-glass windows to go into the house—and I wasn't willing to live with them. He pouted for a couple of days and then he changed the design. The same thing happened with a design element in the bathroom, which I hated—so sometimes we use our veto power."

Gregor interjected: "Judi wants to bring some stuff from the East Coast that's god-awful. She was raised with this stuff. It's going to cost a fortune to bring it here. But she has an emotional attachment to it. I don't like that dining-room table—I don't feel comfortable with it in our shared space."

Judi retorted, "There's probably no room for it—physically or aesthetically—so it probably won't come."

Gregor replied, "Judi's coming along—just give her time! There's times I've mellowed and times when she's mellowed. I'm more eclectic; Judi's more into art deco. . . ."

I asked them if they could summarize for me what were their preferred kinds of spaces. Judi liked rooms where you can "declare privacy and shut out the world. I guess that means where you can close the door." Gregor preferred "a big, open space, like an airplane hangar!"

I asked each of them to indicate which place in the house they felt most themselves. Gregor listed workshop, studio, desk, hot tub. Judi answered, "Nowhere yet! But in theory my bedroom, when it's finished. It's interesting that neither one of us declared the shared space as where we felt most ourselves, but that's understandable. We're in transition now—and anyway, the shared space will never be where each of us is most private, most ourselves."

The conversation with Gregor and Judi left me somewhat disturbed. Part of that was linked to my discomfort at the thought of living in a half-finished house—kitchen remodeling that took two months was as much as I have ever coped with. Both Judi and Gregor referred to the fact that couples often "come apart" over building or remodeling a house together. The possibility of an end to their relationship was something that concerned them. They had written out a sixteen-page legal prenuptial agreement, which included the fact that if a separation occurred, Gregor would stay in the house and Judi would leave—since it was largely his "blood, sweat, and tears" invested in the house. And they had deliberately planned one room in the addition that could—if necessary—be made into a kitchen. Thus, if the relationship ever broke up, the addition could be transformed into a self-contained rental apartment.

The work on the house moved slowly, both because of cash-flow problems and because they wanted to ensure that *every* decision was adequately discussed and agreed on. This very slowness, however, put a strain on both of them, as Gregor saw his building weekends stretching out into the future and as Judi worried about how long she would wait for her space to be finished. Ironically, however, the process of planning and building together was seemingly allowing Gregor and Judi to come to terms with each other's needs and differences. The fact that they now shared, and planned to share, more spaces together than they originally deemed possible seemed like a good omen. How would they relate—I wondered—when all this work was finished? Was the building such an intrinsic part of both of their lives that there would be some kind of letdown when it was all over? For some people, living in space together is the main challenge—creating that space just an irritant along the way; for others, the creation of space together is the relationship.

This story ended in tragedy. On Sunday, October 20, 1991, the combination of hot weather, tinder-dry vegetation, strong winds, and a small grass fire that apparently had not been totally put out led to a conflagration in the Oakland-Berkeley hills of devastating proportions. The urban forest of eucalyptus and Monterey pine trees that attracted so many to these steep hillside lots was a major component in the rapid spread of the fire. The attractive narrow, winding roads, including the one that led to Gregor and Judi's still-unfinished house, were a significant impediment to the rapid response of the fire department. Gregor's body was found in the backyard; he died trying to save the house. Judi, on a business trip, was out of town. The depth of her grief at losing her lover, her home, and all her possessions is impossible to imagine.

Making a Home Together: Communication, Compromise, and Creativity

In a story with a happier outcome, we will look at the life of two women who have successfully created a home together, using clear communication, compromise, creativity, and humor.

Carolyn and Charlene share a very ordered, attractive, and comfortable house dating from the California craftsman era. It has polished oak floors, wooden beams and trim, and built-in china and book cupboards with leaded-glass doors. In the living room, there is a large stone fireplace, comfortable settees, and flowered curtains; the dining room is furnished with oak furniture and a built-in china closet. Off the dining room is a smaller sitting room with overstuffed blue-and-white chairs, a TV (hidden in a white closet), and Charlene's desk. The bedroom is very simple and serene, with very little furniture besides an old oak bed with a white bedspread, a Georgia O'Keefe print of a flower, and a little "altar" to their cat of twenty years who died—her photo, a pink rose, a ceramic cat. The kitchen is neat and functional; an old oak table with a bowl of fruit sits in its center. Off the kitchen—and farthest away from the front entrance—is Carolyn's study, very neat with drawing board, computer, bookshelves, and file cabinets. There are elegant Japanese flower arrangements in every room, well-tended plants, furniture in place, counters and tabletops clean and empty. It appears to be a dwelling of two people who care deeply about orderliness, aesthetics, and creating an atmosphere of calm.

The two women have been a couple for eleven years, the first eight of which were spent in a rented apartment. Three years prior to our conversation, they bought this house in a middle-income neighborhood of a small city. Carolyn came from a large family and spent much time in her childhood working with her parents and siblings on the decoration of a very large house near Pasadena. She had a tremendous interest in interior design and the environment and took the lead in much of the work on this house. She liked to do the "research" and came home with paint chips, fabrics, patterns, books, and so on. She asked Charlene's advice and then checked out various options with two or three friends whose opinions she valued.

They had had "tussles" over a few issues—the living-room curtains, the dining-room wallpaper, the sitting-room furniture—and Charlene admitted to feeling overridden at times by the opinions of some of Carolyn's friends. But each issue worked itself out, and Charlene (who by her own admittance is less interested) was nearly always pleased with the end result.

Charlene lived much of her adult life in a religious order; the first three years were spent in silence. After that, she was involved in community activities—work that she continues today. During all the years in many convent houses, she had no experience of personal space. The colors, the furniture, the pictures, and so on were taken for granted; evaluating or changing the environment was not even an issue. Even if changing the environment had been permitted, none of the sisters had any personal money. With their very different background experiences regarding the environment, it was not surprising that Carolyn had taken the lead in the remodeling of their house. One issue was money. Since Charlene lived without money for many years, any expenditure on the house seemed difficult; for Carolyn, used to a moderate income and coming from an upper-middle-income background, most purchases seemed like a compromise—she would have liked to have spent more money!

For Charlene, a self-confessed extrovert, the house seemed most important as a container of social encounters, mealtimes, and relationships with friends and animals. When asked to free-associate to the word *home,* Charlene wrote down immediately, *warm, retreat, sacred, center,* and then added *people, person, meals, friends, animals.* When recording her feelings about the house in a visual image, she depicted a light-filled and light-penetrated enclosure with several discernible places within it, the dining-room and kitchen tables, and mealtimes with friends. She particularly liked the entry hall—"I like to receive people—I think of all the people who have come in and out of the house since it was built in 1912."

The form of the house (size, age, rooms) was not unlike Charlene's childhood home in Kansas City, and the various convent houses she lived in for twenty-seven years. In her study over her desk is a mandala painting she commissioned for her fiftieth birthday; at its center—like the hub of a wheel—was a realistic rendering of her childhood home. "The artist kept wanting to make it into a symbol—but I said, 'No, here's a photo, I want the real thing!' Which is strange, because usually I like to be very abstract. My fifty years of life have been very intuitive—I've done a million things! This mandala was to bring it all together, which it does. It's interesting that I insisted on the house—as it actually is—at the center of the mandala. I'm so abstract, I need focus in my life—I need to come down somewhere, sometime!"

At the start of our conversation, I asked both women—separately—to put down some kind of picture or graphic image of what the house means. Carolyn perceived the house as an open bowl with a roof, the whole surrounded by the earth: "this little plot of earth—not much, but very special to us." She filled the bowl with the color of light (yellow), the soul of the house (gray), and blue-green for the softness and beauty of the interior and her life with Charlene in this house.

"When I finished this picture of the house, I realized it looked like the earth—half an earth. This is our world, a precious place to me—I've never felt this close to a place before—except the house I grew up in."

She called the house "Earthbowl Altarplace." When I asked Carolyn to speak to the house, she said: "I love you very much. I'm so happy to be here—in a way, I feel honored to live in you. From the first moment, I saw you as a very gracious being—tall and proud and strong. I was so ready to bring your spirit forth. All those weekends of stripping and painting—I guess I liked being that close to you, so intimate."

When asked if the house reminded her of any other place she'd lived, Carolyn responded: "All my life I've been searching to re-create the experience I had growing up in this gorgeous, huge house where I lived until I was fourteen—when my father left and we had to move. We had twenty-seven rooms! And we all helped—it felt like creating a home together. So living here and doing the work we've done—the fact that the house needed work was okay with me. Whatever it took, I figured it out!"

When Carolyn and Charlene each depicted their perception of the "ownership" and use of space in the house, it was clear that they were in as much accord about this as about the other topics we discussed. There was almost total agreement between them as to which was Carolyn's space (her study, her closet, a particular settee, her side of the bed); which was Charlene's space (her desk, her closet, a particular chair, her side of the bed); which space was shared (virtually all the rest of the house); and which was waiting to be developed (the attic and part of the basement). They both also indicated small areas of the house that belonged to their cats, including small "nests" they had created in closets and drawers for a pregnant cat who was about to give birth. What was intriguing was the way in which they each depicted these spatial appropriations of the house. Carolyn drew a roughly accurate architectural layout of the house, including doors and closets. She indicated specific locales as either hers or Charlene's, and depicted almost all the rest as "shared." Charlene, on the other hand, drew the rooms as dis-

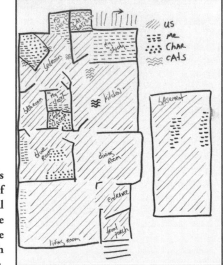

Carolyn's image of territorial claims in the house she shared with Charlene.

crete "boxes" (not a connected layout) and colored each with some of "her" color and some of Carolyn's color, in proportion to the amount of time each spent in a room. At various times in our conversation, Charlene indicated that particular *occasions* were important to her rather than particular *places;* it seemed clear that Carolyn thought spatially whereas Charlene thought in a more temporal mode. For example, she indicated the entrance hall as more her space than Carolyn's, "because I spend more time there, greeting and saying good-bye to guests."

When moving into the house, there had been very few problems about the use of space. As in most older houses, the rooms by their location, size, and detailing indicated the function intended (sitting room, kitchen, and so on). There had been some discussion over who got which closet and who would get the study behind the

Charlene's view of territorial claims in the house she shared with Carolyn.

kitchen, but this was fairly quickly agreed upon as Carolyn's workroom, since she needed space for doing stained glass and for writing a thesis. "I don't need much space," Charlene added, "so I took a desk in the 'blue room,' and if I need to bring work home from the office, I spread it out on the dining-room table." They were sure they'd easily agree on the spaces "in waiting" (attic and basement): "The only constraint is money!"

There was, however, an ethical question for Charlene: "I work with poor people who can't afford a home, who are sleeping on the streets—so there's always an issue for me about having all this space."

When I asked Charlene and Carolyn to tell me where in the house they each felt most herself, Carolyn said, "The whole house—when here alone or just with Charlene." After a pause, she added, "Also my study and my side of the bed."

For Charlene, to name a place was difficult; it was more "moments" that were special: "Talking to my family on the phone, parties in the dining room, a really good conversation—those happen often around the table—but the place is not as important as the occasion, the people."

They agreed that this represented the difference between them: Carolyn, more herself when alone and more aware of the environment; Charlene, more extroverted and less aware of her environment. Overall, these two people have created a calm, beautiful, welcoming house which has room for both to express and be who they are—as individuals and as a couple.

Living and Working at Home: Randy and Marcia

When any couple decides to live together in a space that was formerly his or hers exclusively, a lot of issues regarding territory or privacy will have to be worked out. But when one or both also *work* at home, another layer of potential complications may arise.

Randy and Marcia live in a small, cedar-shingled, one-story house in a racially mixed residential neighborhood of single-family houses. Their front door opens into a small redwood-paneled dining/living room with a fireplace, large dining table, and stained-glass windows made by Randy. On the wall are watercolors by Randy and two samplers; one says "Home Sweet Home. V.G. '39'," and the other reads:

> *Dear Little House—Dear Shabby Street—*
> *Dear books and beds and food to eat—*
> *How feeble words are to express—*
> *The facets of your tenderness. C.M.*

Leading off this room is a smaller kitchen/breakfast room with a red linoleum floor, round dining table, and a collection of wooden cows and chickens on the windowsill. On one wall is a large painting of birds done by Randy as a child. Over the sink is a wooden sign: "Marcia's Starlite Nouvelle Mexican Cafe." The other two downstairs rooms are offices with desks, computers, and file cabinets, decorated with many plants, ornaments, pictures, and, in Randy's case, rocks collected from many places he has visited.

A major transformation of the house since they moved in was to fit a tight spiral staircase into a closet space, leading up to a newly created attic bedroom. Beige wall-to-wall carpet, clean white ceiling angles, and wood-framed skylights create a serene, very private retreat space. No visitor could stumble onto this bedroom by chance—it is hard to find the staircase, let alone negotiate it.

The kitchen table where Randy and Marcia eat all their meals looks out onto the backyard—a view they both enjoy. This is not an average American yard; it looks more like a farmyard. Along one edge is a chicken coop and a series of wooden hutches for rabbits. A huge Monterey pine shades the yard most of the day, its fallen needles forming a deep, soft mulch over the entire space. During the day, a dozen or so chickens and one Muscovy duck scratch and cluck and sometimes attempt to enter the house via the back door. A rough stone path from this door leads to a large, freestanding wooden garage/barn which Randy and friends have converted into a rustic office-working space. Here, each day, Marcia and one or two employees work on a planning consulting business. Randy, an academic, leaves the house most days for his office at the university.

When I talked with them, Randy and Marcia appeared to have made a good adjustment to the sharing and molding of space; it seemed to have been achieved by a series of step-by-step decisions in which Randy often took the lead (making a proposal, drawing a plan) to which Marcia agreed or disagreed. Slowly, they would move back and forth to a point of agreement. Randy had bought the house before he met Marcia. He had started to make some changes to the barn, to build the chicken coop, and arrange the use of rooms in the house. Not long after this, he met Marcia and she moved in. Quite deliberately, they moved everything out of each room, one by one, and then furnished and decorated the rooms together, moving back those items of Randy's and those of Marcia's which they both agreed upon. In this way, they appropriated the spaces of the house as belonging to them both, as a couple.

That this approach had been successful seemed eminently apparent in the pictures they created for me to express "How I feel about this house." Marcia depicted, in rather subdued tones and thin lines, the exterior of the house and the front garden (her domain); she drew herself and Randy returning up the front steps. In giving the house a name, she wrote down *Ours* with a small heart. Randy's picture was much more bold and vibrant with a large red heart encompassing the house and the immediate neighborhood. He also depicted the chickens, the back-yard, the barn, the house next door that they had just purchased, a neighbor's garden, Marcia planting flowers in the front, car fenders representing piles of junk he collects, and irises he has just planted. A black border on the right side depicted the barrier to the hustle of the outside world which he

Marcia's image of the house she shared with Randy.

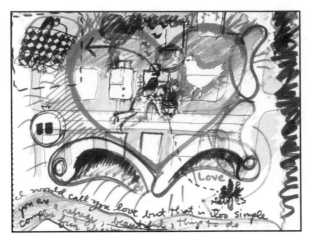

Randy's image of the house he shared with Marcia.

experiences when home. He gave the whole composition the name "Love."

I asked Marcia if she would speak to the house as if it were animate. She said, "I like you very much, and I'm always glad to come back to you. I'm gone an awful lot, and you're a comfortable friend to come home to, to be safe and restful in. I like you particularly now—at this time of year—because you're colorful and you smell good. You're just the right size. You don't take up too much space. This is sometimes a tough place to live, a tough neighborhood, but I like this house."

When Randy spoke to his depiction of the house, he said, "I like you a lot—I like you being tiny and like most of the other houses in the neighborhood. You're a good friend to us—I love you like I love Marcia—you symbolize us being happy together, and maybe me being happy for the first time . . . contented. You seem like a real house in the real neighborhood. Actually, I'm crazy about you! I like you being junky at the back, the way the sun comes in, your view to the back space. I wouldn't leave you for anything. I'm living a better life when I'm here in the house. I'm away a lot, on my work—off 'being important.' I'm happier when I have time to work on the house and garden, when I'm taking care of things here."

In thinking and speaking about the house, Randy grew discontented with his first picture: "You're much more gracious than this picture would have us believe. I want to draw a better one. . . ." He turned the drawing over and did a quick sketch in brown of the house facade—steps, porch, windows, roof, chimney—with two green arms extending from the house as if to embrace the artist, or viewer, or the street in front of it. "You're much calmer than my first picture indicates. You're a very simple combination of natural materials, big chunks of green, and sparkles of Marcia's flowers."

When I asked Randy and Marcia if this house/garden/neighborhood resembled any other place they had lived, Marcia immediately shook her head. "None whatsoever. It's the antithesis of the neighborhood in which I was brought up."

There was no connection, she said—laughing—with her upper-middle-class upbringing in an affluent, segregated Chicago suburb of large houses, large lots, fashionable interior decor, and pristine front lawns. "Every room was done— decorated just so. You couldn't leave stuff out or move stuff around. It was my mother's aesthetic."

"And still is," Randy added. They both laughed.

Marcia continued: "When I left home, I went to live in the depths of the country—in Colorado—nothing like this. And when I was married the first time, I hardly remember any of the places we lived in; it was such a horrible marriage, and my husband was never home. 'Home' was not even home—it was just a house."

In her second marriage, to Randy, Marcia had apparently adapted to a very different environment and style of life, one that was much more an echo of Randy's childhood and early adult life. Randy had grown up in two small houses (within a block of each other) in a racially mixed, working-class neighborhood in Roxboro, North Carolina. Here, in a house he lived in from three to ten years of age, his family kept chickens in a pen in the backyard, except one chicken—his personal pet, Henny-Penny, which followed him around the neighborhood "just like a dog" and laid one egg every day on top of a sack of chicken feed in the barn in the backyard. "Just like our barn here—just the same kind of functions." He laughed at recalling this home and how much he had re-created it in his backyard in Berkeley. Marcia smiled and remarked how very much she enjoyed feeding the animals and collecting eggs; she had not been allowed animals as a child.

At ten, Randy and his parents moved a block away from their first house, and he recalled happily the flower garden his mother made and the large vegetable garden created on a second house lot his father purchased next door. Randy also saw a marked resemblance between his current neighborhood and an African-American neighborhood where he had lived in Raleigh as a young, single faculty member at the University of North Carolina.

For some years, Randy and Marcia had been in the habit of discussing their use of space in the house by each color-coding a plan as to which parts they saw as Randy's space, Marcia's space, shared space, and anonymous space. I asked them to do this for me, and the ensuing discussion brought forth a few current disagreements, particularly over the purchase of the business they jointly ran from the house and how they might use the house next door that they had just bought.

Both agreed on the spaces of the house they now inhabited: The bedroom and kitchen were both shared space, with small subareas belonging to one or the other—the sink was Randy's because he always did the dishes; the stove was Marcia's because she did most of the cooking. They also agreed on the two office rooms in the house—one clearly Marcia's and one Randy's. The front dining room, which had always seemed to me, as a visitor, somewhat ambiguous as to function, indeed appeared that way on their plans. It was usable for a dinner party, but this was not their way of entertaining. Marcia sometimes used the table for her work or for meetings connected with the business. On cold winter mornings, Randy and Marcia would huddle by the hot-air vent near the front door to drink tea before starting the day. They both indicated the space as a mix of shared and anonymous.

The only issue of disagreement in the current house was that Randy felt the business intruded too much onto his need for "home as refuge." Randy left the house each day and had his major working space at the university. He wanted the house to be a sacred and very private refuge. Marcia, who was the full-time, energetic force behind their jointly owned consulting business, had no trouble blending home and work. She alternated between working at the dining-room table, at a desk in the barn, or at a desk in her office in the house—also used by Randy and one or two employees, as it was where the computer and copy machine were located. It was her space, but not exclusively. A regular employee arrived each morning about 8:00 and—somewhat to Randy's consternation—came through the house while he was still in the bathroom or shaving. During the day, Marcia and one or two co-workers walked back and forth from the barn-office to the house. This would not have been a problem, but for the chickens. "They keep tracking chicken shit into the house, and I *hate* it," Randy remarked. Surprisingly, the nicely brought-up girl from the affluent suburb was much less disturbed by this than the farm boy from Carolina.

The garden and yard space, like the house, had portions that were "his," "hers," and "shared." The barn and backyard were shared. A flower garden at the front of the house was Marcia's domain, but planting in a strip next to the street was Randy's responsibility. A narrow planted side yard to the south, where daffodils had just finished blooming, seemed to be a mix of "his" and "hers," while an even narrower strip beside the house on the north had just been claimed by Randy when he planted miniature wild irises there, transplanted from his parents' farm in North Carolina.

Randy loves to collect things—particularly rocks and abandoned artifacts (car bumpers, for example), which he stores in piles in various places until he's ready to do something with them. He recalled, nostalgically, wandering for hours with his mother on beaches in North Carolina, collecting beautiful stones or pieces of driftwood. Marcia, who is not a collector, finds the collections somewhat irksome, but sees them as part of who Randy is.

Decisions about the newly purchased house next door were very much in their minds as I talked with Randy and Marcia. A month or so earlier, just after they purchased this house, they had spent part of their seventh wedding anniversary sitting in the new house discussing how they would occupy it. It seemed clear that it would become the business half of their lives—no more chicken shit in the kitchen! One room would become Marcia's exclusive office. A front room would become a conference/meeting space, and another front room would be a smaller meeting room with easy chairs. The yard space of the second house was more problematic: Should the chickens be moved over there, leaving the home yard as a garden? "But it's too shady for a garden, and I love to look out and *see* the chickens." Perhaps they would move the fence between the two properties and contain the chickens in a large enclosure instead of giving them free run of the yard.

What would happen to the barn when the business moved next door? As Randy talked about the barn, it became clear that this was the space that held the most emotion for him. As a boy, he had helped his father erect a barn on a farm they rented; he remembered it with great feeling as a rite of passage, the time he became a man. Many years later, Randy purchased this house, and an academic colleague, Don, moved in temporarily while separating from his wife. Together, Randy and Don had converted the barn into a live/work area by raising the roof and adding loft space and skylights. It had been a time of profound male bonding for these two friends used to intellectual collaborations, now working together with their hands. Not long afterward, Don was killed in an automobile accident. For Randy, the barn took on an even more intense meaning, not only a memory of a rite of passage with his father, but now, too, the concretization of his friendship with Don. Ironically, he spent little time there, as it was the heart of the business in which he was only partially involved. Perhaps, he mused, with the business moved to the neighboring house, he would reclaim the barn for special uses of his own.

Working at Home

Randy and Marcia are indicative of a growing number of households in which one or both adults work partially or exclusively out of the home. A 1985 U.S. Bureau of Labor Statistics count indicated that more than eighteen million people perform some or all of their regular work at home. Of the two million (by now, no doubt many more) who worked exclusively at home, two-thirds were women. A national poll conducted by Yankelovich, Skelly, and White in the early 1980s showed that one-third of American workers would *prefer* to work at home. Home work encompasses people of varying income groups, races, and geographic locations. The type of work ranges from computer programming, graphic design, freelance writing, and psychotherapy to word processing, data input, telemarketing, and piece work.

If you or another family member is planning to work at home, it would be worthwhile to pay attention to the conclusions of two recent studies about the pros and cons of this arrangement. A critical issue to bear in mind is that all of us, consciously or unconsciously, consider our home to be a *refuge*. It is *the* place in the world where we can recoup from the vagaries of the outside world. When people start to work at home, varying levels of conflict arise as to the separation of work and home—traditionally separated by geography. In a study by architect Sherry Ahrentzen, those who reported being most satisfied with working at home almost all had separate rooms where they could close the door and be cut off from the potential distractions of people using the kitchen, watching TV, and so on.[7] People appreciated being close to a bathroom, being able to look out at the landscape of a backyard, and being able to take a short walk to the kitchen to make coffee or a sandwich. Those whose work brought clients to the home appreciated the image of a well-kept neighborhood and the privacy of a separate business entrance.

But working at home is not all roses. Although setting one's own pace and schedule is appealing, some people miss the camaraderie and social life of the workplace. For many people, the neighborhood becomes critical; home-based workers appreciate being able to go for a walk, visit a cafe, and see people on the street. In a study of home-based workers in the San Francisco Bay Area by city planner Penny Gurstein, those who were most satisfied with working at home were those who lived in an older suburb (built up around 1905 to 1920), with plenty of corner stores, coffee shops, amenities, and pedestrians on the streets. Those who were least satisfied lived in relatively new single-family suburbs, where there are rarely amenities within walking distance and where people walking by were a rarity.[8]

Sherry Ahrentzen highlights the sentiments of some of these dissatisfied home-based workers in her study of the home as office: "Home is not a refuge now—I can get trapped here," responded one woman who lived alone. "Home used to feel like a sanctuary. Now I sometimes feel trapped because I'm here all the time," said a woman who was also a wife and mother. A man who worked at home while his wife went out to work reported, "It's difficult to detach from things at home. I must get physically away."[9]

Thus, for those who began to feel isolated or trapped while working at home, getting out to go for a walk, to go to lunch, or to visit the library or post office became of vital importance. When asked what facilities and services had taken on added importance now that they worked at home, more than half of those in the San Francisco area study mentioned wanting to be close to a post office and a copy center; one-fifth or more mentioned an office-supply store, library, pleasant views, quiet, good working conditions, and convenience to downtown. In short, the social encounters and useful amenities at the workplace (copy machine, stationery supplies, outgoing mail box) must now be sought in the neighborhood around home.

Ahrentzen also mentions that while many people in these studies reported feeling "chained" or "trapped" working at home, others reported feeling that their home was less of a refuge now that it was "invaded" by clients. "I used to feel the home was a more personal place. Now it's not because other people are coming into the home, walking through it and seeing my family. People who come into my house to see my [work] demonstrations also come into my privacy."[10]

Women, who have traditionally been identified with home, may tend to feel these intrusions more acutely and may tend also to be more sensitive to the conflicts between family and work. Ahrentzen reported, "One homeworker felt that her relationship with her home was stronger when she was home alone. When her family entered the house the feelings of refuge disintegrated. Another homeworker saw her home as 'her castle' during the day, and, as she put it, will do anything to 'defend it' then. Her husband had a disability for an extended period of time and was home during the day—her working hours. Even though he spent most of the time upstairs while she was working in a downstairs office, she felt he was intruding."[11]

Many friends of mine who work at home have made varying adjustments to meet these problems. A woman who is a psychotherapist has converted a former garage into her office with an adjacent waiting room and bathroom. Clients approach this place via the driveway; to go to work, she walks down a set of steps at the back of her house and across her garden. Physical separation is also the solution for two men I know who work from their homes; both use converted garages, one for an art studio, the other for a small mail-order business. A woman architect friend has solved the problem by buying a house across the street from her home and has turned this into her design studio.

Whether your need is for a separate structure (Ahrentzen found in her study that less than 10 percent wanted this), or a separate room in the house, the issue of spatial, visual, and aural separation is critical. People remarked: "The office is my refuge"; "My workspace is more of a haven"; "My office is my space. I don't like my family in here. I like having a door to close."[12]

Although futurist writers have sung the praises of the return to home-based work and the emergence of the "electronic cottage," the California study found that by no means everyone was happy with this arrangement. Gurstein interviewed fifty-two home-based workers and found that many worked long hours and rarely had time for other activities. Women sought home-based work in order to be closer to children and maintain family responsibilities, and men wanted more control over their work and scheduling than they had at the office, but both found that work life had begun to take precedence over home life both spatially and temporally. Daily schedules were organized around work; living rooms were being converted into offices and no longer used for entertaining; home-based workers worked long, irregular hours.

Gurstein concluded: "While the home for home-based workers serves as a retreat from the complex environment outside of the home, it loses its refuge nature as work-related stresses become associated with the home. It is no longer only a personal expression of the private aspects of life but becomes, also, a reflection of the individual (or family's) working life. Home-based workers can never leave their offices."[13]

LIVING AND WORKING:
EXERCISES YOU CAN DO YOURSELF

Working at Home

If these issues seem painfully familiar, you might want to try the following exercise. Each family member should draw a layout of the home (it need not be architecturally accurate) and color or shade in rooms or portions of rooms as to whose territory they are. If children have trouble understanding that concept, you might say: "A place is a person's territory if *other* people have to ask permission to come in, or to leave their stuff there, or to speak to the person who is there" (the school principal's office might be an analogy they will understand). When everyone has done this, it is instructive to compare how each sees the home as "divided up."

If in your home, the home-based worker and other family members have different perceptions of spatial boundaries and privacy needs, this is a good place to start a discussion. When the family starts to really *hear* the conflicts of roles experienced by the home-based worker, they may more readily agree to abide by mutually agreed-upon rules, for example: Mother is working from 10:00 A.M. to 2:00 P.M. and cannot be disturbed for anything short of a crisis; Father is speaking to clients on the phone from 8:00 to 9:30 P.M. every evening, and you cannot expect him to pay attention to you at that time. It is critical, if space permits, that the home-based worker have a room of his or her own. George Bernard Shaw went to work each morning in a shed he had made into a simple office at the bottom of his garden. Dylan Thomas wrote much of his poetry in a tiny shack-with-a-view, perched high up on a hillside above his house in a South Wales seaside village. Don't you, or your home-working partner, deserve as much?

Children's Territories

If, in conducting the preceding exercise, it becomes apparent that your children have some dissatisfactions regarding space *they* can control, this is worth looking into. Perhaps two siblings share a room and squabble over territory; this is a familiar story. Although there is nothing inherently wrong with sharing a bedroom (and many children *have* to do this), helping them work out an agreement as to which space is whose may alleviate arguments. If one half of the room is perceived as "better" (for example, has a window or is closer to the bathroom), a plan whereby each person has a turn every six months to occupy this half might be a solution. If both halves of the room are equally attractive (or unattractive!) and the problem is one of territorial incursions, perhaps a line of masking tape across the floor, indicating the "boundary," might help. If one wants to be quiet and read while the other wants to watch TV, engage the children in helping to work out a solution. Perhaps the parents' room or living room can be designated for evening TV-watching, and the shared bedroom for quiet study, reading, writing, and so on.

Three critical components of feeling you have control over a territory are:

- Choosing the furniture, or paint colors, or drapes yourself
- Being allowed to hang up personal photos or pictures
- Being responsible for cleaning the space

We all know what fireworks the latter can evoke with our children—or our parents! But the truth is that when anyone takes on the responsibility for maintaining a space—a child for his or her room, a homeowner for the sidewalk in front of his house, a neighborhood for maintaining a local park—the work involved seems to bond person and place in a powerful way. And being bonded to a personal or group space is an important aspect of individual or group identity. So insist that your child, when old enough, cleans his or her room; it may be the first step on a journey of positive self-identity.

For similar reasons, it is important to let your child express him- or herself in his or her territory: Provide a bulletin board or chalkboard, or have the child accompany you to the store or flea market to buy curtain material or a bedside lamp. Buying something expensive or having the room professionally decorated is not the issue. Allowing your children to be part of the decision-making process that affects where they live is what is important.

Be prepared for them to change their minds, however! Childhood and adolescence are times of constantly evolving preferences and values. I was so proud of myself when I encouraged my eleven-year-old daughter, Lucy, to choose the colors of her bedroom. The combination of deep purple, sky blue, and white would not have been my choice—but I swallowed hard and set about cleaning walls and window frames and painting it her way. Two or three years later, she bemoaned the fact that I'd let her choose; by this time, she regarded the colors as "yucky." I told her this time she could repaint it herself.

Couples and Territory

Perhaps you and your spouse or partner are feeling some tension over the use of your shared home. If you have a sense that it has something to do with territorial control, you might experiment with the following exercise. Do this only if you're prepared to work out some solutions and listen to each other's point of view. The exercise is likely to arouse a lot of emotion!

Take a large sheet of paper and some colored pens or crayons. First, draw a simple plan of your house or apartment with room and furniture sketched in, roughly, to scale. Now place it on a table and sit opposite each other with the paper between you. Each select a color, and start to shade in those rooms, parts of rooms, and pieces of furniture that you feel "belong" to you. Anything that you share—and feel good about sharing—leave blank. If your partner starts encroaching on "your" space, or vice versa, notice your feelings but try not to say anything. In fact, it would be better to do this whole exercise in silence until a kitchen timer or watch set at, say, fifteen minutes, reminds you to stop. Be prepared—this experience may bring up a lot of feelings. How you express yourselves on a sheet of paper may well be a microcosm of how you deal with each other and the environment in real life. If this exercise reveals unexpected differences that are difficult to deal with, it may help to seek the professional assistance of a marriage counselor.

The Need for Privacy

Finally, and most important, moving in together is bound to "press some buttons" about privacy and control unless these are discussed openly and frankly. The need for privacy is a normal, healthy human trait, not one that should be looked on as threatening by either partner. Discuss with each other not only the kinds of rooms and spaces you'd like to share, but also what you each like to do alone. I like to garden, read, and write alone. You may like to read alone, but see gardening as a chore to be done with someone else. Your partner may sometimes like to go to bed early and watch a movie on TV alone. You may already know these things about each other, but it doesn't hurt to verbalize these needs and—if you're looking for a house together—to make sure each of your needs for private space will be met.

EIGHT

Where to Live?
Self-Image and Location

Home can be a room inside a house, a house within a neighborhood, a neigh-
borhood within a city, and a city within a nation. At each level the meaning of
home gains in intensity and depth from the dialectical interaction between the
two poles of experience—the place and its context at a larger scale . . . Home is
a place of security within an insecure world, a place of certainty within doubt, a
familiar place in a strange world, a sacred place in a profane world. It is a place
of autonomy and power in an increasingly heteronomous world where others
make the rules.

—KIMBERLY DOVEY, "Home and Homelessness,"
in *Home Environments*[1]

I feel extraordinarily fortunate to live in a house and a neighborhood where I
feel secure and totally at home. My house sits at the end of a quiet, one-block
residential street. A large backyard and smaller front yard allow me to engage in
my passion for gardening. A short walk and I'm in the midst of a cluster of neighborhood shops on College Avenue. A large, sunny Laundromat is where I do my
laundry. I guess I'm odd in that I love going to the Laundromat and have never
owned or wanted a washing machine. I enjoy the quiet camaraderie of doing a
mundane task in the company of others; perhaps in my genes I recall joining other
people at the village well to collect water. While the clothes are bouncing around
in the $2.50 machine, I walk across the street to a bakery for coffee and a pumpkin
muffin. It was here that I edited much of this book—sipping the strongest French

roast you can find in Berkeley, sometimes dreamily watching people and dogs passing by outside the steamed-up windows.

Later, I might take my film to the photo store, stop by the post office, pick up lightbulbs at the hardware store—and walk home. Likely as not, I'll bump into someone I know, or be embarrassed to meet a long-time ex-student whose name I cannot recall. Tired after two decades of cooking for a growing family, I now often suggest to friends that we can eat at a local restaurant and then walk home for tea and dessert around the fire. On one October weekend each year, two blocks of College Avenue are closed for a street fair. When a rent increase threatened the fountain at the corner drugstore, the neighborhood rallied behind a commercial rent control proposal—and the drugstore was saved.

If I leave my house and walk in the opposite direction from the shops, in fifteen minutes I am in my office on the Berkeley campus. Two days a week, I walk through People's Park and along Telegraph Avenue to a campus gym, where I attend an exercise class. I love to see people on the sidewalks. Although the density of people on Oxford Street in London is now difficult for me to take, and the density of pedestrians in Shanghai actually caused me to fall ill with stress, Telegraph Avenue in Berkeley feels just right. I like to see the varied vendors and pedestrians; I like to listen to snatches of conversation as I pass by.

This is where I live. I love to be in a neighborly, pedestrian-oriented community, and to not have to get in my car to buy a quart of milk, or a bunch of bananas, or a take-out burrito. I love to have houseguests and show them my neighborhood. It says as much about who I am and what I value as the house in which I live.

For most of us, the type of setting we live in is as important as or more important than the type of house. A study conducted by architect Roberta Feldman in the state of Illinois and the city of Denver showed that the vast majority of respondents identified themselves with a particular kind of settlement: "They were a 'city person,' 'suburbanite,' 'small town person,' or 'country person' ('country/mountain person' in Denver), with only a small minority indicating that they did not identify themselves with 'any kind of place. . . .' Respondents were likely to have lived in the type of settlement with which they professed identification in the past and present, and indicated desires or plans to maintain their residence in that type of settlement in the future."[2]

This identification with or rejection of a particular kind of setting may stem from childhood experience—for example, happy or painful memories of a suburban upbringing. It can also stem from a stage in the life-cycle—for example, a young adult's preference for city living with its greater choice of jobs and recreation, or an older person's need for public transportation. It may stem from intrinsic personality traits as well—for example, the rejection by a convivial extrovert of a quiet rural lifestyle. Most likely, our preferences for a particular type of location stem from a complex mix of all three. Small wonder that when two individuals, each with their own unique life experience, decide to live together, the issue of location may loom as a major obstacle, regardless of the house itself.

Indeed as the following stories suggest, residential setting along with aesthetic style and territorial privacy have to be part of a couple's discussions when deciding to live together. To not do so is to court later conflict.

A "Visitor" in Someone Else's House: Lucy's Search for Her Own Place

I met Lucy one weekend at a workshop on the coast of northern California. She heard me telling someone about my work and, at the end of the weekend, asked me to stay on and talk with her about a problem she was having with a house. The conflict she felt in—and with—the house she shared with a partner reflected two very different sets of values about city and country life.

The house was situated in a bleak and rocky landscape with a view of the Pacific, approached down a rutted dirt road and quite remote from any other dwellings. Perhaps remodeled by a former owner, it had the feel of a large rustic cabin with exposed beams, hardwood floors, and redwood paneling. It was the home of her lover, Tony, a sculptor, and was his choice of dwelling and location. Lucy had lived in the house for two years, commuting a long distance

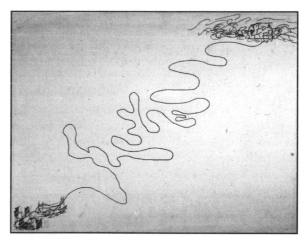

Lucy's depiction of the home she shared in the country with Tony, and her long drive to a job in San Francisco (bottom left).

once a week for three days of work at a part-time job as a social worker in San Francisco. Increasingly, she had come to realize that this was not the right place for her—she did not feel at home in the country. Tony, on the other hand, could not abide the city for long. The conflict here was not one of contrasted aesthetic values—they both liked the house, per se. Rather it was a conflict over lifestyles. Tony, more introverted, loved the quiet expansiveness of the country, long walks, lack of neighbors, and the space to work on his large-scale wooden sculptures without interruption. Lucy loved the energy and excitement of the city—cafes, music, friends dropping by. Her anguish was that she loved Tony but couldn't any longer live where he wanted to live. The interview was frequently punctuated with tears; Lucy felt at the end of her tether. Here is how she described her experience of being "a visitor in Tony's world":

"This house holds Tony and my heart, but not me. It's very isolated. I don't feel like it's me. And I feel guilty when I try to put me in it. It feels like Tony's. And maybe when it's really just his, I can visit and share it without being so torn."

I invited Lucy to try to tell the house why she doesn't feel at home in it: "You're too isolated. [Long pause] I can't just walk outside and be with people or go to places that I want to go. To get anywhere from you is a big deal, a long trip. And you're small. I don't like living without closets and without places to put things. I love your bathroom, but sometimes I really resent that I have to walk outside when it's freezing at night. I wish you had more natural light. But you're real pretty. I like you especially at night, when there is soft lighting and everything looks real cozy. And I like all your wood. And I like looking out the windows and just seeing green. I like the frog that lives in the bathroom and I like all the animals around [suppressing tears]. I'm afraid to be here alone. I'm afraid I won't get a fire started and I'll be cold. I don't know what to do with you."

I asked Lucy if she felt she could learn what to do with this house: "Probably. Yes, I am sure I could. I resist that. I won't let myself love you. You feel like some place to visit but not to live in."

Lucy then began to speak as if she were Tony—how he felt about it: "I feel good here. My dreams were very much to have an 'ours.' Any place I have means a lot more to me if you share it with me, but I'm finally coming into my own and feeling right about the way I live. I won't give that up. I have felt 'not at home' for so long, and it's nice to feel at home. And I wish that could include you. And I think it can, but maybe not as much as we thought. I want you to feel good in this house. But, if this isn't it, I want you to find what you do need, and, when you come here, maybe you'll be refreshed and feel fulfilled."

I asked Lucy about the setting in which she had grown up. She described a suburban house and neighborhood where she had also never felt quite at home, a setting where she felt safe and happy only with an older brother. As she described her childhood, there seemed to be some remarkable parallels with her present life with Tony. Though now in a very different physical setting, it was one in which she didn't feel at home, where she felt she was a visitor, where she felt secure only with the protection of an older man.

"I grew up in a real nice home in a suburban kind of area. It was real comfortable. It was warm when it was cold outside, and it was a good place to be sick in—and I was that a whole lot [snickers]. But, except for the attic, it didn't feel like me. I always went to little nooks up in the attic or down in the basement, and that's where I felt most comfortable. It was a pretty street, on a slight hill; we rode sleds in the wintertime. In the autumn, all the leaves fell and crunched as we walked, and that was real nice. I remember the smell of burning leaves. I wasn't a real well-liked kid. There were lots of kids in the neighborhood, but I was sort of scared of them, and they didn't like me [in tears]. It was a world I would like to have been a part of. But when I was with my brother, then it felt like mine. I felt safe with him. He is five years older than I am. Everybody on the street loved him, and he sort of made them be nice to me. When it was just him and me, then it felt real good. We played a lot of make-believe fantasy stuff, and I loved it [starts to cry]. I think about my brother sometimes, but I haven't thought about living in that house and growing up there. It was almost safe there, but not quite."

I asked Lucy if it seemed more like her brother's environment than her own. "No, it seemed like my parents' environment. We both were kind of [a moment's hesitation] visitors; but, when we were together, it was okay. I have never lived in a place that feels really like me. So I make the best I can with either living with someone I love in their territory, or living by myself and making that okay."

I asked Lucy if she could draw a picture of how she would ideally like to live. She drew a "country cottage" set amidst city skyscrapers with the words *friends, dance, school, writing,* and *people* scattered around her house. A long winding cord, not unlike an umbilical cord, or "the end of my tether," connected her house to a small dwelling in the top-right corner of the picture: It was Tony's house in the country with a red heart at its center, and many letter *T*'s covering its walls like shingles.

Lucy's image of her ideal environment in the city.

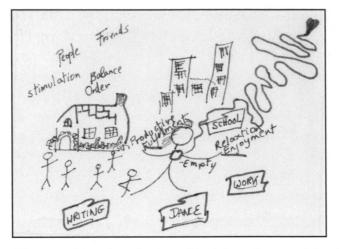

I asked her to imagine she was already in that country cottage in the city. She started to describe her life there:

"I feel balanced and full of possibilities. If one thing doesn't feel right, there are other things to try or places to be. It feels a lot safer and more exciting. There are things I am interested in doing: classes and dancing, and, hopefully, work is gonna come together better. I like walking or riding through the streets and just looking at all the people and all their little homes. And I feel part of a world, part of a community. It feels real good. But there's a big, empty place too. I dream about Tony coming to the city. [Laughing] I imagine wearing something he'll really like and opening the door and him coming into my world and our having nothing to do that whole weekend but be together. And I picture making a nice dinner and making love a whole lot and getting up late in the morning and going to do something we both like to do—going to a movie, a play, or a harpsichord concert. There are a whole lot of things that we both like to do: If my cup runs over for those two days, I have everything I want. I will feel very, very special."

I asked Lucy if she could continue speaking as Tony, if there was anything more he'd like to say to Lucy: "Well, I sort of wish you'd get on with it. It's real hard being in this limbo place. I don't exactly know what I'm supposed to do, how to help you, how to take care of me. It's all really up in the air. You sometimes make me feel guilty about being happy, and I really resent that. I am not happy that you are unhappy. I am not happy that this is happening, but I am happy, damn it, and I want to feel good about being happy. I don't feel very close to you right now. I don't feel real sexually turned on. I feel distant, somehow. But I don't see that as any great big thing. We've gone through this before, and I feel very tied to you, real connected, and I love you a whole lot. And somehow this is all contingent on your making this damn move. So make it, so we can start dealing with it. We're both stuck. And we're waiting for you."

The story of Lucy and Tony personifies the dilemma of many couples who meet, fall in love, and then discover a marked preference for quite different life-styles. At root, the preference for city versus country living may have less to do with liking or not liking the country than with the need to be around a lot of other people or not. Most of us experience fluctuations, even within a single day, in our need for company versus solitude. Lucy and Tony were two people drawn together from opposite ends of the city/people versus country/solitude continuum.

Six months after this dialogue, I met them at a Christmas fair in San Francisco. They both appeared radiant. Lucy had moved to the city. Tony had stayed in the country, but came down often on weekends and was beginning to enjoy the city more. Some sense of balance was beginning to surface in both their lives.

House as Burden: Anne's Isolation in a Rural Setting

Anne is the attractive wife of a successful San Francisco businessman and the mother of a ten-year-old son. I use these words guardedly: Her identity is that of wife and mother. She has no career of her own and is beginning to feel exceed-ingly restless and frustrated. A lot of her anger, just now beginning to surface, has become focused on the house. It feels like a prison to her, located in a rural area just beyond the city and suburbs, where the architect-designed homes of upper-middle-class professionals vie for ocean-view lots.

"When my husband chose this house, it was a means for him to make his mark on the world. He had to do something big that was satisfying to him and showed other people that he was successful. He wanted it to be big, impressive, and mas-sive. He also wanted a beautiful home and one that was comfortable. He thought that would be a good thing for the family. He seems to recognize now that I wasn't part of the decision; he acted like I was at the time, but I wasn't. In retrospect, I wish I had moved out at the beginning. I wish I had said, 'If you want this marriage to last . . .' But I didn't trust my feelings enough. I thought something was wrong with me. Here he's built this beautiful palatial place that everybody else thinks is good, and I can't bear it. I kept trying to fit in, you know, like a square peg in a round hole."

As we talked further, it became clear that it wasn't primarily the house per se that was the problem—it was the location. As in most suburban or ex-urban locations, a trip to go shopping, or sit in a cafe, or browse in a bookshop meant a drive of twenty to thirty minutes. Anne asked me where I lived, and I described my neighborhood in Berkeley. Her eyes lit up: "I used to live there when we were first married," she said eagerly. "Oh, yes, I remember it now." She looked wistful and sad again. "How could I have forgotten that I like to live in a neighborhood like that?"

When it comes to marriage, buying a house, and raising children, many of us, it seems, do forget; even more so if one partner has stronger feelings about house location, or we don't feel able to challenge the prevailing myths about where it is socially appropriate to build a house or raise a family.

Since the rise of industrial and commercial city centers in the mid-nineteenth century, the suburbs have been perceived as the domain of domesticity, family values, femininity, and security. Urban centers, on the other hand, tend to be perceived as more masculine, the domain of power-plays, assertiveness, competition, risk taking, even danger. Men would traditionally return from the cut-and-thrust of the workplace, be thankful to put their feet up, sip a martini, relax from human interaction, and watch the evening news. Meanwhile, the woman, perhaps cooped up all day with infants or small children, couldn't contain herself from recounting the activities of the day. The stage was set for frustration and misunderstandings.

More and more studies are suggesting that women are more affected by the location of the home than are men. At a time when more and more women are entering the work force and are also primarily responsible for home-making, any organization of the urban environment and infrastructure that makes it difficult to combine these roles will adversely impact women.

The sheer distance of most newer residential neighborhoods from shops, work, services, child care, and so on make such settings especially problematic for women. A study that looked at white middle-class couples in northern California over a forty-year period found that the lives of women were more affected by accessibility to urban services than were those of men. Women who in older age lived in remote suburban or rural locations were more likely to be unhappy or "poorly adjusted" than men in those locales.[3]

A study by a group of environmental psychologists of attitudes of middle-income families in New York found that men in the city were likely to emphasize the role that home played in providing a retreat from the stresses of urban living. Many such men felt that suburban life would, for them, provide a desirable degree of segregation between home life and work life. Women living in the city, however, stressed its importance in providing options for full- or part-time work and that they would be cut off from these opportunities if they moved to the suburbs.[4] Two New York psychologists, investigating similar issues, concluded after interviewing more than two hundred couples in upper-middle-class sections of Stamford, Connecticut, and New York City, that in their sample of urban men and women and suburban men and women, the most satisfied group was suburban men. "The two contrasted environments, plus the commitment of a wife to household tasks, provided a balance of adult work activities and a satisfying family-centered environment."[5] Nevertheless, men living in the suburbs spend significantly less time with their families, as well as with their children or wives alone.[6]

When middle-income families in a successful and well-liked New York City apartment block were interviewed regarding housing choice, more men than women expressed a desire to move to the suburbs. When couples did agree on a move, it was the women who expressed more concern: "I was afraid of isolation, intellectual stagnation, and boredom" was a typical response. After the move, half the women said they suffered from a lack of stimulation; one-third reported feeling lonely. Many were discouraged about finding a job; many felt they had become more boring.[7]

Although this last study was based on a small sample, similar problems of women in the suburbs have been reported in much larger U.S. and Canadian studies.[8] New York psychologist Susan Saegert reported: "Suburban women who located in more dense suburbs, or near already established friends, experienced less difficulty with isolation."[9] A Canadian study by sociologist William Michelson which followed the move of families to either city center or suburbia found that suburban women were generally the least satisfied with their residential location; their husbands the most satisfied. In short, women are caught between a rock and a hard place.[10]

Although women recognize that a suburban location may provide the family with "more home for the money," their children with greater freedom (and perhaps better schools), and their husbands with a greater sense of home-as-refuge, at the same time the move will distance women from the stimulation, work opportunities, and choice of social relationships more available in or near the city. Many make the choice in favor of children's and husband's needs; many feel the loss of options deeply, especially when their children need them less. Loneliness, depression, and tranquilizers are not far behind.

The good news is that the exclusively residential nature of many suburban areas is changing: Many suburban centers are turning into so-called edge cities, and more and more employment opportunities have moved out from city locations. Women can find work closer to home. The not-so-good news is that many of these jobs are lower-paying office jobs. And while the emergence of "edge cities" has brought some urban amenities closer to suburban neighborhoods, the paucity of child care, public transportation, and other services still render women's lives there more problematic than men's.

The Saegert study concludes poignantly: "Where does this leave women who value their homes, who want them to be meaningful centers of the family, and who want to expand their roles outside the home? Looking at the same issues from the male point of view, it appears that men prefer residential environments that reinforce the public/private distinction. This may be an inadvertent consequence of the bonuses of suburban life—retreat, outdoor activities, homeownership, relief from the pace of the city—or it may be partially motivated by the perhaps unconscious desire in many men to assure that their home will be taken care of by a woman with few other options."[11]

In her much-discussed book on gendered language, *You Just Don't Understand,* linguist Deborah Tannen describes the contrasting needs of many husbands and wives on returning home after a day at work. Men, who are more likely than women to use language as a means of determining who is "on top," and who use it this way particularly in the workplace, want to have the option on returning home of saying nothing, of not having to "prove" anything through language. Women, on the other hand, are more likely to use language to establish and nurture relationships, not to maintain a "one up" position. Returning home themselves, or welcoming husband and children home, women's need is to foster relationships through the medium they are most comfortable with—conversation. Hence the classic cartoon situation of the husband behind the newspaper or in front of the TV while his wife is trying to engage him in conversation.

Ironically, these language-style differences are mirrored in men's and women's house-location preferences. The studies quoted above suggest it is more often the commuting male adult in a family who wants to move to the suburbs, and that this type of location and density is least supportive of women's needs. A man's need to come home and be quiet is reflected in his preference for the privacy of suburban living. A woman's greater need for social involvement is reflected in her preference for urban living or older suburbs with neighborhood shops and street life.[12]

Settlement Identity

We live in a very mobile society. Most of us move when we leave our parental home, go away to college, and take our first job. Though marriage or partnership may not prompt a move, child rearing very often does. Divorce, widowhood, and retirement are life stages that also often lead to a move. Research suggests that though few of us remain living in the same specific locale throughout our lives, many of us have a tendency to prefer living in the same type of setting—older suburb, new suburb, city, small town, and so on. We tend to feel most comfortable in a particular type of place, its values, lifestyle, and image; we each have a "settlement identity."

Investigating this phenomenon via residential autobiographies of a number of Chicago residents, architect Roberta Feldman describes how the great majority of them expressed "intense and deeply felt bonds with only one type of settlement. . . . Their residential autobiographies are filled with volunteered convictions about the best or only place for them to live in the past, present and anticipated future."[13] Many felt it appropriate at certain stages of their lives to live in settings that were not their preferred ideal, but did so for the sake of spouse and/or children. At some period, almost inevitably, they returned to a setting that was congruent with their settlement identity. Feldman recounts the experiences of Joan, who described herself as a "confirmed city person." She was raised in a Milwaukee suburb, but "never felt quite comfortable. It was nothing tangible. I never had a really bad experience. Just a feeling like I didn't fit in. I never felt like I belonged."

On a childhood vacation to New York City with her parents, she discovered her settlement identity; she loved city life. Subsequently, she spent most of her adult life, before and after her marriage, living in downtown Chicago. On becoming pregnant, she reluctantly moved to the suburbs, but after eight years in two such communities, "I just had to move." Moving back to a large, old lakefront apartment in Chicago not only permitted Joan to juggle career and family, but was also "liberating." Suburban residence had been alien to her concept of self and her aspirations for her children's developing self-identities. In Joan's own words:

"I love the involvement of a city. It feels like I am a part of the world and I love that. I want my children to be part of the real world—to become worldly people."

Though the majority of people in this study had a consistent settlement preference, like Joan, there were a few who seemed able to adapt to many different settings. Fred, for example, grew up in a small town, enjoyed young adulthood in a city, married and moved to the suburbs, divorced and moved back to a downtown high-rise, remarried and remained living downtown. On his wife's retirement, they moved to a small place in the country. He foresaw a possible move to Arizona or Florida. "I've lived in a lot of places, but I wouldn't want it any other way. I always felt like I belonged, you know, in all my homes. It was who I was at the time."

Thus, Fred made various moves at different stages in his life and was able to feel quite at home in each one of them. Perhaps he represents someone more able and willing than most of us to be "in the here and now." He felt comfortable in each setting because he was in a different stage of his life and "it was who I was at the time."

When my husband and I began to look for a house, we were—happily—in total agreement about what we felt to be an ideal neighborhood setting. Interestingly for both of us, it reflected an aspect of where we had grown up. Stephen was raised in an older, working-class neighborhood of St. Louis, with houses and apartment buildings dating from around the 1920s, with tree-lined streets, corner stores, buses, and street life. From his upbringing in a warm, boisterous Jewish family, with both sets of grandparents within walking distance, he inherited a totally positive attitude about this kind of neighborhood. For my part, after evacuation in the Second World War, our family returned from the country to London, and I spent my teenaged years in an inner suburb dating from the 1930s, with lots of pedestrian activity, nearby shops and bus routes, and a half-hour subway ride to the center of the city. I could bike to school, run errands to the shops, walk the dog in a brookside park, or go into the West End with friends to browse in bookshops, go to the theater, or imbibe the latest chic Italian import-espresso. As an adolescent and young adult, I loved the freedom of exploring London by public transport and having easy accessibility to a whole range of shops and entertainment. This setting suited me perfectly, just as the countryside had been ideal for me as a child.

Upon marriage and starting a family, Stephen and I were in total agreement about where we wanted to raise our children—in a neighborhood where they could walk to school, friends' houses, and to shops as soon as they were old enough; where he and I could indulge our enjoyment of walking to a local cafe or bookshop; and where, in time, our children could independently move about by public transport. By the age of eight, our son and daughter were both comfortably traveling by bus and subway alone to their school. They have grown up to be exceptionally mature, curious, world-traveling adults. They, in turn, I would not doubt, will probably choose to raise their children in a neighborhood similar to the one in which they grew up.

Thus, our settlement identity is passed on from one generation to the next. Given that children or adolescents are comfortable and at home in the setting in which they are raised, it is more than likely they will choose a similar setting for raising their own children. If, however, those early years were not happy, and they felt ill at ease or bored in the setting their parents had chosen, it seems likely they would choose a contrasting setting—as did Joan, quoted earlier, who never felt comfortable in the suburb in which she grew up, and became a "confirmed city person."

Neighborhood Landscapes as Communication of Social Status

When we start to consider one particular type of settlement—for example, semirural suburbia—it becomes apparent that there are many subtle variations in the residential landscape that offer clues as to the values of the particular group who lives there. In a study of neighborhood settings in Bedford, New York, geographer James Duncan showed that subtle variations in the landscape taste of two groups of people of high socioeconomic status were significant indicators of group identity. "In a society which does not officially sanction social stratification, individuals provide covert cues (such as speech, dress, and landscape tastes) rather than overt cues to their social status."[14] He examined the residential settings of "old money" residents, who tended to be members of an Episcopalian church, the country club, garden club, and/or local historical society. Their preferred landscape was one Duncan described as "rural but sophisticated." Roads and lanes were narrow and twisted, overhung with maples and oaks, and lined by dry stone walls. Gardens, roads, and houses appear to be old and "natural." Houses are set back and separated from each other by screens of vegetation. They are eclectic and rambling in style, though most are nineteenth- and early-twentieth-century versions of traditional colonial dwellings. The residents of this landscape appear to value the "English upper class style of studied seediness."[15]

In contrast, the "new money" settings in Bedford comprise paved straight streets; open, symmetrical front gardens; nearly perfect reproductions of New England colonial houses all built since the Second World War; and traditional American accoutrements, such as carriage lampposts, eagle ornaments, rustic signs, and ornate mailboxes.

"The degree of openness of the landscape appears to be central to each group's image of the landscape. A member of the alpha [old money] landscape wants to stand in his garden and feel that he is out in the country, surrounded by nature, not by other houses. . . . In the beta [new money] landscape, however, the spacing of the houses and the openness of the landscape suggest that the resident wants to stand in his garden, to see and be seen, while a streetful of expensive houses similar to his own mirror his prosperity."[16]

No doubt, residents of most metropolitan areas of the United States can supply similar examples from their own observations. In the San Francisco Bay Area, the fear of residents of an "old money" landscape that their neighborhoods would take on the appearance of a "new money" landscape were passionately expressed after the devastating Oakland hills fire of 1991. The rustic landscape of half-hidden houses, narrow streets, no sidewalks, and minimal street lighting was what appealed to the community of academics, artists, professionals, and writers who chose to live there. As discussions on rebuilding after the fire gathered momentum, and old neighbors found each other through the pages of a postfire newspaper, the common dislike for a particular "new money" landscape began to emerge. People did not want their rebuilt homes and neighborhoods to look like Blackhawk—a nearby spec-built, walled and gated community of one- to three-million-dollar homes, clustered around a country club and golf course. Like the "new money" landscape of Bedford, New York, houses are very visible to the street and to each other, in a setting of orderly landscaped yards and ornate mailboxes. But unlike Bedford in the 1970s, Blackhawk in the 1990s displays a jarring array of house styles from French château and Mediterranean patio to English Tudor and New England farmhouse. It was the size, ostentation, and visibility of these "monster homes" that horrified the residents of the burnt-out Oakland hills as they discussed plans for rebuilding.

As houses are being rebuilt amid burned tree stumps and reseeded hillsides, the residential setting is taking on the appearance of a tenuous cross between California-style "old money" and "new money" landscapes. Around 40 percent of former residents have chosen not to rebuild; memories of what once was are too painful. Often, when something happens to change the neighborhood setting in which we live, we bring it to the forefront of our consciousness and realize how critical it is to our sense of feeling "at home." In the story that follows, we meet a woman who was profoundly disturbed by changes around her home—in particular, intrusions on a panoramic view that she had unconsciously appropriated as part of her home space.

Neighborhood Change as a Violation of the Self

Sylvia's mother and father had built a small house in the Berkeley hills in the late 1940s. At the time, there were few other houses within view. Sylvia and her friends used to play Robin Hood and Maid Marion on the forested hillside.

Sylvia's parents built a second house next to the first in 1965 and lived there for twenty years while Sylvia lived in the original cottage, on and off, as she went to college, married, and returned to graduate school. After both parents died, Sylvia moved into their house. It was in this house—looking out from the hillside at a panoramic view—that I talked with Sylvia, two years after this move.

Since Sylvia's childhood explorations in the forested hillside around her home, there had been many changes. Houses had been built, road access improved, and a trail above and behind the house had become a popular place for bicycling and jogging. "It's not so much their using the trail that bothers me, as the fact that so many joggers stop right here—just above the house—to look at the view or the sunset. They seem to be looking right into my living room, and they spit! It's disgusting; I feel very violated. 'You can't come and spit in my territory!' I want to tell them. Then I started noticing all the litter and dog shit along the trail, and one day I pushed it all out into the middle of the trail so people could see what an impact they had. Now there's an epidemic of bicyclists cutting through the forest. People don't know how to walk softly on the land."

At the other side of her house is a panoramic view of San Francisco Bay. It is a view Sylvia has enjoyed since childhood. This too is now being "violated." A year before our conversation, a neighbor just below had started to build a second-story addition that is blocking part of Sylvia's view—not only by the structure itself, but also by the addition of a skylight and driveway floodlights which, at night, light up the area around the house, masking views of distant lights around the bay. She referred to this building project and the extreme emotions it aroused in her as "the most awful thing that has ever happened in my life. I mean, I watched my mother die of cancer. It was very difficult, but this is worse. It's caused almost an existential crisis. This is where I was born."

Sylvia's anger is directed at the owner of the building, at the city and its politicians, and at certain neighbors who have "let this happen." Despite her anguished pleas to the building's owner, appearances at public meetings, and meetings with neighbors, the city granted him a building permit. The view being disputed felt like a violation of Sylvia's memories, of her connectedness to this place.

Many people choose a house or apartment with a view (if they can afford it) because of some quality of peacefulness, serenity, or "getting things into perspective" afforded by its contemplation. In virtually every culture, neighborhoods with views command higher prices, especially if the view includes water. In the San Francisco Bay Area, such sought-after settings include Telegraph Hill, Pacific Heights, Russian Hill, Twin Peaks, and houses in the Berkeley, Oakland, and Richmond hills. When a new building threatens to violate a familiar view, a political battle is virtually guaranteed.

As a visitor and relative stranger, it did not appear to me that the neighbor's relatively small two-story house had, in fact, obstructed more than a very small proportion of what was still a very panoramic view. But clearly, Sylvia's feelings had little to do with the extent of the violation. I asked her if she could speak to the view, to tell it directly what it meant to her.

"This is hard. View, you are such a changing creature. Some days, when it's foggy, you aren't there at all. You're so wonderful to watch and just let my mind go—not thinking about anything in particular—just admiring the beauty. I never look at you and think: Oh, that's over in San Francisco, or that's the Bay Bridge toll plaza. I never think of you as what you really are. You are like a painting or a dream—you change colors, you change moods—it's almost as though you are alive and [sobbing] I don't want you to die! I don't want you to die!"

From the degree of emotion expressed, it seems clear that the view and its violation are touching on some profound developmental issue in Sylvia's life. Perhaps the key to its symbolic meaning is her reference to it as "a dream." Many of us, to some degree, are struggling with the balance between left-brain, rational, linear thinking and right-brain, connective, intuitive awareness. We need both strands of thinking to be whole. For Sylvia, this view has come to symbolize, perhaps, permission for her more imaginative self to flower. Immersed as she is in an academic career, the view is an invitation to engage in imaginative daydreaming, a necessary balance in her life. An intrusion on that view is far more than a structure spoiling the picture; it is a threat to a way of being and experiencing the world that she desperately wants to keep alive.

As we continued to talk, it became clear that Sylvia's mother had been engaged in the same search for balance and had similarly seen intrusions on familiar views as personal violations. During her life, Sylvia's mother had been involved in a variety of political battles over zoning, views, and lot sizes in the hills. She had particularly enjoyed the view to the back, from her bedroom, upslope to the hillside and trees. A house there had drawn Sylvia's mother into bitter political battles with the builder and the city twenty years before. When the new owners of that house built a deck looking straight in her window, she covered the glass with plastic rather than look at their house. When, in later years, she developed cancer, it was in this room that she lay ill and eventually died.

As Sylvia talked about her mother's life, she suddenly gave a gasp of recognition: "I never thought of it before, but my mother came down with cancer when the people in the back added a hot tub to their deck—it was only a few feet from her bedroom window. And it was the first case that violated the very zoning ordinance she and others had fought for, and implemented, years before. There were huge battles; the neighbor at the back had late-night parties and violated the use permit by putting in the hot tub—I can't help thinking that that conflict had caused her cancer. There's so much unknown about what causes disease and ill health. I'm sure she put her anger into her body. She was very, very attached to this place; perhaps even more so than I am."

The irony of this story is that Sylvia is pursuing a Ph.D. in public health, with a specialization in epidemiology—the study of the causes of disease, and was considering writing her thesis on case studies of the risk factors in environmental change. "Obviously people aren't dying because a house is being built next to them. But, on the other hand, I know how I feel. The more I talk to people who have gone through this kind of experience, the more I see how my feelings are not unusual. I can remember when I was a young child. We used to go to Stinson Beach maybe twice a year. It was a very long trip; we had to take the ferry. I remember watching the Richmond Bridge being built and feeling very sad. You don't normally think of a five or six year old as experiencing loss through environmental change." She also told me of a neighbor who, on fighting the construction of a house too close to his, had had a heart attack right after the city meeting at which he lost his appeal.

We returned to the picture Sylvia had drawn. I asked about the depiction of herself crouching as if in a cage. She remained silent a long time, staring at the picture: "It's as though—no matter how much writing I do and no matter how many phone calls I make or how many city council meetings I go to—it's a feeling of being powerless, a feeling of being trapped."

I asked if there was anything she could do to break out of the cage. "That's the $64,000 question!" She started to laugh. "I could leave—but I have to feel that something is pulling me—not just pushing. Not long ago, I was a delegate to the Democratic State Convention in Sacramento—one of the spin-off advantages of having gotten involved in these environmental battles!—and I ran into this Democrat from Orange County; I think there are probably three Democrats in Orange County! He is a very spiritual kind of fellow, and I told him about this battle, and he said: 'It's a gift. It's been given to you in order for it to be a challenge for you. You have to learn to accept it as a gift instead of fighting it as a trauma.'"

That was wise counsel, for an obsession is nearly always a signal to us that at its core is a personal problem we need to deal with before moving on. In the case of Sylvia and her mother, their passionate concern with intrusions into what they perceived as their territory had taken on the aura of an almost life-or-death battle. Perhaps for them, despite all the frustrations, it was preferable to direct their attention outside rather than consider what inner issues these might symbolize.

Neighborhood as Metaphor: Peter Living in a Self-Imposed Prison

Consciously or unconsciously, we all place ourselves at times in social, emotional, or physical settings that test our limits and challenge our image of ourselves. Perhaps we do it to wake ourselves up: the spouse who leaves a comfortable but boring marriage, the young person who takes off with backpack for parts unknown. When people move into a neighborhood that is the antithesis of their settlement identity to live among people they feel to be quite unlike themselves,

Peter's boarded-up storefront apartment in a run-down neighborhood.

they may be doing it unconsciously to jolt themselves out of some complacency or rut; the unfamiliar setting may be a reflection in the outer world of an unrecognized, shadow aspect of their own psyche that needs to be confronted.

Peter is a young musician who, at the time I talked with him, was very depressed. He had been referred to me by his therapist, because part of his problem appeared to be his living situation. Though well educated and with potentially marketable skills, he was living in a very low rent, run-down, converted storefront in a depressed and dangerous neighborhood. There was peeling paint on the door, which was approached via a glass-strewn sidewalk and three rickety steps. Peter had no friends in the neighborhood, and few of his friends from elsewhere ever dropped by. He worked at home, repairing musical instruments; he supplemented his meager income with a paper delivery route. It looked like many of them were never delivered; they were stacked in piles beside a moth-eaten couch. There were dirty dishes in the sink, clothes on the floor. The only touch of beauty—perhaps hope—was a colorful fabric wall-hanging, the center of which was a stylized red heart.

I asked Peter to put down graphically his feelings about his current home. He immediately took a black pen and drew the rectangular layout of his small apartment; around its perimeter, he drew barbed wire. In the surrounding streets he drew a gun, a spent bullet, a body, and the words *anger* and *rage*. Finally, he drew a yellow, almost dovelike figure in the middle of his dwelling: "That's me when I meditate; when I put white light around me." He talked of the danger outside and of his need to protect himself. Then he shaded around his home in yellow.

"The yellow is the energy field around my house, like white light. It's supposed to be the Holy Spirit; some kind of guiding principle. The only way I can protect myself is some kind of unseen power. I added the fence; I feel I need to have an actual fence. But this is what's really doing it—light around my house. Keeps me from getting ripped off, getting killed."

As we talked more, he began to articulate his problem with other people. "I need to get myself straightened out so that I can be around people. The thing that keeps me away is either that I'm not good enough or the people aren't good enough." As he started to describe the setting in which he lived, it became clear that he had placed himself in an urban wasteland, where a lack of contact with other people was virtually guaranteed. He has placed himself in exile: "I am in the middle of a desert. It starts about eight blocks away, the hopeless land in America. It's populated by people who don't care, who have no sense of power, who are just angry, alienated from everything. There's no sense of community. People are in constant fear of being ripped off, and nobody talks to anybody. It's just like hell. I don't know whose fault it is; I mean, whose fault is it?"

We were talking in Peter's workshop. It was an old storefront; the former

Peter's image of his defended home surrounded with rage, fear, and violence.

shop windows were now whited out with paper taped over them. Unlike the disarray in the living spaces of his apartment, Peter's workshop where he repaired musical instruments was relatively neat and ordered. Fine woodworking tools were arranged carefully on the wall over his workbench. He continued to talk as he buffed the back of a guitar. Then Peter stopped buffing the guitar, sighed deeply, and looked off into space.

"I've been through all this before and I don't know

why I do it. I hear part of me saying: 'I had to do it this way. I'm a victim just like the rest of these people.' But you know, I'm starting to see that that isn't an answer; that's hopeless. There's no way out of that one. But I hate taking the responsibility for getting

Peter's ideal—a music camp in the mountains.

out of it. When I look at it from afar and see all this stuff that's standing between me and what I want, I have a great temptation to just lay back, wait for it to be all over. It just seems too hard. I don't know where that comes from, whether I'm angry at my parents and I'm proving to them that I'm gonna fuck up just to prove to them that they fucked up. I just feel real scared. I don't trust myself enough; I don't believe in my own power enough to think that I have the means to create my way out of here."

Peter talked about his underutilized talents as a musician and a woodworker, how he'd never earn enough to get out of his present fix. He was adamant that he would never become a nine-to-five wage slave. "And I'm also real lazy and weak. I feel like I'm a man between two worlds. I know that I still have a whole lot to get straight inside myself. I'd like to move more into the center. 'Cause out here—it's just like going into exile."

He sighed again and remained silent while he resumed polishing the guitar. After a while, he continued. "That's so much bullshit, I mean, I could be right in the middle of a fucking paradise where people interacted, and I wouldn't be interacting with them. I just put up my walls wherever I am. It's hopeless. I might as well kill myself. I love to suffer—that's a big one. I really love all this isolation. It's like dangling all this power and creativity in front of people and then fucking up behind it."

At the time of this conversation, Peter was a very frustrated man; trapped in a part of town where he felt alienated and mistrusted, he apparently did not have the strength to leave. Although he ostensibly moved to this storefront apartment to have low-rent space for his work, it appears as though he has chosen an outer milieu of frustration, rage, and powerlessness to reflect what he feels inside. Was this psychologically necessary in order for him truly to recognize his own "stuck-ness"—to sense these feelings both inside and out? For some people, it may be the contrast between inner emotions and what is happening around them that high-lights their dilemma and may eventually motivate them to change. For Peter, it was as though he has sought an outer mirror of his own "dis-ease," to magnify his pain, to prevent any escape.

In Jungian terms, Peter was in a state of alienation—of separation from the higher Self. Since the health of the ego depends to some degree on an awareness of, and connection to, the broader objective psyche or Self, a person who has lost that connection is in a state of mental imbalance or depression.

Before his move to Oakland, Peter had been in therapy and had certainly dealt with the painful realities of depression. His decision to live in this particular setting was—I believe—a deliberate (if unconscious) move to surround himself with hos-tility and danger, as if to bring home to his conscious mind his own self-destructive path. He needed to immerse himself totally in a metaphor for his own inner state of being. Only then—and after more painful self-reflection—was he able to take the next step and move to a more nurturing milieu.

Some years later, I heard from a mutual friend that Peter moved out of his storefront, went back to school, and is now a family man with a wife and children, living in a suburban tract house and working as a computer programmer. In his child-rearing adult years, Peter has returned to the type of setting in which he was raised. The move to a dangerous neighborhood in his angst-filled young adulthood served its purpose; he learned to face, and live with, the demons inside.

But what of those who have no choice? Although this book is based principally on stories of psychological development and its relationship to home, I feel it is incumbent on me to speak briefly about another facet of my work. Over the past few years, a colleague, Carolyn Francis, and I have worked with teams of architects and engineers on the modernization of extremely run-down, poverty-stricken, and crime-ridden housing projects, not unlike the neighborhood of hopelessness described by Peter.

Garbage and broken glass litter the dirt areas between buildings; abandoned automobiles rust away in oil-streaked parking lots; vandalized play areas have long since been taken over by drug dealers selling crack or heroin to resident-addicts and to middle-class customers who cruise by in BMWs and leave quickly for the freeway. Mothers rarely let their children play outside, and teach them to fall prone on the floor at the sound of squealing auto tires. Drive-by shootings are a daily occurrence; innocent bystanders—even children inside houses—have been killed. All this is happening no more than twenty minutes' drive from the boutiques and corporate headquarters of downtown San Francisco. Most people do not know of the existence of Hayes Valley, or the Sunnydale housing project, or Geneva Towers. These are the hidden shadow side of our cities. We as a society don't want to deal with this forgotten underworld any more than Peter wanted to deal with his own inner wasteland. So forgotten is a place like Sunnydale that the police delay in responding to emergency calls, and the local newspapers relegate reports of shootings to brief paragraphs, if they are mentioned at all.

While many more-affluent San Franciscans might be appalled at these living conditions, they might be even more amazed to hear that most residents want to remain where they are living. This, despite all the problems, is home. "Get rid of the dealers, the crime, and fear," one woman told us, "and we can make this place into a paradise." This is just what the residents and teams of architects are trying to do. And though Sunnydale housing project may never be "paradise," it can be rehabilitated, redesigned, and replanted to be a 100 percent better neighborhood than it is right now. The residents and their children know what needs to be done. The federal government is supplying most of the dollars. Prior experience in other projects, in other cities, tells us that people's relationship with their housing neighborhood changes dramatically when they are given the power to take control of their lives. When, conversely, people feel powerless, intimidated, and relegated to a forgotten wasteland of the city, the repetition of riots like those in Watts and in south-central Los Angeles are a distinct possibility.

Whether by choice or not, where you live and what you see around you are a reflection of who you are—or who society says you are. Making neighborhoods safe, secure, beautiful, and socially nurturing is not just some pie-in-the-sky aesthetic dream. It needs to be an essential component of urban policy, a high-priority expenditure of tax dollars. If the place where you grow up is as critical to your psychological development as I have tried to communicate in this book, imagine the damage to the next generation of youngsters who cannot freely play outside their homes for fear of being shot.

When we asked the children at Sunnydale to draw pictures of how they'd like their neighborhood to look, like most youngsters of eight or nine, they drew storybook houses with peaked roofs, smoke-curling out of the chimney, and flowers in the garden. But under their pictures, they wrote in childish script—*Get rid of the dealers, Stop the shootings,* and *Tell people to stop taking drugs.*

When we think of home, it encompasses much more than the house or apartment in which we eat and sleep. Home embraces also the neighborhood, and if that fails to nurture and protect us, to express something positive about who we are, it matters little how beautiful or spacious our house is. Like any living being, humans need not only a nest or dwelling, but a whole ecological setting in which they can feel "at home."

SELF-IMAGE AND LOCATION: EXERCISES YOU CAN DO YOURSELF

Your Ideal Neighborhood

The following exercises may assist you if you're feeling dissatisfied with the setting in which you live; if you are not quite sure if it is the setting or dwelling that is the problem; or if you're planning to move, buy a house, or build a house and want to be clear about the kind of setting that is right for you.

Take a sheet of paper and some crayons or felt-tipped pens and draw a simple sketch, map, or diagram of your ideal neighborhood. It might be a good idea to represent your home as a small square in the center of the page. We're not concerned here with the details of your house or apartment, but rather with what is around it. Start to put in other houses or buildings, roughly indicating how far apart they are: Do you want to see other houses from your own, or do you want to be in a rural setting? Do you imagine yourself and others in this setting mostly driving back and forth to home, or do you imagine walking to some places? What would those be—a park, a beach, a church, a movie, a grocery store, a coffee shop? How close would you like these amenities to be? If you have children, how close might they like them to be? And what about when they are teenagers: Are you prepared to drive them everywhere they want to go, or would you like them to have the freedom to walk to shops or take the bus to the library?

How urban—or rural—do you imagine your ideal neighborhood

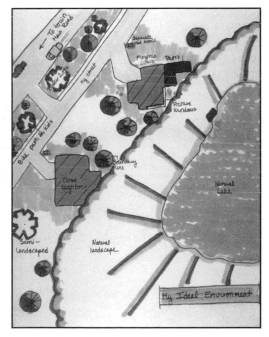

A young woman's image of her ideal environment.

to be? Do you want uninterrupted views of farmland or mountains, or do you like to see houses, and people passing by through the filtered greenery of street trees?

What about privacy? Most of us need two kinds of privacy. One is within the house—the ability to go into a room, close the door, and be alone; the freedom to decorate a small space that is just ours. But privacy from neighbors and passersby is equally important. Some people like to drive into their garage, close the garage door, walk into the house, and be seen by no one outside the family, and to have neighbors who do likewise. Others enjoy seeing people on the sidewalks and may even garden or work on the car out front as an "excuse" to chat with neighbors or passersby. Elderly people living alone, in particular, often like to sit on a porch or balcony within view of the street; to see other people, even if they never speak to them, is to engage in a kind of vicarious socializing. What kind of house/world connection appeals to you? What level of privacy from the outside world do you require to feel comfortable? How far are you willing to commute to work? What about other employed adults in the family? Put an arrow on your drawing to indicate the time it would take you to get to work from this neighborhood. If you'd ideally like to walk to work, what are you willing to compromise on in order to do that?

What kind of exercise or recreation appeals to you? If you like to go to a gym for a class or to work out or play squash with a friend, how close to home (or work) would you like this amenity to be? If you like to walk or jog from home, how close would you like a walking trail or track to be?

Don't let yourself be sidetracked by a rational judge in your head who says: "Oh come on! You can't really have everything you want." Although your ideal neighborhood might not exist in all the particulars you have outlined, you may be surprised at how many of the qualities you value can be found in an existing place. Once you have really thought about the kind of residential setting in which you would feel totally "at home," go exploring and look for it! Ask a knowledgeable real-estate agent where neighborhoods like the one you have drawn are located. Once you have found neighborhoods or settings that appeal to you, start to look for a house or apartment or building site. You can always fix a house, but it's hard to fix a neighborhood.

Your Preferred Residential Setting

If the previous exercise was enlightening or affirming, you might want to delve a little more deeply into your preferred residential setting. East Coast city planner Sydney Brower has developed a simple but extremely useful typology of residential settings, which he terms *Big-Town, Small-Town,* and *Out-of-Town.* He argues that the settings we choose to live in comprise an arrangement of "near-home spaces" which add to or extend the capacity of an individual dwelling to satisfy our housing needs. The individual house or apartment fulfills such basic needs as shelter (accommodation for sleeping, eating, entertaining, and so on) and facilitates for home- and self-maintenance (storage, utility room, bathroom). But each of these needs can, to some extent, be met by the wider, neighborhood setting. You may wish for the shelter and protection of your individual house to be backed up by formal or informal residents' associations; you may feel more protected in a walled and gated community, or you may find this superfluous or even repugnant. You may look to the immediate neighborhood for services to relieve housekeeping tasks—take-out delicatessens, laundromats, attractive playgrounds—or you may find the resultant blend of land uses not to your taste. The more one enjoys satisfying certain residential functions outside the home, the smaller and simpler the dwelling unit need be: An efficient apartment in a downtown setting would be a case in point. Contrast this with the domestic setting of, say, a wealthy aristocratic family in England in the "good old days." The house and its estate setting might well have incorporated, besides normal residential functions, a library, chapel, orchard, greenhouses, swimming pool, tennis court, riding stables, servants quarters, nursery, bakery, and so on. There were few amenities near the home, because the home provided almost everything. Brower suggests that "lack of amenities in near-home spaces may be offset by adding amenities in the unit, just as inadequacies in the unit may increase dependency on the near-home spaces. Housing satisfaction requires a suitable balance between the functions satisfied in the unit and those satisfied in near-home spaces. There are many possible points of balance, ranging from heavily unit [home]-dependent to heavily setting [neighborhood]-dependent combinations with all shades in between." [17]

To simplify understanding of "all shades in between," Brower suggests a three-part typology of preferred settings—Big-Town, Small-Town, and Out-of-Town. Rather than the more standard definitions of places based on proximity to the center (urban/suburban/rural), or on size and density (city/town/village), this typology is organized around the quality of residential experience. Since this book is about the experience of places, it is a particularly appropriate way to sort out what kind of place-experience you are looking for. Here in Brower's own words is a summary-description of each. As you read them, be aware of which seems to resonate most favorably for you, with your tastes and at your particular stage in life.

- Big-Town settings emphasize near-home spaces that are active, lively, varied, changing; places to see and be seen. Facilities are regional, and a great many of the users come from outside the area. It is the type that attracts self-styled "city people," people who enjoy activity, diversity, fashion, and new ideas. This is the place for chance discoveries. It is the place to live if one wants to change one's life, meet someone new, try something different. It includes a large representation of young people who are starting out, and older people who are starting again. Because it is open and tolerant, it offers many opportunities, but it can also be uncontrolled and dangerous; it is stimulating but it can also be crowded and competitive; it offers companionship but it also offers anonymity and the risk of loneliness.

- Small-Town settings emphasize near-home spaces that blend home and social life. Facilities, institutions, eating places, and meeting grounds tend to be settled, familiar, stable, and locally run. Service is personal, shopkeepers call customers by name, and banks do not ask for identification. Residents are not necessarily all of the same income or class, but they get along because of accommodations that have been worked out over time. They tend to hold on to established ways and resist change. This type of setting offers companionship and support, but it discourages non-conformity.

- Out-of-Town settings use near-home spaces as a backdrop for the unit and a buffer between the unit and its neighbors. The appearance and spaciousness of near-home spaces, as seen from the unit, are therefore important. Out-of-Town settings are effectively removed (although not necessarily distant) from the hustle and bustle of city life. There is little pressure to socialize or join anything. Being off the beaten track, residents depend upon relatively self-contained units and good transportation. Out-of-Town settings are for people who want to be alone or to enjoy, undisturbed, the company of family and friends; for those who are self-sufficient, introspective, detached; for seekers after a slower pace, a simpler and more direct way of life, or the natural order. In exchange for privacy, they accept inconveniences in getting to other people, stores, services, and cultural and educational facilities.[18]

Did one of the above descriptions particularly appeal to you? Or, conversely, did one or more seem definitely not your kind of setting?

It is important to remember that such settings may be found in unexpected places. For example, one would expect to find a Big-Town setting in a downtown area, but it may be absent from some downtowns or seasonal resorts. Small-Town settings would likely be found in small towns, but not in all of them; sadly, some have had the "small town-ness" bled out of them by anonymous out-of-town shopping malls. Small-Town settings can be found in some inner-city enclaves; I know many in London, and a few in San Francisco. I live in one in Berkeley. They may be present in some suburban areas, where new development has engulfed an older small town. But beware of suburban subdivision advertising that assumes you will "love the traditional small-town atmosphere of Oakridge Village." Likely as not, there are no corner groceries, small stores, cafes, people of mixed backgrounds, or pedestrians on the streets. Without these, a Small-Town setting will not evolve, however convincing the architects' plans or the developers' hype.

Out-of-Town settings, as the name implies, are likely to be found in rural areas, but not in all of them. They are traditionally found in planned suburbs; and if you are willing

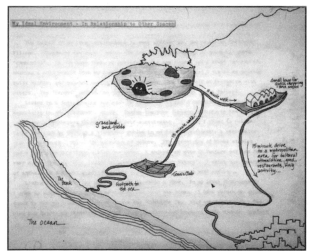

A young man's depiction of an ideal place to live.

to drive to most services and amenities and don't especially desire informal social life and activity close at hand, this may be the setting for you.

As Brower reminds us, "No one type of settlement is inherently better than any other. No one combines either the advantages of all or the disadvantages of none. Each has its advocates (also its zealots) and its detractors. Together they represent the types of places that people, ideally, would choose for a permanent or temporary home, their choices influenced by such things as income, experience, lifestyle preference and stage in the life cycle." [19]

If you are planning to buy or build a house with a spouse or partner, it is important that you do an exercise like this together. If one of you is a Big-Town type and the other an Out-of-Town type—as were Lucy and Tony, discussed earlier—you will need to do a lot of talking and probably compromising, before you find a setting in which you'll both feel reasonably comfortable.

Familiar with the broad place-types in Brower's typology, it may help if each of you makes a list of what is essential to your happiness and peace of mind in a setting and what is negotiable. If privacy is crucial, as it is to most people, remember that a large spatial distance between houses is not the only way to achieve it. So long as you cannot see or hear your neighbors (or they, you), you are likely to feel private. A downtown high-rise can be more private than a suburb of detached houses. If one of you yearns for an Out-of-Town natural setting but the other would like easy access to a Small-Town setting (the conflict for Anne and her husband, described earlier), there may be a possible compromise in a very green, overgrown, older neighborhood within walking distance of a Small-Town setting of shops and cafes. Go for exploratory drives on weekends; look at places or neighborhoods you've never considered before. Consult knowledgeable real-estate agents, but don't necessarily rely on them. Their job is to sell you a house, not to ensure that both of you are comfortable in a particular setting. House and setting must be thought of together; they are as intrinsically interwoven as the nest of a robin and its territory, the lair of a lion and its range.

NINE

The Lost House: Disruptions in the Bonding with Home

Houses have their own ways of dying, falling as variously as the generations of men, some with a tragic roar, some quietly . . . while from others—and thus was the death of Wickham Place—the spirit slips before the body disintegrates. It had decayed in the spring . . . By September it was a corpse, void of emotion, and scarcely hallowed by the memories of thirty years of happiness. Through its round-topped doorway passed furniture, and pictures, and books, until the last room was gutted and the last van had rumbled away. It stood for a week or two longer, open-eyed, as if astonished at its own emptiness. Then it fell.

—E. M. FORSTER, *Howard's End*

Those of us fortunate enough to own or rent a home that fits our needs may never realize the depth of its emotional significance until we lose it, through divorce, natural disaster, or old age. In this chapter, we consider the stories of a number of men and women who—through marital separation or divorce—had to leave the family home, or remained there alone after their partner left. As just one example of loss through natural disaster, we hear the poignant stories of some of those who recorded their feelings in writing after losing their homes in the disastrous fire of October 1991 in the Oakland-Berkeley hills. Finally, a Swedish study comprising interviews with elderly people after a move into housing for the aged communicates the complex emotions and parallel health problems that often accompany what for most will be their final move.

Divorce and Dramatic Changes of Feelings toward Home

The trauma of divorce is a crisis that occurs in many of our lives, and one which often triggers a profound dislocation in person-dwelling relations. The home may have been shared for many years; patterns of territory, privacy, and personalization established; and memories of the past enshrined in objects, rooms, furniture, and plants. When children are involved, the shock of adjustment may be even greater: The partner remaining in the house with dependents may have to juggle housework, child minding, maintenance, shopping, commuting to day care, and/or paid employment on their own whereas previously there was some degree of shared responsibility. The house that was once perceived as stable, nurturing, and calm may now be seen as oppressive, stressful, even unsafe. For a partner who leaves, there is the anxiety of establishing a sense of self in a new physical setting, separate from children, spouse, and family memories. In the long run, it is probable that both partners will make a positive adjustment, and home—wherever it is—will again become a benign refuge and expression of self-identity. But at the time of separation, one or both partners may experience a profound change in their familiar, often taken-for-granted relationships with home.

Increasingly, neither partner in a divorce remains in the original home; both have to deal with reestablishing home bonds in a new setting. Under early divorce laws, the mother usually received custody of the children and was almost always awarded the family home. Under today's no-fault divorce laws, the family home is much more likely to be sold. U.S. National Census data indicate that in the first year after separation, only about 45 percent of divorced mothers stayed on in the family home. Three years later, the figure dropped to only 26 percent.[2]

Barring the Doors and Windows: Vulnerability and the House

If there was one event in my life that motivated me to work on this book, it was my own divorce and the subsequent adjustments I had to make in feeling secure in the family home after my husband left. My relationship with our house after his departure astonished me and, in my later years, triggered my exploration with couples and divorced persons of the deeper memories of home. Stephen and I had met in

Berkeley in the turbulent late-sixties, when I was a young, beginning lecturer and he was a long-haired graduate student. He came to see me in my office hours with pamphlets about the evils of white sugar and the merits of goat's milk, his faithful dog, Chester, always in tow. Though I was not much interested in his nutritional advice, I was intrigued by this tall, strikingly handsome young man. Our markedly different backgrounds and personalities seemed to draw us together.

In the mid-1970s, after six years of marriage and the birth of two children, our relationship became severely strained. My career was becoming established; Stephen's career as a designer was, at the time, more problematic. Despite considerable effort to reach a state of mutual understanding with the help of marriage counseling, the resentments felt by both of us escalated: I resented the exhaustion of being homemaker, mother, wife, and primary wage-earner—all at the same time; Stephen resented my work and the limits on the time I could spend with him.

After many threats to leave, Stephen finally moved out, leaving the family in the four-bedroom house we had recently purchased, and leaving me with the primary responsibility for the care of our two preschool children. My change in attitude toward the house was dramatic.

I had never felt such a profound degree of insecurity, pain, grief, and anger all rolled into one. Each day felt like an insurmountable burden—logistics of child care, work, shopping, evening meetings, preparing lectures, and phoning baby-sitters became a nightmare. But most stressful of all, the house seemed to change dramatically, or, rather, my attitude toward it changed. When Stephen was there, we had worked on it together—painted rooms, hung pictures, chosen material for drapes. As a designer, he had had a lot of ideas about the house, and I happily deferred to him on many things. I felt he knew much more than I about color, light, and the potential of different rooms. A lot of the objects in the house were his. He had lived in Colombia for two years in the Peace Corps and had traveled in Central America; he had lots of colorful masks, fabrics, and paintings. When he left, there were reminders everywhere—I wanted his stuff in the house but I also resented it.

But worst of all was how I felt at night, a carryover of nighttime fears from my wartime childhood that came back in spades when Stephen left. I was terrified that someone would break in and kill me or try to kill my children. It didn't make any sense; it wasn't Stephen I feared. It was some kind of unknown "other" who would creep in at night. I tried to talk myself out of it; that didn't help. Every night—two or three, sometimes five or six times—I'd go around checking every door and window to see that it was locked. I'd go to bed, knowing that everything was locked, then I'd have to go downstairs again to check. In the middle of the night, I'd wake and swear I'd heard movements downstairs, and go down, my heart pounding. There never was anyone there; the doors and windows were always secure. But still it went on—I was a wreck. I don't think I slept through the night for two years.

Eventually, the house began to feel secure, warm, and nurturing again. But for that period in between, I felt under siege; the house seemed permeable, vulnerable. Every time Stephen came and retrieved some of his belongings—and he did that painfully slowly over a couple of years—it felt like another blow to my heart, another nail in the coffin of our marriage. Yes, he really was leaving for good. And every time, my fears of nighttime returned. The house wasn't taking care of us like it should. My own extreme sense of vulnerability had been projected onto the very fabric of our home.

Although I can recount only my side of this story, Stephen's reactions on periodic visits to the house are indicative of his pain at separating from the family environment. Through words and actions—all of which angered me considerably—he continued to lay claim to the house: He left many of his possessions there for a long time; he criticized any changes I made; he admonished me for not keeping the garden up, and always inspected it with clippers in hand, chopping off pieces of shrubs and trees as he went through his rounds.

In a study of the housing environment and divorce, interviews with psychologists counseling separating couples reported: "The feeling that non-custodial parents [usually men] are being evicted from their homes is fairly common and it can be very destructive. For example, in one of the clinical case histories, the mother decided to embark on a series of home improvement projects once the separation from her spouse had occurred. In fact, her ex-spouse's failure to assume any of the house maintenance responsibilities was one of the major reasons for her wanting the separation. Despite her objections, however, the father was constantly attempting to involve himself in these home improvement projects. It was simply too painful for him to surrender his sense of territoriality towards and identity with the former family home."[3]

The story of my own changed attitude toward my house illustrates dramatically how intimately our feelings of identity and self-esteem are intertwined with our dwelling environment. My whole sense of self-worth was shattered by Stephen's departure. I felt a failure as a wife and companion. I felt resentment at being "abandoned." I reverted to insecurities of childhood—to fear of the dark, of a dangerous enemy coming into the house at night. I projected my own psychological vulnerability onto the physical fabric of the house, reflected in the fear of intrusion via unlocked doors and windows. It took time, counseling, and the slow reemergence of self-esteem for my benign relationship to the house to resurface.

In my story, we see a sequential pattern of, first, an almost unconscious, taken-for-granted attitude toward the house; then a clinging-to and insecurity about the dwelling, after the trauma of separation; followed, eventually, by a reestablishment of a calm, benign, and again taken-for-granted expectation of the house as a place of security. A relatively long-term disposition to do, think, or feel a certain way in certain circumstances has been termed "emotional disposition" by psychologists James Russell and J. Snodgrass. In reviewing the stories shared with me, it seems clear that most people tend to have an underlying emotional disposition vis-à-vis "home" and that certain traumatic life-events are likely to bring this disposition into sharp focus. It is as though the disposition was the ongoing, often unconscious association of home with certain affective states (contentment, security, or sometimes negative emotions such as anxiety), and that it is brought into conscious emotional awareness by such events as moving, marital separation, children leaving home, death, or loss of employment. Once the particular event begins to sink into affect-less memory, a state of relative emotional equilibrium is reestablished, and emotional disposition becomes again largely unconscious.

In the next story, we meet a woman who had separated from her husband and, when I met her, was struggling to reestablish her identity in their formerly shared home.

Reclaiming the Family Home: Madeline's House as Anchor

Madeline lives in a wood-and-brick house on a quiet cul-de-sac in the Berkeley hills. The house is situated on a steep site with entrance gained via a long wooden stairway. Large old oaks surround the house, and there are spectacular views to San Francisco and the Golden Gate Bridge. The overall feel of the house is light, comfortable, and calm. The large-beamed living/dining room has a warm, yellow polished floor, redwood-paneled walls, an old piano, beige drapes, and beige and green upholstered furniture. There are books lining the walls; many of them look very old. There is a mellow, green feeling in the room, both because trees are visible from every window and because large potted ferns and a vase of lilies decorate the interior. As we began to talk, Madeline kept referring to the house as "warm"; to me, that description seemed altogether apt.

Madeline was in her early fifties and had lived in this house for thirty years. Three years previously, she and her husband had separated. Since then, the house had become an enormously important anchor or "island" in her life. As we went on a tour of the house, she pointed out various minor ways in which the environment had changed since her husband moved out; there were not many. She always thought of it as his house and his garden, since he had made most of the decisions. She hadn't been able to touch the garden since he left, but was glad that the two student renters were putting in a few flowers. She had barely altered the living room except to add some plants "to make it seem more alive." Even though it had been three years, only recently had she been able to refer to it as "my" house, rather than "our" house.

"This house is so warm and comfortable, I don't know what I'd do if I couldn't live here. For three years, I've lived almost as if I were living in a museum. Ever since John left, I've been sleeping on my side of the bed and changing the sheets regularly each week, although half of them weren't used. Just recently, I've started to use the whole bed. So many people keep at me to move; they think it would be best. My friend Kathy thinks I have too many memories. 'Madeline,' she says, 'you must not be too attached to this house. If you moved to a brand-new location, you would have more chance to see life afresh, to make more friends, and begin a new life.' But I don't want to move until I have someplace to move to, and I don't think I'll be ready to do that till the house becomes mine, legally. I don't feel the house is holding me back; I feel I am holding me back. I've had a lot to survive these past three years—my husband leaving, then my younger daughter ran away. For eight months, we didn't even know if she were alive. So it's been . . . [starts to cry] . . . The house is the only thing that's left.

"I had to have some real-estate men appraise the house for the divorce settlement. I just felt so terrible having them estimate . . . [cries] . . . you know, what my life is worth. I felt like saying, 'You think you're looking at a house, but what you're looking at is the history of a family' [cries again]. My husband doesn't care about the house. He wishes I would sell it, buy a condominium, find a new boyfriend and lead a new life. That's what he's doing! Oh, how I hate condominiums! They're so totally impersonal; they have no character. They have a swimming pool and a sauna, and all interchangeable. It would be like living in a motel, and motels have always depressed me. I've always felt if I ever committed suicide, it would be in a motel."

Madeline's experience is typical of many women of her generation. Raised before the era of feminism and changing gender roles, Madeline had to reassert her individuality within an environment formerly controlled by her husband. This she was doing, slowly and painfully. To keep a house just as it was before someone left—or died—is a way to hold on to their memories, to make-believe they will soon return. It is also a way of easing oneself slowly through the transition. Just as most people cling psychologically to the familiar settings of their lives in the face of a natural disaster, so Madeline holds on to her house.

When Madeline reported disagreeing with her friend who advised her to leave the house, she was probably acting wisely; a study of seventy-six divorced families indicates that those women who stay in the family home together with most of the familiar household furnishings and appliances tend to maintain their self-identity better than those who are forced to leave. For divorced men who leave the family home, the loss of a familiar environment is compounded by the loss of family life and memories. Many such men are left with few household possessions, sometimes rendering their new environment unpersonalized and reinforcing their sense of loss.[4]

A Place of Her Own and a Place to Share: Carole's Changed Relationship with Home

Carole is a woman in her midfifties. When we talked, she had been divorced for two years and was sharing the family home with her nineteen-year-old daughter. The house is cool and elegant, with white walls, polished wood floors, and oriental rugs. It is set on a quiet, tree-lined street in an upper-middle-income neighborhood.

Carole was raised in Budapest, where her father was a lawyer, and her mother a traditional and, Carole speculates, quite frustrated stay-at-home wife and mother. After Carole's marriage and the birth of three children, the family emigrated to Australia. Carole became qualified as a social worker; her husband died in an accident. Eventually, she remarried and moved with her new husband and three teenaged children to California. They purchased the house where Carole now lives; a fourth child was born.

In describing the issues between herself and her husband that eventually led to divorce, Carole talked about her need for more privacy as well as her need to make changes in the house without her husband's constant negation of her proposals. I asked Carole if she could imagine the house to be animate and to start to talk to it. She paused for a while, then spoke:

"Mmm . . . I really can't separate the house and my life. You've been just as much trouble to me as people have. I struggled with you maybe more than with people, because with people I'm used to being accommodating, trying to be tolerant. I guess all the struggles that relationship gave me, I projected onto you, house. Many times I wanted to push your walls around. Many times I got angry. There are obstructing walls I can't change, and it felt so hopeless and difficult. Sometimes I made peace with you, and there were moments of great delight just looking at you and saying, 'How very nice and beautiful!' But it would never last very long; I would start all over, trying to make changes—like a challenge!"

Carole had still said little about her husband but implied that the struggles were also with him. I asked if it was a problem of liking different styles of creating a home. "No, not so much that. He really didn't have any specific likes and dislikes. He liked to live through my pace and energy. But he had to boost his male ego by just saying 'No!' to everything I proposed. If I quietly persisted, he came around and then—to my astonishment—he'd take guests on a tour of the house and show them proudly the very things he'd given me such a hassle over and say, 'Look what we did!' He was always sending me double messages; he had to say 'No' to be important. So, it was a drain on my energy—but it also gave me a vicarious incentive, you know? He said, 'No, it can't be done,' and that was a challenge. I didn't realize until later that while I was working against his 'no,' it was within the safety of this outer circle of our relationship."

Carole began to think about some kind of separation in which her husband could express what he liked and didn't like without Carole's feeling overwhelmed. She began to feel a vague urge toward growth and change, but didn't think of it in terms of an end of their marriage. Several times she traveled alone to give herself space to think. On returning to the home, she fantasized about a little bachelor apartment, where she and her husband might alternately stay for a few weeks or which he might want to have as his own space for five days a week, then they would share the family home on weekends. Her husband felt panicked and threatened by this suggestion and, while Carole was traveling with a daughter in Europe, he served her with divorce papers through the mail and tried to instigate a court order to prevent her from returning to the house.

Eventually, the divorce proceeded, and Carole and her daughter returned to the house. To her surprise, however, she now felt totally paralyzed to do anything in or for the house. "There was this struggle—and when it came to an end, the house just seemed to collapse and slip away. It was a terribly difficult time. Wherever I looked, there was another room, another box—I could never get through it. I felt I would never be able to physically attend to the house—or financially make it. You know, it's like when you really appreciate someone most when you almost lose them. It was like that with my house. I went through two years of not knowing what to do with my life; now I had space and time to myself, and I felt paralyzed. When I had to make a decision in the house against my husband's negative attitudes, there was this kind of outer circle beyond which I couldn't go. Once you're all alone, you make your own outer circle—there are no bounds—and you become sort of paralyzed. I had to question myself again and again—'what's important and what's not?'—and then watch myself with disgust. I wouldn't be surprised if a lot of women go through this kind of loss, especially in a traditional marriage. I always reckoned myself a very independent woman; I assumed a lot of responsibility. I never realized how much I relied on the protective outer circle against which I could move so seemingly independently—it provided a safety of some kind."

After almost two years of near paralysis, Carole did climb out. With great joy and energy, she started to change the house through painting, taking up carpets, exposing wooden floors, and changing the function of rooms. She was doing what many of us do, albeit unconsciously, in order to bond to our place of residence. She was touching, nurturing, beautifying, paying attention to her environment. These acts create an affectionate bonding, just as nurturing and paying attention to another human being establishes a similar bond.

In Carole's case, she also turned the house into a source of income: A large front room was transformed into an art gallery, where she had invitational open-house shows several times a year; a cottage in the back became a bed-and-breakfast accommodation for musicians visiting the Bay Area. Finally, there was her kitchen—which she depicted in a graphic expression of her feelings as the "heart of the house." Here she drew on her culinary skills and started to give cooking lessons. She began to realize that her struggles with the house and with her husband had been expressions of a struggle within herself to be more than "just a housewife."

After eighteen years of putting energy into her setting, she wasn't prepared to start again somewhere else, although friends advised her to get a smaller place. "They didn't understand that this house was more than just living in it and having shelter. This house represents both my need for a small space all to myself, where nobody interferes or touches anything, and my need for a center, where people come and share the space and make everything messy. Very few people understand that an environment for a woman is not just somewhere to sleep and have a roof over your head, and a sink to wash your things in. It means your life. I feel at peace with myself now—and with my house."

Whereas Carole, Madeline, and I represent the experience of spouses who remained in the family home without their partner, the next two cases represent those who did the leaving and had to learn to disengage from the family dwelling. It is not just as simple as "moving out." In both cases, there were mixed emotions about the home as a place of past memories of good times and the present experiences of tension and separation.

A Transitional Home: Alice's Move toward Independence

Alice heard me speak to a women's organization about my work. She asked if we could talk, and, a few weeks later, I went to her current home. It was a bland, stucco apartment house on a pretty, tree-lined street in the flatlands of Berkeley. She had been living here for five months since separating from her husband of twenty-four years. Her daughter was away at college; her son in high school had remained with his father. While she is slowly transforming her motel-like apartment into a comfortable, personalized home, Alice has returned to the family house on occasions—to retrieve possessions, to pick up her son, to meet with her husband over the divorce settlement. The visits were very painful.

I asked Alice if she could put down in a picture her feelings about the family house she recently left. First, she drew a lot of blue, squiggly lines, which she said was the only way she could express the feelings of emptiness, sadness, and confusion she felt when she returned to the house. Then she added splotches of rosy-pink to represent the rhododendron and the rose garden she had planted. "I thought of the happiness and joy there. I thought of the flowers that are all in bloom now. So I feel some joy—but also sadness because the joy is over, and I don't know why

Alice's depiction of conflicted feelings for her former house.

it has to be over. I also have a lot of heavy feelings when I go over there—so I put some brown and black in the picture."

I asked Alice if she could imagine speaking to the house and what she had to say to it: "I feel I'd like to start over. Maybe I didn't take enough care of you! I want to be able to say good-bye to you, and I've tried to do that but it's not quite over because you're still there. My family is still there. I don't see much of me there. When I go there, I don't see much of me."

At this point, Alice started to cry; after a few minutes, she continued: "It seemed like it was never finished. It was a burden—I always had more things, more work to do. I guess now when I think about it, there was a lot of tension in the house over whose house it was. I guess it was never quite mine—it was more like Gerald's house—a little austere, very formal, and dignified. I tried to temper it with a lot of color and confusion, but basically it was orderly and formal, and I resisted that a lot. I want my next house to be more comfortable and informal."

Alice sighed and remained silent for a long time. Then she continued: "As long as it's sitting there, with my husband and son in it, the house sort of haunts me. I know sometime it will be like all the other houses I've ever lived in. I'll be able to think of it pleasantly—a scene of happy times and really difficult times, coming to terms with the growing up of the family, and the breaking up of the family. While it's still 'unfinished,' I really know how it's going to come out. It's going to come out okay."

The apartment Alice now lived in was small, compact, and sunny, with off-white stucco walls and pleated drapes, an acoustic ceiling, and a green sculpted carpet. It was a standard 1960s apartment, renting at a standard middle-income price. The living room opened onto a sunny balcony with white garden furniture and poppies in a planter box. The apartment had a spacious appearance since it overlooked a strip of open land being transformed into a park. Through a lacy silver birch there were glimpses of rooftops and of San Francisco Bay.

The living room had a warm, cozy feel; there was a white wicker rocking chair with flowered cushions, antique tables with plants and flowers, an old bookcase overflowing with books *(Existential Imagination, The Courage to Be, The Joy of Cooking),* a big handsome desk, macramé hangings, and many original lithographs and oil paintings. It was a mix of old and new. It felt like a lot of care had gone into these rooms without their appearing studied or decor-conscious. At the upright piano, a book of Chopin sonatas was open with penciled notations in the margins.

In contrast to the semiabstract swirling lines depicting her former home, Alice's drawing of her current apartment was almost an architectural layout. She drew the rooms carefully, trying to get their relative size and connection "right." She put in the furniture, her plants, the balcony, and the view. The picture was as light, colorful, and ordered as the apartment itself. She described the start of her process of creating a new home:

"It was hard to do; all those decisions whether to take this or leave that. Every time I went over to the old house, I felt that heaviness; I just couldn't move very fast. I had to sit down a lot. I would cry and just stare out of the window. Then

Alice's image of her current apartment providing a calm transition point in her life.

when I came over here, I felt light on my feet. I danced and put things away and felt a lot of energy and joy. I felt an obsession to get some plants on the balcony, get some pictures framed and the furniture the way I want it. I realized I had to have some place to start from; I had to have a home. I do feel this is my home. I like to eat on my balcony, to take sun baths, to watch people on their bicycles. I like that I don't know my neighbors; I want to be really alone and know what that's like. My life has become scaled down like this apartment; a lot calmer and more peaceful. This apartment is helping me to simplify, to learn how to be self-sufficient and independent. I can express myself here in music and energy and color and tears and courage. The apartment seems to be teaching me about inner contentment; it just sits here, facing the world, taking in the sunshine, and the rain against its windows. It's a good transition place. I guess I'm coming to terms with the loss of so many things—my house, my marriage, my family, my youth—all at once."

Alice is in the midst of a grieving process. Although we are familiar with the experience of grieving for people who have died, there is equally deep grieving for a relationship that ends and for the place identified with that relationship. Despite the tensions and differences in environmental expression (and thus of deeper values) that Alice and her husband become conscious of in that house, it was nevertheless the place where the family grew, where she planted a rose garden, and where she lived her life for many years. The grief is real. So is the relief at starting a new life. Alice's inner wisdom knows that ultimately, with time, "it's going to come out okay."

Much as design critics may decry the featureless apartment buildings that have sprouted up in many U.S. cities since the 1960s, such settings provide an important milieu for people who are in transition. Whether that transition is from student life to adult life, from living with parents to living alone, or from the tension of an unsatisfactory marriage to the relative calm of life alone—the very form of the dwelling environment may be supportive of this transitional stage in life. Someone else (the landlord) is responsible for maintenance and long-term care; someone else (the designer or builder) has ensured that the dwelling will function relatively smoothly from the day you move in. The white walls and functional layout expect nothing from you. There is no garden to keep up, no porch to sweep. Behind the bland and anonymous exterior, a person in transition can begin to articulate an emerging self-image via the moveable objects with which she decorates and furnishes her apartment. It may not be satisfactory forever, but during that critical period of change experienced by someone like Alice, the setting of a neutral apartment can be a significant "screen" onto which new images of self can be projected, reflected upon, manipulated, discarded, or, perhaps, eventually embraced.

For some people who have lost their home through divorce or natural disaster, the move to a neutral transition place—a rented room, a furnished apartment or house—may be just what is needed in terms of a dwelling that provides security and shelter, but not much else. The psyche is in shock. The trauma of loss and the stress of dealing with insurance claims or divorce proceedings is more than enough to cope with. A ready-made home is just what is needed. In time, as healing imperceptibly occurs, the need for self-expression in the choice of home and how it is decorated and furnished will begin to reemerge.

Bob's Return to the Family Home

Particularly poignant and confusing emotions arise when one member of a separating couple has to return to live in the now empty family home, redolent with memories. Such was the case for Bob, an academic in his early fifties. Bob had owned this house for ten years, and, until a year before our conversation, had lived there with his wife of twenty-five years and two college-aged daughters. When he and his wife decided to separate, he moved to his own apartment a few miles away. For a year, he visited the house by appointment to discuss the divorce. Then his wife left the house to take a job overseas, and Bob moved back in. The divorce was not yet final, and there had been no decision as to what would become of the house. When I spoke with him, Bob had been in the house for four months; he had rented a room to a graduate student and had occasional visits from his daughters.

The small, cedar-shingled house sits up, one floor above the sidewalk, with a garage and large basement underneath it. It is a light-filled house with polished wood floors and throw rugs from the Middle East, where Bob lived and worked for many years. The furniture is a compatible mix of contemporary leather and old wooden rocking chairs, chests, and fabrics. The house feels quiet and calm, with a sense of being lived in but not of frantic activity or disorder. Although situated only a half block from a busy city street, the setting is peaceful, with birds singing in the many trees around the house. Pendulous blooms of white wisteria cascade from the front porch; an orange cat sleeps on a wooden bench by the front door.

When I asked Bob if he could depict his feelings in some kind of visual form, he found the task very difficult. The separation and impending divorce, though self-instigated, had rendered him very defended in terms of emotions. Eventually, he drew a simple house-shape and inside it recorded the words: *empty, deserted, incomplete, damaged, not mine.* Outside the house, he wrote: *too big, too proper, too uniformly white, needs repairs, wants attention, cracks, paint.* Underneath the drawing, he added: *Possibilities: light, air, space, fireplace, hearth, brick, music, food.* And then, as if to emphasize that these potentials in the house were no longer of interest to him, he wrote, *Not now.*

I asked if he could tell the house something about his feelings. He said: "I'm feeling very ambivalent about you. I don't really belong here; some of the time I don't want to be here, inside you. It's hard to be here and feel as though I'm in a different time of my life; I feel connected with past years' living here—the furniture, almost everything is connected to past times, which are pretty mixed up in my head. It's hard, not knowing what I want to do with you—whether I want to hang on to you or sell you."

Bob felt he would like to do more for or to the house, but didn't have the motivation to follow through; he didn't know whether it was worth the effort: "I don't feel it's the right time for me to pay attention to the house, other than keeping it clean and reasonably attractive for myself." The house "responded" that it felt neglected, not particularly well taken care of, and uncertain about the future.

When asked if he could recall how he felt about the house when he first moved in, ten years previously, Bob recalled that it was the first home he and his wife had owned. They had spent some years as graduate students and as a young married couple in rented apartments. "It represented a kind of dream. It had possibilities. I always liked the attic and basement spaces, but never found the time to do anything to them. A room in the basement was going to be a study for me, but didn't prove workable as it was dark and I could hear everything from the kitchen above. I thought the basement might become a workshop, but it became completely unusable, filled up with the unused accumulation of family stuff. Then the attic became a space I thought I might fix up for me, or as a studio for my wife, but neither ever materialized."

Bob mentioned several times when he had seen a lot of possibilities in the house, but none of them were realized. "Gradually, I lost interest in doing anything with the house, except low-level maintenance, minimal repair work, and painting. And then I left. I don't think the house was ever really an expression of my self. The most I ever did was to move furniture around, but that always upset my wife—she didn't like any kind of change. But she began to take over walls and doors and dark spaces to put up posters of her shows and photos of her artwork. . . . One summer, when she was gone in Europe, I took over our bedroom as my study, moved our bed out into the smallest room, moved her study into another room downstairs, and gave one of our daughters another room. When she came back, she was shocked. Other than that, I never really shaped the house for myself."

The room in which Bob had the most positive memories was the kitchen. After the first year or two, the family ate all their meals there: "That was nice because it was a small space and it brought us together." After he moved back into the house, that was the room where he felt most himself. The simple round kitchen table was one of the few pieces of furniture Bob felt attached to. He had chosen and refinished it himself.

"The kitchen was the best-used space, where we worked best as a family, over meals. I did a fair amount of cooking, so I spent a lot of time there. When a marriage is becoming unraveled, maybe the kitchen is the last place where it comes apart. When you've become distant in other ways, at least you come together for meals. The kitchen, at least, felt like there was still some dynamic—the other rooms felt like they'd been abandoned. When I moved out, I had few feelings about the house. It had come to be identified with a stability which had become very sterile. Our marriage was going nowhere; I was feeling pretty stuck in my life, so leaving the house was escaping to some kind of freedom, to a place that was going to be my own place—no responsibilities, no emotional unhappiness."

On moving back to the house after his wife's departure, Bob had found it hard to reappropriate the house, to feel comfortable inside it. Initially, he slept in a sleeping bag on the settee; he didn't feel comfortable in any of the bedrooms. Eventually, he moved upstairs and rearranged his study as a bedroom–sitting room–study; this was the room (other than the kitchen) where he spent most of his time. Significantly, on renting a room to a student, Bob moved the double bed that he'd shared with his wife into the rental room. The room that had been his and his wife's stood empty for several months; right after quitting a job he disliked and beginning to make other changes in his life, Bob reorganized it as a guest room. Meanwhile, downstairs, he made a few small but highly symbolic changes: He moved his papers and files into his wife's former study and he moved an "extra" chair out of the kitchen so that the table was set up for three (himself and his daughters) rather than for four. By degrees, in a series of physical changes, Bob appeared to be ejecting his wife from the house—and from his life. But Bob had little inclination to stay on permanently in the house. "I don't think any new dreams are going to take shape in this house. When the time comes, it will be better to let it go."

Compared with some people of his age, Bob had spent very few of his adult years living alone or being responsible for shaping a place to his own needs. He was married quite young to someone who liked things to be "set"—both spatially and temporally. His wife kept a calendar with daily schedules laid out weeks, even months ahead. Bob, on the other hand, didn't like to plan too far ahead; he liked to do things spontaneously and he liked to rearrange furniture. Their temporal and spatial styles were at odds and perhaps expressed a deeper division which neither could articulate. When I asked Bob to give a name to the house he was living in but would someday leave, he paused for a while and then in small script in the bottom corner he wrote: *Brown box.*

The human spirit is remarkably resilient. Grieving is a necessary process after deep loss. How long that period of healing needs to last may differ from person to person. What does seem to be universally true is that problems occur if grieving is suppressed or truncated. If we listen to the inner judge who tells us, "Don't be a wimp—get on with your life and forget her," or to the well-meaning friend who says, "Get out of the house and its memories," before we are ready to move on, the pain and anger, which is part of grief, will return. Though Madeline seemed to be preserving the house as it had been during her marriage, and though Carole was temporarily "paralyzed" in the home she had always wanted to mold to her own needs, both were going through a necessary period of grief and readjustment. And both, eventually, were able to find happiness again and a home that expressed who they had become as single women. Alice recognized that eventually she would leave her neutral apartment for a larger home and garden. Bob admitted the need to start again, away from the memories embedded in the family home.

Death of a Partner and Attachment to Home

Marital separation and divorce are two kinds of severance from established bonds of attachment to a home-place. Another is death of a partner or spouse. Financial difficulties may force the sale of a much-loved house; or the home may become such a symbol of the deceased partner that nothing is changed or altered; or a gradual adjustment may take place as the surviving partner modifies the home to express who he or she is alone; or a voluntary move to a completely new setting may allow a healthy break with the past and an embracing of life as it flows. The next two stories of Leonie and Jack portray two different responses to death and the attachment to a previously shared home.

Trapped by Grief: Leonie's Decision to Live Again

I met Leonie while I was visiting Australia on a consulting job. She is an extraordinarily brilliant young woman. In her early thirties, she was already head of an academic department at a university in Sydney and the author of four well-known books in her field. She is attractive, vivacious, fond of body surfing (like so many Australians), sociable, and a gifted scholar. However, she was hiding from all but her closest friends an almost debilitating grief at the death of a lover three years previously. Much older than her, her lover—Ian—had died in her arms after a sudden heart attack while they were playing with friends at a beach party. At one level, her life had come to an agonizing halt with that traumatic event. The halt had become manifest in her house.

Leonie lived in a charming gentrified neighborhood of inner Sydney, beloved by young professionals and academics. But as I approached her house for the first time, I was immediately aware of a puzzling double message: Although close to the street and apparently approachable, the pathway to her front door was almost totally blocked by the luscious unpruned growth of a fig tree. Squeezing around this hurdle, I entered a somewhat dark and lugubrious interior. Weighty antique furniture of dark wood and deep brown leather upholstery sat heavily in the living room, as did an antique desk, grandfather clock, and old bookcases— all in somber tones. At first glance it seemed a very masculine house. The tone of the furnishings, made even more somber by poor natural lighting in most of the rooms, seemed to be in contrast to Leonie's vivacious style and colorful clothes. The rooms felt lifeless and cluttered, especially since every available wall was hung with pictures—lithographs, etchings, originals of cartoons, portraits, abstracts. In corners were piles of additional framed pictures for which there was no room. The house had the feeling of a dark and cluttered art gallery.

As we talked, it became clear that the house was a memorial to Ian. Virtually everything in it—furniture, ornaments, pictures—had been selected by him. Leonie was quite aware of this and was just now, after three years of feeling nurtured by these tangible reminders of her lover, beginning to feel irritated and held back by the past. She had chosen her current house so that it could contain all that she had inherited from Ian. But it was too big for her, and its decor was not expressive of who she had become. She began to talk of selling most of the heavy antique furniture and buying a few pieces of her own choosing—light, natural pine, pioneer style. She thought about giving away or selling most of the art collection. Without these artifacts, which had now become encumbrances from the past, she could begin to think of moving to a smaller, lighter house, more expressive of her own opening up to life again. About six months after this dialogue, she made such a move. She selected a modern, light, white condominium apartment with an expansive view of Bondi Beach and the Pacific, and just enough room to contain the furniture and artwork retained after a major moving sale. Leonie was ready to start a new life.

Coming to Terms with Loss: Jack's Creating His Own Place

Jack lost his partner, Stephen, to AIDS in 1989. They had never fully lived together; Jack maintained a small townhouse near his work in Silicon Valley, but spent long weekends with Stephen in his San Francisco duplex. Jack decided to move to San Francisco to live in the house where he and Stephen had shared so many happy times. I asked him if that had been a difficult decision.

"Yes, I had a lot of doubts. I was hesitant in case I was holding on to memories and times that couldn't be again. Right after Stephen's death, there was so much to do . . . I would go back to my apartment thinking I wouldn't have so many memories there, but I did. It was harder to be there than here; it felt like a hotel room. So then I realized I could move into Stephen's place and it wouldn't feel like shutting a door so abruptly on that chapter in my life . . . I didn't want to run away from it or escape. There are so many good neighbors around who knew us both."

Gradually Jack changed the interior of Stephen's house to reflect more who he is. Stephen had been the more exuberant and charismatic of the two, and

Jack's image of his home six months after the death of his partner, Stephen.

expressed his character in bright colors and exotic paintings. After his death, Jack painted over a red room and a blue room, and made them both white, "which suits my more subdued character." He moved a rattan couch and chairs into storage and replaced them with his own traditional upholstered furniture. He gave several of Stephen's vivid Hawaiian jungle paintings to his family and replaced them with art that he had collected himself. "I couldn't stand the lamp he had in the bedroom; a new lamp was the first thing I brought in." The primary aspect of the environment which Jack maintained just as it had always been was the garden. Stephen had been a talented landscape architect, and this garden, which he had created, was his living memorial.

It has been five years since Stephen's death and Jack is still in the same house. I asked Jack what his feelings were now. His response confirmed my impressions: The house continues to provide him with a great deal of support. He is surrounded by remembrances of the rich life they had together, and of that which continues for Jack. Pictures of Stephen, family, and friends remain displayed, as well as mementos from their travels. The garden is still where Jack feels especially close to Stephen, and it remains very much as Stephen planted it.

In these stories, we see individuals holding on to the memory of their partners, now gone, through aspects of the domestic environment. So long as a particular house, item of furniture, picture, or ornament is around, a connection with the much-loved partner is retained. If indeed, as human beings, we find one means of expressing our ego-self in the form of the dwelling and its contents, it would seem perfectly reasonable to do the same for a significant other, now deceased. When this material expression has become a burden or barrier to connections with other, living people, the dwelling and its contents may have become a type of trap.

To some extent, the dwelling-as-trap is a manifestation of a self-image no longer relevant. Initially, the self-expression manifested in the current dwelling and its contents is embraced, because it offers comfort to a very shaky ego. But in a healthy path of personal growth, the home will eventually have to be changed—or abandoned—to permit the flowering of the partner left behind.

Loss of Home and Possessions in a Natural Disaster

Faced with an unintentional loss of treasured possessions, most people experience a profound sense of diminishing of the self. Thus, when possessions are lost to theft, burglary, or natural disaster, many people go through an experience of grief, similar to losing a loved one. Interviews with flood victims found that six weeks after the disaster, many could not speak of the event or cried while attempting to do so. Field notes from one interviewer included this account:

"The losses that concerned [the flood victim] most were those of his record collection . . . a first-edition book collection . . . the tools that his father—the cabinetmaker—had used . . . the ceiling and paneling of the basement that he had installed with the help and advice of his father, and (upstairs) the hutch, lowboy and stereo cabinet that his father had made."[5]

For the more than three thousand families who lost their homes in the October 1991 fire in the Berkeley-Oakland hills, many reported that their most wrenching losses were of irreplaceable photo albums and items given them or made for them by other people.

In a book of personal reminiscences about that fire, *Fire in the Hills: A Collective Remembrance*, a professional writer recalls his feelings at having lost his home and possessions to fire for the second time in two years: "Every hour or so I am devastated by the pang of something left behind. I saved my snapshots but not the Super-8 film of my two sons as children—touching scenes which I can play in my imagination, though I have not, I remind myself, seen the footage in eighteen years. Why didn't I think to copy this film onto VHS, as well as the old reels of my brother and me as kids, that were mistakenly left in my care fifteen years ago? I could have grabbed all these and thrown them in the car in half the time it took to have the fax machine fall apart on me. I lost all the personal letters anyone ever wrote me—when it would have been so easy to pick out the ones

Searching for fragments of home after the Oakland hills fire.

close to my heart and put them in the safe deposit box. I lost the old records I had lovingly taken from my mother's apartment in Indianapolis when she died, including . . . a scratchy 45 of my father at Ft. Davis, North Carolina, about to be shipped out and singing 'Take Good Care of Yourself.' I also lost, among other birth, death and marriage mementos, a tiny initialed baby ring given to my first son when he was born—a treasure I've been holding for him ever since—though he has never seen it and would not know what to do with it.

"In my manic mood I felt relieved because I didn't have to carry this baggage through life anymore . . . Do I feel this all the time? No. Would I feel it if I hadn't rescued my dog or if I had been like the painter in his sixties getting ready for his first one-man show, who had every painting turn to smoke? . . . But everything we hold on to will go anyway—a fact that defies the unthinking assumption of daily life. We live, we must live, mostly as if we don't believe this. The difference with my house and possessions is that they went all at once, with me there to see them going.

"As I walk down at dusk from the ashes of my house, I pass a new Infiniti pulled over to the side of the road. A lonely rich guy, having finished his day at the office, plods in deserted shadows with an open can of liver scraps, softly calling the name of his lost cat. Cooing cries of pet owners rise in the murky stench, echo along purple canyons gleaming brighter than ever in the polluted gorgeous sinking of the sun."[6]

A writer, musician, and artist who similarly lost everything wrote in her journal: "This fire is full of lessons: about ending, about continuing, about the grace of surrendering, the kindness in goodbye, about beginning, about choosing to create from nothing, over recreating from the ruin. . . .

"In this fire, the metal twisted out of shape. Some melted into pools. Hollow things collapsed in upon themselves; glass exploded, melted, bent; most everything just entirely evaporated—the table and chairs that became a shadow, the armoire and silk robes I may have inhaled this morning.

"In the basement, I had a case of 1954 dry Sauterne, bought cheap in 1975, now worth maybe over a hundred a bottle. As near as I can figure the miracle, the bottles exploded and leaked their dear contents onto a box full of my creative writing: letters, poems, song lyrics, maybe even an early short story or two. The liquid soaked the pages, and when the fire moved through, it was all too drunk to burn."[7]

A woman recalled taking leave of her house as the fire raced closer: "When it was time to leave, I sang to my house. I composed a sort of Gregorian chant as I moved through rooms, stuffing precious items into paper bags. Letters from my grandmother. A christening gown. The glass cylinder of shiny stones my husband and I had collected on a lonely beach long ago. I sang loudly: 'Good-bye bedroom, where we comforted one another and where we dreamed. Good-bye little boys' rooms that cradled my babies and held them through the night. Good-bye study, where I hung my heart. Good-bye rooms, where we lived the quiet moments of our lives.' My chant lapsed to a lullaby. 'Good-bye house that held us safe. Good-bye, sweet house. Good-bye sweet house . . .'

"Through the night, tossing in an unfamiliar bed, I imagined my house fending for itself, like the little house in the Laura Ingalls Wilder books. At dawn, when the fire had moved south of our neighborhood, we awoke, and my husband dialed the bulky hotel phone next to the bed. I heard the clear sound of my voice on our answering machine. After the beep, my husband whispered, 'Hello house, we love you.'"

The fire stopped one lot away from their house, and a few days later they were able to return home.[8]

Studies of people's responses to burglaries report reactions not only of anger and rage, but also of violation and grief. Clearly, people who have experienced such loss perceive it as a loss not just of material possessions, but also of part of the self. It is not uncommon after a burglary for people to clean and scrub their house, as if the body itself had been violated. A violation of one's larger home— the neighborhood—can provoke similar emotional responses. Researchers in Boston in the 1960s found that residents involuntarily removed from a West End neighborhood designated for urban renewal experienced profound feelings of loss and grief. Connections to important extensions of the self—neighbors, streets, stores, familiar places—had been severed, and the very human reaction was one of mourning.[9]

Aging and Memories of Past Dwellings

The loss of a house, through divorce, death, urban renewal, or natural disaster, is a traumatic experience, as devastating for some people as the loss of a loved one. The best one can do is nurture its meaning, as author Nancy Mairs describes in her book, *Remembering the Bone House:* "No, I'll never get the house back . . . I must content myself with another kind of possession altogether. My task is to house this house which has vanished from the waking world, as it once housed me, to grant it the deed to my dreams. In the biochemical bath of my own body . . . I preserve and perfect the yellow house on the coast of Maine. As long as I do, I get to dwell in it immemorially."[10]

For many people, the longer they live their lives in one place, the more they become attached to it—particularly if the time spent in that place included fulfilling human relationships. The place and the people who lived with and around us become intertwined in our memories. Moving from an affectionately remembered home may be successfully accomplished when the move is to "something better"—leaving the family home to go to college, emigrating to a new country full of hope, moving to a larger house due to more available income or additions to the family, and so on. But for the elderly, the decision to make a final move from the family home due to failing health is often a highly emotional experience. Some research indicates that there is a marked rise in mortality among those who move—sometimes involuntarily—into a geriatric institution; the shock to their emotional system is too great.

In a study to understand the complexities of this move, Tadashi Toyama, a researcher in Sweden, interviewed fourteen couples and single adults. He met with them just before a move into housing for the elderly, just after the move, and approximately a year later.[11] Their reactions varied all the way from quite positive to very negative. Those who moved only a short distance were better able to cope with the change. For example, when one elderly man moved only 500 feet from his old home to a new housing project for the elderly, which he had seen being constructed while on his daily walk, the move was quite positive. And for seventy-three-year-old Mr. Bengtsson, the move was largely positive because the elderly housing scheme was located near his childhood neighborhood.

"He adapted to the new environment quite smoothly and was feeling at home in the new place within a very short time. He enjoyed his early morning walk immensely—the streets, fields, and lakeshore where he used to play brought back pleasant memories, and he even met a few old friends from an interval of over sixty years."[12]

Also experiencing the move as positive were those who were able to re-create the interior of their old home in the new apartment, or who found a familiar layout of rooms—and therefore in their daily routine. Mr. Knutsson had a great love of nature and animals, and was happy when his new apartment very much resembled his old home, with floral patterns on the sofa and bedspread, large tropical houseplants, views of landscapes, and photos of endangered animals. Similarly, Miss Lihnas, at eighty-eight, was happy in her new flat because of her almost daily phone conversations with a network of friends from Estonia (her native country), and because she was able to re-create the special atmosphere of her previous home of twenty years with a large collection of Estonian textiles, carpets, and handicrafts.

Conversely, Mrs. Davidsson became disoriented in her new apartment, because rooms were not in the same relationship to each other as before, and an oblique view of the walls of a factory was much resented, compared with a much-loved view of the forest from the house where she had lived for twenty-three years. The adjustment for Mr. Fedrikson and Mr. Karlsson was similarly difficult, because each had made so many physical improvements and changes in the flats that had been home for twenty-eight years and forty years, respectively. For these two men, space had been appropriated even more profoundly than for those who might inhabit space in a more passive mode. Mr. Karlsson's second wife, however, had never felt their flat was "home"; she adjusted quite quickly to their new apartment in an elderly project, developing a daily temporal and spatial routine that she enjoyed and claiming the kitchen as her space. Her health and looks improved after the move. Her husband's health deteriorated, however; he started to smoke more heavily and lose his memory.

Those elderly people in the Swedish study who had a more active role in both the decision to move and the actual moving process were much more likely to adjust well. In the case of one couple, deterioration of the husband's health motivated his wife to make arrangements for the move without consulting him, but the whole event backfired. The man was disoriented and very unhappy in the new apartment; he didn't understand why they had moved. He died within a month. Racked with grief and a sense of guilt, his widow avoided staying in the apartment or thinking of it as home. She visited her adult children, traveled, refused invitations from the new owner to visit her old home of thirty-six years, and—significantly—spent much time at the summer home she and her husband had enjoyed for many years. Here—in a setting they had created together—she gradually adjusted to her loss.

In conducting these interviews with elderly people, Tadashi Toyama took photographs of the original home and produced them at the time of a second interview, six months or so after a move into elderly housing. He noted: "Without exception, the photos called forth deep feelings, and the subjects made many comments. Some of the subjects rearranged the decorations in their new living rooms to match the photos."[13]

On moving to a new apartment, some people had to dispose of furniture because they had less space. This was often a very difficult decision; most objects or pieces of furniture had vivid associations with people or times in the past. However, when furniture was passed on to a relative or close friend who understood the emotional connection it had, the separation was easier. When objects had to be disposed of commercially, the wrench was much greater. This was the case with Mrs. Jakobsson.

"She had sold some furniture to a second-hand dealer, and missed her rocking chair. . . . When the interviewer showed her photographs taken in her old apartment, she smiled (the only time she smiled during the interview) and was very glad to find her old rocking chair in one of the photos. The interviewer invited her to choose some of the photos as mementos, but she took all of them."[14]

Although approximately two-thirds of the U.S. population over sixty-five continues to live in their own home of many years, it is likely that an increasing number of the current aging population may end their days in a nursing home or housing for the elderly. We now have considerable information from social surveys about what works and what doesn't work for them in terms of the physical environment. Pertinent to our discussion of home and self-identity, every study reports the critical importance of allowing older people to furnish and decorate their rooms with the furniture, ornaments, mementos, and photographs that represent a lifetime of memories. As the Swedish study indicates, the move can be traumatic in and of itself. If the new place has little within it to reflect back to the residents who they are—and were—the result can be life-threatening. There is a marked rise in mortality, for example, in the first year after a move into a nursing home. Unlike a private apartment or house, a room in a nursing home is often shared with a stranger, and the atmosphere of white walls, fluorescent lights, linoleum floors, and metal furniture speak forcefully of hospital and illness, and not at all of home.

If you have to select a nursing home for an aging relative, you can greatly ease the transition of the move by choosing one in which her room is not shared with a stranger and where you and she can furnish and decorate the room with meaningful objects, pictures, and furnishings from her previous home. After all, if the prison system recognizes and condones the right of convicted criminals to personalize their cells, should we not insist on the same rights for our aging loved ones—and for ourselves?

An elderly person who is moved from a much-loved home of many years may yearn not only for its familiar rooms, views, and furniture, but also for the feeling of comfort and security it evoked. Feelings occur in space and inevitably become associated with various highly charged places; feelings cannot occur "out of space" any more than they can occur "out of time." Thus, any discussion of emotion and place must return to the observation that the two are inexplicably connected, not in a causal relationship, but in a transactional exchange, unique to each person.

In the sense that memory of place is a universal human experience, we are all alike; in the sense that each person's memories are unique, accessible and meaningful only to him or her, specific memories embedded in place cannot be fully experienced by anyone else. As E. M. Forster so beautifully writes in *Howard's End,* "To them Howard's End was a house; they could not know that to her it had been a spirit, for which she sought a spiritual heir. . . . Is it credible that the possessions of the spirit can be bequeathed at all? Has the soul offspring? A Whych-elm tree, a vine, a wisp of hay with dew on it—can passion for such things be transmitted . . . ?"[15]

DISRUPTIONS IN BONDING WITH THE HOME: EXERCISES YOU CAN DO YOURSELF

A Shrine for the Lost Home: Grief and Reconciliation

Let us suppose your situation is that you have chosen or been forced to leave a house due to divorce, or that you have lost a house due to fire, earthquake, flood, tornado, or other natural disaster. You are experiencing terrible pain and grief, not only for the loss of the physical place and its contents, but also for the memories anchored there and the future events that will never take place there. Dreams of this house persist; you find yourself driving back there despite the loss. If the loss is through a sudden, natural disaster, you are plagued with thoughts of "If only . . .": If only I had saved the photographs . . . If only we had been at home that weekend . . . If only we had paid attention to the weather forecast. . . . You constantly replay, as if rerunning an old movie, how it was before the disaster, what happened on that day. Or, in different circumstances, you remember special celebrations before the separation, or just uneventful family weekends in the house before the end of the marriage. You have lost a deeply significant portion of your life, and it is totally appropriate to grieve. If you find yourself in this period of grief, the following exercise may help.

Choose a quiet corner of a room where you now live and create a simple altar of memories. You might place a small table in your bedroom and put on it a photo or self-drawn picture of your house, some mementos, some fragments recovered from the ruins, if loss was due to a natural disaster. And then add a small vase of flowers; the flowers are the symbol of hope, rebirth, growth—just as they are on the grave of someone you love who has died.

When it feels right to do so, spend a little time each day, sitting, looking at the shrine. Let whatever feelings emerge have their place; if you feel grief, let yourself cry; if you feel anger, tell the house what you feel about the loss; if you feel nothing, or just numbness, let that be, too. Nothing is required of you; there is no way you ought to be. But it is important to give yourself the gift of a time and place to be with your feelings, whatever they are.

Return to your shrine, change the flowers, rearrange the mementos as often as you want to—just as you might visit the grave of a loved one. No one need know about your shrine. It is there for you, to serve you, as long as you need it. We all need a time and a place to anchor and express our grief. Funerals, memorial services, gravestones, cemeteries—they are present in every culture; grief is part of the human condition. Give yourself permission to grieve for your lost home; your connection to it may be every bit as deep and complex as your links to human companions. Denial in the face of catastrophic loss is a human reaction, but in the end we have to face the fact that what has happened has happened. The shrine is our place to do this.

Adjusting to Loss through Divorce

If you are the partner in a divorce who remains in the family home, you may want to experiment with one of the following scenarios. Take all of your partner's belongings and stack them away in a storeroom or basement until they can be removed. Or, change nothing in the house until you feel you have passed through a period of grief and anger. Or, select one room and make this totally yours—with furniture, pictures, ornaments, plants, and so on that are exclusively your possessions. By spending time in this room, you may come to experience what your values are, separate from your former partner, and, gradually, you may be able to expand your sense of self into the rest of the house.

If you are the partner who has left the family home, the temptation may be to start fresh, with no reminder of times past. Though the move to a transitional apartment or condominium may be a healthy decision, it is unwise to cut all ties with the earlier home, for the grief embedded in those ties must be experienced. To not do so is to court future disaster in which the same pattern is repeated; unacknowledged emotions tend to reemerge. One way to express those feelings to yourself might be to conduct a dialogue with your former home, represented by a photo or drawing. Tell it all that you are feeling—positive and negative—and repeat this exercise as long as feelings continue to reemerge.

Beyond the House-as-Ego:
The Call of the Soul

A tourist from America paid a visit to a renowned Polish rabbi, Hofetz Chaim.
He was astonished to see the rabbi's home was only a simple room filled with
books, plus a table and bench.

> *"Rabbi," asked the tourist, "where is your furniture?"*
> *"Where is yours?" replied Hofetz Chaim.*
> *"Mine?" asked the puzzled American. "But I'm only passing through."*
> *"So am I," said the rabbi.*
>
> —*Tales of the Hassidim*[1]

We are more than our ego-selves, more than our social selves. Each of us is striving also (though less consciously) to feed our spiritual soul, that indefinable essence or core of our being that lives in our deep sensibilities, our passions, our pain.[2] It is, as the Zen saying goes, our face before we are born. The voice of the soul is not necessarily comforting. It offers a challenge; it may demand a change. It is often a part of us we disregard or betray, but it never ceases in its struggle to be recognized and redeemed.

Throughout our lives, we are all in the process of emotional growth. One of the most subtle and profound struggles we are likely to encounter is that between the ego-self demanding recognition of our individual place in the world, and the transpersonal Self or soul, reminding us of our connection with all that is. As adults, we may fear the call of the soul; it seems to demand that we give up something—our long-standing image of who we are. As children, before our natural self was overlain with the expectations of parents, society, and the judgmental ego, we were often perfectly in tune with our soul. We were in tune when we climbed a tree and spoke to it as a friend, when we found comfort in a simple den or fort we built for ourselves, when we stared up in wonder at the stars, listened with fear to approaching thunder, stood in delight with bare feet in a puddle of water.

Those profound, unselfconscious soul-experiences of childhood, for the most part, fade away with the onset of adolescence and adulthood. We become busy with school, relationships, figuring out who we are, what our role in life might be. Soul connection fades for many of us during the necessary process of developing a healthy ego, making our way in the world. But the demand of our soul for recognition is never totally absent. It may reoccur, unacknowledged, in dreams or fantasies, or in unexpected emotions, as when a panoramic view lures us into a state of contemplation, or a piece of music brings tears to our eyes. The call of the soul, first encountered in childhood, is reencountered again and again through life. Often we repress or ignore it, passing on to what seem more pressing demands. Our ego-self is the most conservative element of the psyche—resisting, fearing change, it contrives to ignore the call of the soul. But there comes a time when the soul's insistence cannot be ignored; it is a voice seducing us into a fuller life.

While immersed in the early stages of this book, stressed from teaching full-time, advising students, and mothering my two energetic children, I was definitely in a period in which I had forgotten the importance of nurturing the soul. A wise graduate student, Kim Dovey, who had himself written insightfully on the meaning of home, asked me one day if I had ever conducted an interview with myself about my home. "No, I haven't," I answered, somewhat surprised at his question and at my response.

"How about if *I* interview *you?*" he said. So, a week or so later, we sat in my living room, and he asked me the kinds of questions I had asked other people. I was astonished and a little embarrassed at the result. Talking about, or as, the house was not especially difficult or surprising. But when he said quietly, "And what about the garden?" I burst into tears. The garden felt neglected, was calling me, had much to impart. I engaged in a dialogue with myself to try to understand what the garden needed to tell me. It was a conversation with an ignored but insistent part of my psyche which I called "Outdoor Clare" but which sometimes confronted me as the Child Within, or the Forgotten Soul. It reminded me that I had abandoned the spiritual, intuitive side of my nature.

Indoor Clare (IC): Where are you? *Outdoor Clare (OC):* I am in the daffodil field in April. I am under the horse-chestnut trees when their blooms—like white candelabras—are standing tall. I am in the bluebell wood. I am under the tree where the scillas grow. I am in the courtyard, planting pansies. I am picking primroses and violets in the woods. I am always outdoors. I would like you to get to know me just a little. *IC:* Oh, all right—so long as you don't expect too much of me. I guess I have neglected you. *OC:* I don't easily give up. Are you willing to go on an adventure? To let me take the lead? To leave a whole lot behind? *IC:* Well, not too much. *OC:* We'll see. Everything is negotiable. We will find a way to work together, don't you think? *IC:* Even as I talk with you, I feel something imperceptibly lifting from my chest. I feel a lightness returning. "Lose your mind, and come to your senses," Fritz Perls told us in the sixties. The garden is for my senses. I *am* sensing—a feeling, sensing person. Somewhere, sometime, I got diverted into my head. I lost it—the other half of me. *OC:* Oh, yes—yes! That's why you keep looking out of the window at trees and clouds during faculty meetings—catching glimpses of what might be. Be courageous—come out and *claim* me. I won't let you turn back now. I will turn your eyes toward the garden, your heart toward the ocean. I will prick your eyes with tears, your body with heartaches. I will send you dreams and fantasies. I will throw synchronicities in your path until you cannot turn away and ignore me. Even if it causes you anguish, sleepless nights, you can't turn back now. *IC:* I am losing touch, losing touch with who I am. I feel cast adrift—as though I am on a raft somewhere—no sight of land, no one with me. *OC:* I am here—long ago and far away. But I am here. I am the girl who raised rabbits for food for the family, the girl who grew vegetables and collected berries and mushrooms and firewood. I knew the names of dozens of wildflowers, trees, and birds. I could navigate long distances through woods and fields. I could walk home alone in the dark, in the blackout. I was afraid, but I did it. *IC:* Perhaps you can help me . . . *OC:* Yes, I can! But first you must recognize and acknowledge me. When you came into the garden this morning to pick an iris and a narcissus in the rain and put them in a vase in the kitchen—that is a beginning . . .

And so it was.

What is curious about this dialogue, looking back on it more objectively, is that the forgotten soul, asking for recognition in the garden, speaks in images from my past. The bluebells, scillas, primroses, horse-chestnuts—all are fond memories of an English countryside childhood. This is no coincidence, nor is it just wistful nostalgia. The innocent openness many people experience in early childhood places a soul-seed in our unconscious. As we grow up, become educated, and make our way in the world, the seed is often forgotten. But it is still present, quietly germinating beneath layers of consciousness and outer, material symbols of our ego and social selves. At some point, its presence subtly sifts into consciousness. The turning point may be a crisis or a slow awakening. It may occur when we are young or very old. Most often it occurs in midlife, for, as Jung observed, the work of the second half of our life is the recognition of the salience of spirit or soul in our lives.

In keeping with the theme of this book, I am most interested here in the environments that seem to trigger that poignant reconnection. Each of us has to find the place of our soul—in our memories, our imagination, or in the material world. For some people, this place of soul nurturance may not be in the home at all; it may require spending time in another place or—over a lifetime—in varying soul-nourishing places, each appropriate to a particular stage of emotional development. When we start to feel not totally at home in our dwelling or, conversely, when we seek a broader home in another place, it is likely that the soul is demanding recognition.

The Tree House and the Desert: Pat's Places of Soul Connection

If we accept the Jungian notion of individuation as a gradual but insistent striving toward the transpersonal Self or soul, then the life of a person dedicated to a religious vocation may offer especially salient clues as to how the environment may be used as a symbol at different stages of the journey. Pat is a Roman Catholic nun in a noncloistered order dedicated to teaching and community activism. I talked with her on two occasions, in 1977 and 1987.

Pat was born in New York City and spent most of her childhood in New York State. Her father was a Vermont "country boy" who had run away from the farm and eventually became a financier on Wall Street. He clearly had had a profound influence on Pat's life and values. In particular, he had taught her how to seek challenge and peace in the world of nature. He had bought a summer cabin in the mountains of upstate New York. It was there—between the ages of six and nine—that Pat had her earliest contact with the forest. The memory of it reverberated through her life, as do those magic places of middle childhood for many people. As a woman in her early sixties, she told me about her forest fantasies:

"I fantasize about living in the forest, living as a person in the woods, my safe and serene place. I never felt afraid in the forest; that was always a comforting place. The cabin my father bought was on the edge of the woods—I once tamed a chipmunk there. The idea of a house in a tree—a tree house is an important image for me, even in adult life. When I can't go to sleep, instead of counting sheep, I fantasize that I'm young and going into the forest. I calm myself. I explore and I'm fascinated by the beauty of all the shades of green, the shadows, and the sounds. It is so beautiful! It was the beginning of my spiritual relationship to the world, going out into the forest as a child."

Pat's memories of the forest are certainly suggestive of that contact with the Self that many of us experience in childhood and later lose. As she described other loved environments of her life, it became apparent that she had a pattern of returning to settings that exemplified the peace and freedom she had experienced in the forest. They were not always forest environments, not always natural settings, but each had the ability to rekindle the spiritual connection she had first encountered near her family's cabin in the woods.

In her thirties, Pat lived in a convent in Tucson and worked as a teacher. She was not particularly happy with her dwelling-place, especially with the other sisters who were, then, her "family." To find peace, freedom, and privacy, she went out almost every day into the desert. She remembered that environment in later years with particular love and longing. The desert accepted her, expected nothing of her. It was strong, could withstand all the vicissitudes of the weather. It seemed solid and unchanging, and yet it changed constantly in many subtle ways. It was a perfect setting for Pat to experience the immanence of God and her soul.

When I first met Pat in 1977, she had just moved from Tucson to Oakland, California, where a group of sisters in her order had established a house in a very poor, run-down neighborhood. Here, under the successful leadership of Sister Joanna, they formed an organization named Jubilee West, which enables low-income people to buy and refurbish houses. Pat lived at this time in a small, sparsely decorated room in the convent. She felt very confined and unhappy in this space. To counteract the confinement she felt, she looked for an equivalent to the Arizona desert. In part, she found it on trips to the ocean, but it was not as accessible or as meaningful as the desert had been. Meditating on a tree outside the window of her small room helped her connect to the peace of the natural world and bring some of that energy into her life.

When we reconnected in 1987, Pat's living situation had changed. She and Sister Joanna had created a home for themselves in a rented house a few blocks from the convent. The homeyness of the interior, the decorations, and the personalization of the space spoke of a significant investment in home-making. They had lived there for seven years.

"As nuns, we left home at eighteen and entered a convent. In the convent, we were discouraged from claiming anything personal, even from claiming our past history; we were told not to talk about our childhood and family with the other sisters. There was a conviction, at that time, that all that would detract from God. But for many of us in religious orders, things have changed—the normal, natural way of living for every human being is an experience of how God is with you. We want to identify with everything around us and within us, all that is good and beautiful—the friends, relatives, places—and see God in all of those."

Clearly, the move to her own house and the process—still ongoing—of transforming it into a comfortable home had been of profound importance in Pat's psychological growth. Her expression here and elsewhere in our conversation about the hostility and negativity of the outside world was a realistic assessment of how it felt to her, a vulnerable older woman living in a very poor neighborhood in a city with one of the highest homicide rates in the country. I asked her to speak to the house as if it were animate. Her words and tone of voice conveyed the love she felt for this environment:

"House—I'd like to express my gratitude for your being here, for letting me do things to you, for letting me be the way I am without putting constraints on me. You have given me my freedom; you give me comfort, pleasure, security, safety. You give me nourishment and rest and a place where I can be at peace. You also provide a challenge—challenging me to come to you and not bring all that baggage in from the outside world, all the negativity and bad things I experience outside. You tell me to leave those things behind and come here to be refreshed. You help me take some of the peace I find here back to the outside. You are like my imaginary tree house! You let me surround myself with growth and light and beauty."

As Pat continued to speak to the house, the images and words she chose reflected, I felt, some of the ways she now perhaps regarded her own body. She was having various medical problems that were beginning to slow her down. "Take care of yourself, house! You're old and I don't want you to fall apart. I'd fix you up if I could. I need you to be strong. I need you to be here."

I asked Pat if she felt that creating a home had been an important part of her spiritual growth, whereas earlier in life, she had been denied that experience. Was the path to God, as her order had traditionally implied, via denial of the personal? Or was it a path that must lead inward?

"I think God works in both ways. When I went into the desert, I was seeking my own spiritual home, but not looking for it in a house-home. I was being my own home. And now, very definitely, I think of this house as home; I think it makes a difference in the spiritual being to feel the peace here. In the desert, I found the peace in freedom; here, I find the peace in safety and protection. There, I could be—and run and walk and hike and do all those things that express freedom to me. Here, I can be without being torn apart by the actions taken on others out there. It's the protection of this house."

At this point in our conversation, Pat shifted back to talking about the forest of her childhood. Forest/desert/current home were all metaphors for the same thing: a coming back to the soul. And tied in to that initial discovery and continued reconnection to soul were loving memories of her father.

"I have to put my father in here. It was he who encouraged me to ride ponies at our summer home; it was he who bought a horse for me in the desert. And when I was thrown, it was he who said, 'Get back on!' He was a really important person in my life, always encouraging me to climb and explore and just try. It's hard for me to be away from all those outdoor things here—because that's what he taught me. But he'd also say—'Be what you've learned to be, here, here is where your work is.'"

Although Pat now found peace in her house, she also felt the need sometimes to escape the city—house and all—and return to the forest. "The wildness, freedom, spaciousness—the yearning for something that is untrammeled. That is real. There is so much that is unnatural and wrong in cities—for me. In a few weeks, I'll go on retreat to the redwoods to a monastery—the ocean isn't far away. There's a confluence of two brooks on the property. I love to go out there and sit under the big trees and watch the water. It's a very peaceful place—you can be yourself. It will be Holy Week when I'm there. There will be many rituals—and the symbols are water, fire—which come right out of the natural world—the forest, the meadow, the brook. The whole setting is a symbol. That's where my home is. I'd like to live there permanently—but it's not possible. I think of a quote from a poem—I'm not sure who wrote it:

> *Not where I breathe*
> *But where I love—I live.*

And, having said that, Pat returned to the theme of her house in Oakland—the house where she had been able to express her personal needs: "The place you have made with parts of yourself—you leave things in it, they're there because of you. You come back to find parts of yourself. You're better when you're back; you're more whole when you're back. When you 'come home,' you're coming back to yourself. That's what houses should be able to do for people—let them put an imprint of themselves there."

Seven years after this conversation, in 1994, Pat died while on a visit to Vermont, the birthplace of her father and grandfather.

In the journey toward wholeness, some people—like Pat—are lucky enough to recognize unconsciously that a certain environment will enhance their contact with the soul. They physically *go* to the desert or the wilderness, there to experience a certain change of consciousness that assists in the journey beyond ego. For others, the physical journey may not be possible, and so they decorate their dwelling with pictures of this place and retreat into its embrace while fantasizing, meditating, dreaming, or listening to music. Either way, the unconscious, seat of the Self, is quietly insistent on being acknowledged. Like the Garden of Eden, a myth of original oneness for the Judeo-Christian world, the individual in this culture often contacts the Self via metaphors from the natural world—sun, moon, mountain, forest, landscape, ocean, river. For many people, though not necessarily all, it is time spent in natural settings—or reminders of those settings in the form of photos or paintings in the home—that triggers connections to the soul or higher Self.

The conversations that I had with people about their dwellings did not begin with any notion of investigating the soul; rather, I was seeking to understand the ego/dwelling connection. But I was struck by how many times people profoundly stuck in a state of alienation or depression would project this onto their dwelling (hating it, neglecting it, rejecting it); and when asked to draw a picture of where—ideally—they'd like to live, they would invariably depict a scene in the natural world, or at least a picture containing many natural elements. Occasionally, this natural metaphor would appear in the picture of their current, disliked dwelling—but almost as an aside, a footnote, as it did in Marilyn's picture of her refuge-prison with an image of the sun outside the enclosure. When asked to speak to, or as, this element, there is often an immediate change in the tone of voice, a long sigh, or tears. The soul is yearning for recognition; the ego, unconsciously, struggling to frustrate that (re)connection. Let us look at several people for whom this appeared to be the critical issue at the time of our conversation.

The Draw toward Soul and Creativity: Maria's Yearning for an Ocean House

Maria had become alienated from her current home and had a fantasy of a place she'd really like to live. She and her husband, Les, had moved from San Francisco to the wooded slopes of Mt. Tamalpais in Mill Valley, ten years prior to our conversation. They had worked closely with an architect during two years of construction, which they both described as one of the most exciting experiences of their lives. Here they had raised their son, and Maria had established herself as an artist. She depicted the house as a yellow, glowing "mushroom" in a forest of trees. But the house no longer felt comfortable to her. She and her husband were growing apart; their son had left home. The house felt like Les' place, not Maria's. More significant, Maria liked to build, to create; and when the house was finished, it felt like it was time to move on. "The first day we moved in, I recall myself saying—'Oh, you mean I have to *live* here?'"

Interestingly, Maria's artistic creations included many images of houses—in particular, painted wooden bas-relief forms of house facades. To relieve the frustration of having to live in the completed Mill Valley house, she created a tiny, sculptured ten-by-ten-foot cabin by herself on a piece of land in Mendocino. (Despite several requests, I could not persuade Maria to let me see this house; clearly, it was too personal to share.) "This was a house for my heart. It grew

from the inside out, so that the form became a metaphor for my inner feelings. Having a house built for us was an inspiration, but building my own house gave me a sense of security."

But even this "house for the heart" was not enough. It was a retreat, a place for inspiration but not day-to-day living. As we sat talking in the Mill Valley house, it was clear that Maria wanted to move on. She spoke of the redwood trees that were such an overpowering presence in her picture and which, in reality, brushed against every wall of the house.

"I used to go to the woods as a child to talk to the trees and be with the trees. They were real comforting—but at the same time overpowering. They kept me apart from the world. It was a conflict—both comforting and at the same time smothering. I don't have to be with people when I'm with trees, and sometimes I much prefer to be with trees."

I stared at the trees in her painting as she talked. It felt as though they were still keeping her apart from something. I asked, "What is there beyond the trees that you'd like to go to?" Maria responded without hesitation: "The ocean! I feel if I could be near the ocean, I could paint again. I would like to have an ocean house instead of a tree house. Before I die, I would like to live near the ocean."

I asked Maria to close her eyes and imagine being close to the ocean and to speak to it: "I would *love* to be close to you, and to be able to swim in you every day. To wake up and hear you in my sleep. Oh, if only I could be near you and walk on your beach and know that you're always there. I would feel that I had come home. It is not like a house. A house encloses you. The ocean encloses you, too, but it flows, it is wet, it is strong. It's like eternity. The tide comes in and the tide goes out. The ocean doesn't judge you—it's like a lover."

When feelings about an environment are so strongly expressed, the pull toward it so powerful, it is likely that it is the soul—the transpersonal ground of the unconscious—that is calling. Maria did eventually follow her dream. But first she made a radical statement about the trees that seemed to smother her. She rented a chain saw and cut down those trees whose branches scraped against the windows. Eventually, she separated from her husband and moved to a comfortable cottage on the coast to pursue her calling as an artist. The ocean became her solace and her inspiration. She had, as Joseph Campbell expressed it, "followed her bliss."

Not everyone has the freedom or resources to move in order to satisfy their inner yearning for a place of the soul. For some people, in fact, no move is necessary; that connection may be made within the home, however ordinary it may be.

Going Within:
Anita's Finding a Soul Connection at Home

Anita was a successful therapist in her early forties. At the time of this conversation, she had lived for about five months in a newly purchased home. It was a modest, cedar-shingled house on a tree-lined street in a middle-income urban neighborhood. She had been longing for such a home for many years; the impetus to move came when the rented cottage she had shared with her two teenaged daughters was put up for sale. She was immensely happy in her new setting.

I asked her to put down her feelings about this house, and what emerged was a soft, abstract, pastel-shaded "explosion" of colors and shapes. She began to talk about the process of making this visual image:

"I went inside myself, and what emerged was a sigh, a sense of relief and protection, and that's this central part of the picture. It's my inner being, my room upstairs, my sanctuary. From there, I mentally put myself into all the things I do in various places in my house. This is the place where I work; I showed that with a rich, violet color. I also play here in my house—it's a joyous place: gold and sunny feelings. This statement I've written down sums up the whole feeling I have here: *My house is simple—grace, beauty, joy—no big deal, just me.* This really is my self as well as my house, you see? I mean, there's really no separation."

I asked Anita if she would speak as if she *were* the house: "I am really grateful that you've come inside me. I was such a wreck when you first came, and you've absolutely made me over into my true self. I feel so marvelous now. I just radiate!

Anita's feelings about the home where she lived and worked.

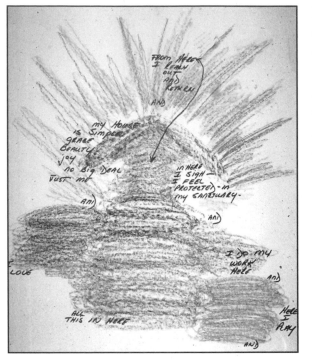

I'm filled with music and change—people changing and growing inside of me."

I asked Anita if the house could tell her how it experienced her: "What I see here is a woman with a very deep serenity in her center, a serenity that is simple and yet profound at the same time. I see a lot of dimensions, a lot of power and excitement and intensity radiating from the center."

She returned to speaking as Anita: "It's a little hard to describe. I am the place in myself that is solid and always here. To actually describe that place, I have to recall some experiences I've had in my life, where I've deeply contacted this place in my self. It is a place I contact when I meditate, when I'm quiet, when I run, when I do my work. I come back to this place unfailingly, inevitably. It's the central place inside myself—my core. And this place is very connected to something I conceptualize as divine."

In Anita's case, the connection to the soul is made via the altered state of consciousness that comes to some people when jogging, or during the course of working, or being quiet and meditative within their house. She describes this core of her being as variously "solid, unfailing, simple, serene, divine." Clearly, she has found a means of continuously reconnecting with the soul; and the setting for that reconnection, the setting that permits her the privacy, the security, the peace of time alone and time to meditate, is her home.

Anita is fortunate; for many people—especially women—the persistent intrusions of family, housework, or social demands within the home make this an especially difficult place in which to withdraw. For withdraw we must, because the soul speaks to us predominantly in times of silence. In the next account, we meet a person whose house and its setting were indeed too busy, exciting, and demanding of attention to allow space and time for contacting the soul. Another place had to be created.

Amish Quilts and Way of Life: Sue's Search for a Lost Part of the Self in the Outer World

Sue was a therapist, an artist, a wife, a mother. When I spoke with her, she had been married for twenty years to a shy and scholarly academic; she described herself as "99 percent extrovert." Her two teenaged sons were about to graduate from high school; her days of mothering were virtually over.

The family lived in a large house in the Berkeley hills, ample for four people and a dog. Yet Sue began to realize that there was little space in the home she could call exclusively her own. She yearned for a studio or work space that would be hers alone, where she could lay out projects and leave them undisturbed. As she put down her fantasy of how the house could be, she drew a yellow work space with rows and rows of uncluttered tables, and was surprised that she had rendered it "regimented, linear, cell-like." In contrast to this was the central blue organic segment of the house that she shared with her husband and sons. As she finished the picture, she impulsively tore a hole in the center of the blue space and thrust into it a piece of yellow paper to signify herself.

"I put myself right smack in the middle. Maybe that's a need in me I didn't realize—I have to be absolutely in the middle of everything. I want all this privacy and yet I want to be the center of the family."

Sue's picture did in fact portray the dynamics of the family—she tended to be more demanding of space and attention in the family than her more introverted husband and sons. Her desire for a place of her own seemed to express her needs at many levels: a need for functional space to pursue her work in ceramics; a need for a quiet, ordered, linear space in contrast to what she experienced as an overstimulating house decorated with colorful art and an extraordinarily beautiful view through trees to San Francisco Bay; a need for a private space where she could experience more self-reflection than she allowed herself in the exuberant communal space of the household. Although scarcely able to articulate it directly, it seemed as though a quiet, reflective side of Sue was yearning for her to take

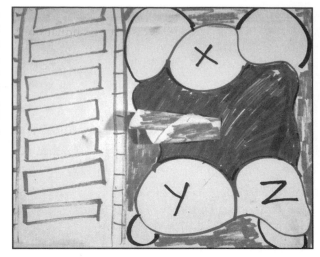

Sue's image of the work space she yearned for, separate from the home she shared with her husband and sons.

time out. Overwhelmed by her ebullient, energetic ego-self, she was seeking a balance—personified in a space that would be hers alone and where communication would be inward, with her higher Self or soul, rather than external, with family and the world. But the thought of this space, so clearly longed for, was also frightening; for, having drawn her studio space, Sue quickly thrust herself back into the communal space of the family. In all the interviews I conducted, Sue was the only person to tear the paper while making a picture.

"It's a struggle for some balance. And it's a scary new journey, and journeys are scary. They don't have any guarantees as to what's at the end of them. But I don't feel I have any choice."

Less than a year later, Sue took over a large garage adjacent to the house and transformed it into a work space very much like the one she had depicted, with long spacious tabletops, no distracting exterior views, and complete privacy from the house and family. Though continuing with her work with ceramics, she found herself exploring with more and more fascination the quilts and artwork of the Amish people—somber colors, quiet centeredness. The patchwork pictures of muted blues and violets that Sue began to create seemed to personify the quiet inner depth she yearned to explore within herself. Her work space in the converted garage was a beginning. Later, almost as if to overwhelm her assertive extroversion Sue felt compelled to visit and live with the Amish, to immerse herself in a whole culture of quiet, ordered introversion. The Amish community was her own garage-studio writ large. The insistent inner pull she felt to visit, live with, and learn from the Amish was both exciting and frightening.

This combination of a setting, situation, or journey that is both compelling and fearful is frequently a clue to the next step on the journey toward individuation. Jungian analyst Edward Whitmont describes it thus: "We cannot get away from it; its pressure to be known will not let us go. . . . It is the intruder, the stranger, who wants to be let in [in a dream]. . . . The call to individuation is contained within this dynamism; if we want to know the next step along the path toward what we are 'meant to be,' we can look for the thing that attracts and frightens at the same time."[3]

Eventually, Sue wrote a book about her encounter with Amish life and culture and, through this medium, both explored her own journey into wholeness and offered an eloquent model for others. Ironically, the success of her book pulled her out into the limelight again, as she did book signings in stores across the country. For Sue, as for most of us, the struggle between ego and soul is an ongoing dance throughout our lives.

Fifteen years after the first conversation, I interviewed Sue again. She read what I had written of our initial meeting. "A lot has changed—but a lot is still the same. A huge introverted component of my psyche has emerged. The Amish were a metaphor. After visiting there four or five times, I suddenly knew I had no more questions. The answers were all inside me. I had never planned or dreamt of a book; I had taken no notes. But while I was churning butter one day, a voice inside me said: Now it's time to tell the story. I didn't want to heed that call—or to write! The book of 117 pages took me five years to write. I stopped working in the studio, stopped all my extroverted activities. I could think of little else. It became like an obsessive love affair with a project, rather than a person."

Sue did, indeed, seem subtly different. Outwardly, she appeared unchanged— the same hairstyle, clothes, jewelry, way of speaking. But there was also a new softness, a vulnerability. The task of writing the book had not been easy. "I had to trust the inner voice which didn't 'make sense.' I was looking for a pattern in my life. Amish quilts were the visual cue; I see the world through artist's eyes."

Since the publication of her book, Sue has had many calls to speak to women's groups. She feels a "missionary zeal" to raise questions about what really matters, to give people the courage to look for the pattern in *their* lives. "The talks I give and the nourishment I gain from the audience are like making another quilt—a spirit quilt. I like to talk to an audience, because I need to be reminded of what really matters by the questions they raise."

Sue is now about to embark on a new project, another task that doesn't totally "make sense." She feels it is time to "come home" and practice what she has learned from the Amish. "It is *so* difficult! I'm trying to sort out my priorities;

I still feel overwhelmed. I'm developing a loving relationship with my home—not just how it is aesthetically. I'm beginning to see home-based chores as part of life, not something that takes me away from the studio. Amish houses felt alive! I'm not quite sure if my home is a monastery—or a fortress, or a beautiful space where my spirit can be expressed! The Amish see life as all ordinary, and all sacred, and that's something I long for."

Like Sue, many of us in midlife have a similar experience. Having spent most of a lifetime sorting out who we are, taking on with varying success the roles of spouse, parent, friend, lover, professional person, one day we start to question what it is all about. Chinks of doubt begin to glint through the fog of busyness that we have constructed around us. Far from denying or covering up these glimmers, we need to recognize and nurture them as messages from that higher state of consciousness which Thomas Moore refers to as "soul power":[4]

"What is the source of this soul power and how can we tap into it? I believe it often comes from unexpected places. It comes first of all from living close to the heart, and not at odds with it. Therefore, paradoxically, soul power may emerge from failure, depression, and loss. The general rule is that soul appears in the gaps and holes of experience. . . . Power pours in when we sustain the feeling of emptiness and withstand temptation to fill it prematurely. . . . The soul has no room in which to present itself if we continually fill all the gaps with bogus activities."[5]

Prospect and Refuge: The View from the House

British geographer Jay Appleton has written of the human proclivity to seek out places in which we feel comfortably protected yet where we also have a view outward. He termed this concept "prospect/refuge" and speculated that it might be triggered by a genetic memory of living on the forest edge (refuge) and perusing the open plains (prospect) for enemies or prey.

For some of us, the move to a dwelling with a view may parallel (or trigger) a changed relationship between self and the world. In the writing of May Sarton, two journals emerged from her renovating an old house in New Hampshire and adapting to living alone in the country. These published journals, *Plant Dreaming Deep* (1968) and *Journal of a Solitude* (1973), focus on her inner journey just as the documenting of simple housekeeping tasks tended to focus on the interior of the house and on unresolved emotional issues rooted in the past. On moving to a new house in York, Maine—a house with a view of the ocean—Sarton documents a more expansive and spiritual awakening in *House by the Sea* (1977), *Recovering* (1980), and *At Seventy* (1984). Commenting on Sarton's work, Suzanne Owens noted: "'Wild Knoll,' a spacious house set back from the shore and surrounded by woods, pulled the writer's focus further away from the confines of the house and yard . . . the landscape is cathartic, a touchstone for emotions . . . The poet's eye turns outward . . . for the writer becoming accustomed to new spaces beyond her doorstep (quite literally, but emotionally too), definition is a process of extension. What grew so deeply inward during the writing of *Journal of a Solitude* was here pushing the limits of private space as far as the eye could see. Outer and inner landscapes joined in her sense of personal boundaries."[6]

While living in this house, Sarton writes in her journals less about the past, her parents, a lost lover, and more about her own coming to terms with present realities, illness, aging, and the unknown future. The ocean—particularly in its tranquil moods—becomes almost a metaphor or reflection of her own occasional states of transcendence. She writes: "I am living under a powerful spell, the spell of the sea. But in one way, it is not as I imagined, for I had imagined that part of the tides, rising and falling. But I do not see the rocks or the shoreline from my windows; I look out to the ocean over a long field, so I am not aware of the tides, after all, nor influenced by their rhythm; instead I am bathed in the gentleness of this field-ocean landscape. Without tension, it has been the happiest year I can remember."[7]

As in Forster's *A Room with a View,* the view outward as something beyond the room or dwelling acts as a powerful metaphor for a psychological expansion of the self. In Sarton's case, it is the start of an expansion into the transcendent realm beyond the personal self; in the case of Forster's heroine—Lucy Honeychurch—the expansion is from a chaperoned adolescence into the burgeoning maturity of full womanhood. The nature of the "refuge" and the "prospect" may be different, but the expanding modes of awareness are comparable.

If the view can be a metaphor for our own expanding awareness, then the emotional reaction of Sylvia to the intrusion on her view by a neighbor's building project (chapter 8) is all the more understandable. So too is Maria's devout wish to leave her home, where forest trees brushed against every window, and seek an "ocean house" with an expansive view. But if a view is a metaphor for widening consciousness, what of Sue, who found the panorama of her home "too much"?

An expansive view over San Francisco Bay from virtually every room in her house had become distracting, outwardly drawing. It is significant that Sue chose as her studio the one space, a converted garage, without a view. Here, in isolation from her family and from the distracting views over city and landscape, her work and her psyche became more focused, more inward-oriented, and much simplified. Depending on our psychological makeup and the development stage at which we find ourselves, our dwelling may need to be all prospect and less refuge; all refuge and little prospect; or a felicitous balance of the two.

The pull to a view seems to be very powerful, too, when people are in a temporary state of grief, sadness, or confusion. In an ongoing study conducted by colleague Carolyn Francis and myself, we have asked many people to recall a time when they felt upset or distressed and went to some place that helped them feel better. One of the most frequently mentioned types of settings was a vantage point which, they reported, helped them become more calm and centered and "get things into perspective." It is not that the environment causes our moods or expansions of awareness; rather, that given the freedom (economic and psychological) to find the "right place," many of us are drawn to settings that appear to parallel and mirror our psychic states or to offer us therapeutic sustenance in times of stress.

Periods of loss or depression, while experienced outwardly as empty and purposeless, are often paralleled by a period of "inner construction"—clearing out old structures, putting up new ones. Dreams may depict construction sites or the building of houses. When, many years ago, I lost a lover in a car accident, I dreamt that night of a man in a white robe conducting me through the ruins of a house, pointing out amid the rubble the location of doorways and rooms. I interpreted this as my wise, inner soul assuring me that even amid the devastation I felt at Al's death, my basic structure was still present and discernible. A few days after this dream, David, a young friend who later became a Buddhist teacher, consoled me and asked me to try to see Al's death as a "gift of growth." At the time, in my grief, I could barely hear his words, but they were wise counsel. Through this profound pain, I began to wake up. This event was the start of a spiritual quest, of searching for something lost but latent in my inner being.

Although depression or melancholy may not be emotions we would consciously invite into our lives, they will arrive, nonetheless, for most of us. If we look upon depression as a harbinger of change, an opening to the soul, we would not be so hasty to wish it away or dull its feeling with tranquilizers. Thomas Moore has written: "When love's sadness visits us . . . it isn't necessary to take a pill or search out a therapeutic strategy to dismiss the feeling, because to dismiss that feeling is to banish an important soul visitor. The soul apparently needs amorous sadness. It is a form of consciousness that brings its own unique wisdom."[8]

A Journey into Wholeness: Sara's Letting Go of the House

Some gardens of the Renaissance had a bower dedicated to Saturn, the Roman god identified with melancholy. Here, a person experiencing the dark mood of depression could withdraw to a remote, shaded place without fear of being disturbed. In the case of Sara, a San Francisco housewife deeply questioning her life, a private room for meditation at the top of her house in Pacific Heights fulfilled this same need.

Sara was in her forties when I first met her; we were both living at the time in the alternative community of Findhorn in northern Scotland. I was, admittedly, a little put off at first by her appearance. Her clothing never varied. She wore sandals and a long white tunic over a pair of loose, cotton pants. She had the look of a wandering Indian *sadhu*. She worked alone in one of the community's gardens; she often sat alone at mealtimes. I was intrigued but also a little intimidated. She seemed so self-contained. Eventually, we began to talk. Her story was fascinating; she was one of the few people I had met who seemed to have moved through all the stages of development described in the Jungian process of individuation. And each stage seemed to have been expressed by a particular relationship to the physical environment.

As a young wife, Sara and her lawyer-husband relocated to San Francisco from a suburban home in Ohio. They moved into what she described as "the right neighborhood" for an aspiring lawyer. They took great delight together in remodeling the house, redesigning the garden, buying pieces of art, and showing off their house to their friends at parties. Sara took pleasure in creating a home, raising three daughters, joining "the right clubs," and supporting her husband's successful career.

In depicting her feelings for this house in a picture, she started with a vibrant swirl of red: "This is the creative energy involved in finding something aesthetically beautiful that my husband and I could both agree on and love—the anticipation of actually buying it and turning it into a home."

After the red swirl, Sara added areas of green and gray and then drew a ladder, a screen, and a vase. These all represented aspects of the remodeling process. The green represented the garden: "My husband and I worked together an entire afternoon digging a trench and planting six magnolia trees. They bloom fragrantly with large, lush flowers every spring."

The screen was an antique, a wedding present from her mother. The vase was a treasure she and her husband had purchased—a Tiffany vase, iridescent with lavenders and yellows. The ladder was built to connect to a sun deck on the roof: "I remember the first day I could climb up and get to the roof—there was the Golden Gate Bridge and the rooftops and chimney pots of all the houses around. We painted the ladder blue to try to match the color of the sky." A patch of blue-gray in her picture was the living-room carpet: "It was soft, soft wool, a sea-color . . . it changed colors . . . sometimes a pale blue, or a pale green, sometimes a light gray. You couldn't quite catch it. It had a silvery quality, and I loved it. To me it represented a lot of peacefulness."

This was clearly the period in Sara's life when it felt appropriate and comfortable to be a householder—to manifest an expression of both the ego-self and the social self in the form, location, decor, and social function of the home. And clearly she had enjoyed all of it. But there came a time when Sara no longer found such pleasure in her home.

"I came to realize that I had done all the things that were expected of me. I had gone to the right schools, married the right man, reared my children, supported my husband's career [starts laughing], given the right parties, worn the right clothes! There came a time when I wasn't satisfied with that anymore. There was nothing to look forward to. My creative itch left me restless. So I bought a notebook and started to write, thinking I would try to be a poet. But actually it became a journal of self-expression—what came out from inside me led to places, thoughts, and feelings I didn't know I had. I came to realize I was a social mess of other people's expectations. Even my husband and I were polite masks to one another. We would never reveal *that* part of ourselves. In the silence we pretended, but we weren't—at home."

This growing awareness became more and more painful to Sara. There was a time when she was afraid to continue writing, and noted in her journal: "I feel as if I'm packing my bags to take a long journey. But I feel afraid . . ."

Sara was about to embark on travels into the unknown, but these were not, as yet, actual physical journeys. Rather, like the meanings behind so many journey myths—*The Odyssey, The Divine Comedy,* the quest for the Holy Grail—her travels were inward, a frightening exploration of her own psyche in search of the elusive soul. First, she had to withdraw from the familiar; this she did by slowly withdrawing interest in the house and what it contained, from her husband, and, indeed, from all that had made up the previous sixteen years. All, that is, except her children and her plants—those elements in her milieu that she knew could not flourish without her love and nurturance.

Even the living room with its beautiful sea-color carpet became, for Sara, "dead space. There was a time in my life when the house satisfied all of my longings and yearnings. Then there was a completion. It wasn't heart-rending. It was as if I'd moved through the rooms which had served so well in the ways I wished for myself, and then I simply came to the end."

Sara moved out of the bedroom she shared with her husband into a small room of her own. It was the end of a role devoted entirely to that of nurturing others and the start of a period of intense self-examination. With generous support from her husband, Sara entered therapy and started practicing meditation. Her room became a very private "temple."

"It was a very nourishing space. There was a gold-colored carpet on the floor and lots of plants on the windowsills. There was a blue futon, where I could lie down at night. Everything was blue. There was virtually no furniture, just two white chests which blended into the wall. I had a picture of Yogananda, smiling . . . the smile came to mean the permission I was receiving from him and from my therapist to give expression to myself, to break out of the patterns and structure around me."

With the profound changes that Sara was going through, she began to yearn to assist others in similar situations. She entered a demanding program in a newly formed school of professional psychology "so that I could be a guide for other people on their journeys." For seven years, she worked and went to school. She and her husband separated, then divorced. Her daughters were growing up; the first left for college. Her husband remarried and created a home for their two daughters. Having withdrawn from much of the house to her own simple, small room, Sara now felt the need to divest herself of the whole house and its contents. She no longer had need of the ego-supports of the "right house," of its socially acceptable location, contents, and function. She felt an increasing urgency to embark on an actual, physical journey that would parallel her inward exploration.

Sara and her former husband agreed to sell the home they had shared. She determined to give away all the furnishings, then remodel and beautify the house before finally moving on. She notified all her friends and for one week stayed at home while people came and took what they wanted. I asked her if she could "speak" to all those possessions—so lovingly purchased and displayed—which she had given away. "Oh, well—all of my interest in you is finished. You were very beautiful and I was delighted with the joy you gave to people. For me, it was exactly like toys. You remember how you liked them, but then the interest is gone. There was no pain in giving them away. I had been anticipating it for some time. You know, evolution is something that happens slowly, so you have a chance to get used to it. It was like opening the door to the universe, stepping into a freedom where my extended world would begin to reflect what my inner experience had been for some years."

When the house was empty, Sara stayed on—sleeping on the floor in a sleeping bag—to supervise the remodeling and preparation of the house for tenants who would move in. She sanded floors, painted, swept, and cleaned up behind a team of workpeople. She had often dreamed of placing a stained-glass window in an opening on the stairs so that you would see the color on the carpet as you went upstairs. She commissioned a young artist to make a window. It was a view of Yosemite, with trees and rocks and water; Sara and her husband had enjoyed many backpacking trips in that setting. She considered it "a gift to the house. It was such a beautiful feeling of fulfillment to not only give everything away, but to make the house beautiful, better than it had ever been before, for the next people who would come to live there."

I asked Sara if she could speak *as* the house, how *it* felt about this leaving: "Well, I'm an old house. You weren't the first to live in me and you won't be the last. You were just another passerby. What's sixteen years in the life of seventy?"

Only one possession felt a little hard to part with. Significantly, it was a painting that seemed to exemplify Sara's break with convention. "It was this huge painting of a nude woman. It represented to me Mother Earth, and I used to drink at her tits every time I walked by. It was a beautiful color of blue and reminded me of Gertrude Stein. I had all these associations with Gertrude Stein as one of the people who gave herself permission—through her art—to let go. When I began to write, I let go of all the conventional rules of punctuation and grammar and got into the words and the spirit and let my own will express itself. It also represented a breaking with convention, because some people—like my mother—were horrified—'What will the girls think?'" She laughs.

As she prepared to leave the empty house, she took the possessions she wished to keep—family photos and personal records—and left them in a locked cubby in the basement. "It was dark and dank down there, but I had a toehold in the bowels of the house, in the guts. I feel a lot of gratitude to myself for making the changes. I nearly didn't make it—it took so much to extricate myself from all that former lifestyle. It was almost more effort than I thought I had the strength to make. But then I came to this time of greatest awakening; so much poured out of me, and all my defenses came down. I felt like an empty shell that was going to go on living until the body died. What tipped the balance in favor of this schism in my life was faith. I didn't even know I had it, but it was this faith in God that made the difference, that lead me through. It was painful. I didn't know where I was going."

I recorded this conversation when Sara had been "on the road" almost six years. She had thought, on leaving her house, that she would make a beeline for a yoga community in the mountains east of San Francisco, where she had visited many times and where she felt very comfortable. But, instead, on the day she vacated the house, she got on a plane for India, with her possessions in a backpack.

"Since that time, I have never been anywhere for very long. I have traveled in the United States, in Scotland, in India, in the USSR, in Europe. I come back every so often to be with my daughters—I want to be sensitive to their needs. They are well established in their father's house—in their new family."

As I listened to Sara's story—and especially as I listened to her account of giving away her possessions and leaving her house—I found myself becoming very uncomfortable. "How does it *feel* to have no particular physical place that you call home?" Her response was revealing, an expression of that striving to find the soul beyond the ego: "I have *every* particular physical place! I tell people 'the home just got larger'! There are all kinds of rooms in my home that I have never seen. The home, the anchor, is so strong inside me that it doesn't matter where the body is. One of my names is Gaia and that means 'the earth.' I very much embrace the earth. I have experienced myself to be a cell in the larger organism called Earth— this is Earth talking to you! It's recycled matter that has been around for a long time and, right now, it's got this particular name and form, that's all. It's accumulating a certain history which I need not identify with too much. That also has to be released because there is something much larger than we are—and if we identify with that person that we think we are, we miss the larger Self. It's a tremendous goal to attain. We overcome the fear of death; we attain our true immortality. And we experience incredible joy (laughing). I don't want to miss the joy!"

With these moving words, Sara was describing the evolution of the psyche from total identification with the ego to an understanding of oneself as *both* the discrete personality (ego) *and* the Self. As described by Jungian analyst Edward Edinger, "The ego is an incarnation, an entity, which participates in the vicissitudes of time, space, and causality. The Self, as the center of the archetypal psyche, is in another world beyond consciousness and its particularizing mode of experience. The ego is the center of subjective identity; the Self, the center of objective identity."[9]

The urge toward individuation does not necessarily connote some kind of removed "sainthood." For many people, it leads from inner, personal concerns to those of the environment, the planet, and of serving society. But first, it seems essential that we shed those trappings of ego-self and social self that often hide—most of all from ourselves—our true nature. As Thomas Moore commented insightfully, "We could all use an emptying out of identity every now and then. Considering who we are not, we may find the surprising revelation of who we are."[10]

Sara seemed to follow this pattern. She did not become some kind of permanent hermit-wanderer in the wilderness. When I spoke with her six years after our first meeting, she was entering the area of service to others through politics. She had assisted in the organization of a peace conference, she had worked on the campaign of Barbara Marx-Hubbard for vice-president, and she had volunteered for a congress entitled "Planetary Initiative for the World We Choose." A few years after this, she relocated to the East Coast and embarked on a career as a psychoanalyst.

Coming Home to the Self: David's Room in a Commune

Contact with our higher Self or soul can take many forms and be facilitated by many different environments. Sara passed through—and experienced her personal identity in—many dwellings before she felt the need to explore her *inner* experience of the self. In the case of David, the process started at a much younger age.

David was in his late twenties when I talked with him. He was a freelance computer programmer and lived in a large old house in Oakland in a neighborhood of middle-class homes on tree-lined streets. The house was a commune; six people each had a private bedroom-sitting room while they shared a large sitting room, kitchen, and bathroom. David's room was at the front of the house, with large sunny windows looking out to a palm tree. Half of the room was taken up by a bed raised on a wooden loft structure, underneath which was a cozy space with bright curtains, hanging batiks, and a stained-glass lamp; in front of it was a low table with books and a collection of shells.

When I asked David to put down in a picture his feelings about this home, he drew an image of concentric circles in bright primary colors with four yellow "tongues" leading out from the center. It was totally symmetrical; at the very center was a small blue dot. He described the red and yellow circles as the "warm, fuzzy nest" of the house; the layers of brown, green, and blue around it as layers of the outside world . . . "as I go farther away, it's less and less appealing."

I asked about the center of the concentric image, where a red circle seemed more emphasized, with a blue dot at its center. "That represents the coolness of solitude, of meditation, peace. The house seems to me in general to be warm. My relationships with the people in the house are warm. And my room is painted in warm colors. The whole thing is kind of warm and alive and moving. But a

very necessary part of that is that at the very center is solitude and quiet and peace and coolness. It's a center in a psychological sense, being very deep within myself and then going very, very far out into the world and then coming back and regenerating. So it's a center in both a physical sense and also in a psychological sense. When I come back here I feel a warmth in my chest."

I asked David to close his eyes and imagine himself flowing into that picture and *becoming* it, and to start saying whatever came to mind: "I'm David's house. I'm large. I'm

David's room in an urban commune.

expanding. I'm yellow and brown. I'm safe. I'm a peaceful and calm center. I'm the center of the universe."

Like others fortunate to have had a relatively stable childhood, David had experienced as a child some sense of the peace and wholeness he now felt in his adult home. In his childhood in Bolinas, California, it was an experience generated by being outdoors on wooded slopes with an expansive view of the Pacific Ocean. Here, he felt a sense of letting go, of exhilaration and awe. As an adult he has, as it were, transferred this experience indoors. He uses similar words to describe similar feelings, this time generated during meditation in his small, enclosed, comfortable room in Oakland.

The concentric circular image divided into four is a classic example of a mandala—a symbolic image of the Self. In expressing his feelings about his dwelling, David drew, unconsciously, an ancient symbol for the central source of life energy, wholeness, totality, the axis of the universe.

One of the earliest and most powerful mandala images in western culture is the Garden of Eden, often depicted as a circular enclosure with four rivers flowing from it, and the Tree of Life at its center. Edward Edinger describes it as "an image of the Self . . . representing the ego's original oneness with nature and deity. It is the initial, unconscious, original state of being. . . . It is paradisal because consciousness has not yet appeared and hence there is no conflict. The ego is contained in the womb of the Self."[11]

With the development of consciousness/ego, we become separated from this original state of oneness. We yearn to return—this time conscious of *both* the ego (individual personality) *and* the Self (transpersonal totality). David was a young man who quite early in life was striving toward this state of individuation. His ego-self had found partial expression in his work, and partial expression in the personal creation and decoration of his room.

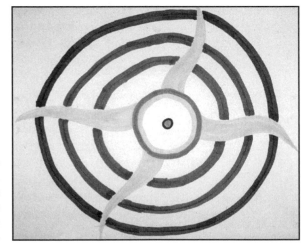

David's depiction of his feelings about his room.

"When I first moved in, it very much felt like creating a space around me, making it part of me, putting myself into it, expanding myself into it. All the little things to be done—light bulbs to be put in, cleaning to be done, things to be built and changed and put away and arranged, shelves to be built, just all the things that go with living here— all those things felt like energy being

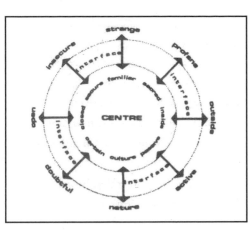

Our homes feel familiar, sacred, and secure in contrast to what is outside, what is "not home."

(Diagram by Kim Dovey.)

put into the house that comes back to me. One of the strangest things when I moved here was a feeling that I'd finally come home, that there was no lease going to run out, there was no plan to move. There was a kind of letting go about the necessity of getting everything fixed just right."

In the creation and maintenance of his small room, David has found a perfect metaphor to express himself, to place around him the colors, materials, objects, and images that have salience in his life. Within that nurturing space, he was able to meditate, and through that practice began to experience the Self beyond the ego. Thus the physical dwelling was a necessary locale of calm and peace from/through which to experience the altered state of consciousness which some describe as dissolving the bounds of ego and merging with a greater wholeness or universal interconnectedness. Some people may seek such an experience through formal religious ritual in a church or temple. Others seek it through spending time in the wilderness. For David, his room took on even greater salience in his life, as it was both his living space and his temple, his place of contact with the infinite. Significantly, on one of its walls he had pinned up the familiar quotation from T. S. Eliot:

> *We shall not cease from exploration*
> *And the end of all our exploring*
> *Will be to arrive where we started*
> *And know the place for the first time.*[12]

Living in the Flow: Beverly's Dome in the Forest

Finally, let us look at the experience of Beverly, an artist in her thirties who, when I met her, shone with a kind of inner radiance which seemed to speak of soul. At the time of our conversation, Beverly was living with her lover, Tom, and his teenaged daughter in a dome they had built for themselves near the northern California coastal town of Mendocino. It was nestled in the forest, "like a mushroom," partly for aesthetic reasons and partly to avoid the prying eyes of local building inspectors who were always on the lookout for structures that didn't meet local codes. I had met Beverly in a women's group in Berkeley, where she came once a week to get a "shot of the city" and to work on her relationship with Tom in a warm and supportive environment.

Throughout our talk, I was struck by a recurring theme of flow and movement in Beverly's words. Asked why she had been drawn to create a round house, she spoke of "the energy that flows up into the center of the space and then comes back down again. You don't lose energy in the corners; everything just keeps revolving."

The original plan had been to divide the dome into separate rooms. But Beverly soon realized she didn't want "any restrictions on the space. I don't want the circle broken."

I asked her if she would speak *as* her house, to articulate what the dome would say if it had a voice. Without hesitation, she began: "There simply is no separation between me and everything that surrounds me. My windows look out in every direction. I am a continuation of what exists outside of me—a reflection of the sky, the trees, the animals. Mostly I reflect the *colors* that are outside—the green, the blue, and brown. There's nowhere to get stuck in here; everything is round and circular . . . [sighs, then laughs] I just love imagining that I *am* this house! I just love this roundness. It's the best part of the house. It's the best part of me! . . . Until about two years ago, I saw myself as a few inches of superperson Beverly— what the world sees—and inside, just a gaping hole. But now, I sense a more solid mass inside—it's smaller, but it's solid! And it's definitely circular. So to be in this house is also to have an absolute sense of myself."

Another theme that recurred in Beverly's words was that of nonattachment or lack of possessiveness. The flow that she felt within her house and between her house and its setting seemed to mirror the flow of feeling that she felt about the land and her own creative activity—making beautiful stained-glass windows. "I don't feel that land can really be owned. Land is something that is simply enjoyed and used by everyone. So I don't feel any deep attachment to

Beverly in her dome in the forest.

it. I feel the protection of the land is my responsibility, but not just this twelve acres. When we have finished this house, I can see leaving it; I feel it is some kind of transition for me. I feel about it the way I feel about windows I have made: They are beautiful things, and if someone else wants them, that's great because I created them. It's the creation that's most important, not the living in it."

In describing the process of making a window, the image of *flow* again surfaced. It was clear that this basic mode of relating—to house, to land, to forest, to creative work—permeated her being.

"My stained glass has really changed since my first window. My feeling now is that if I can just stop thinking about doing it and just *do* it, I become some kind of creative channel and the window becomes exquisite. I don't know where that energy is coming from. I don't see it as some little knot inside me that all of a sudden is becoming expressed. I feel that some kind of energy is flowing through me and *becoming* that window."

Everything in her life had not always been so flowing, so apparently easy. She talked of earlier years with Tom, when they lived in a standard suburban house near San Francisco, and Tom's daughter joined them. There had been a lot of tension. Tom built an extra floor on the house for his daughter. He and Beverly had separate rooms. The three of them spent a lot of time apart—in the same structure, but apart, with doors closed. Now, if a problem or tension emerges in the dome house, she and Tom deal with it immediately while walking in circles round and round inside the house, circling the stove, "the heart of the house."

I asked her what seemed the obvious question: "Do you think this space helped you relate in a different way, or were you relating in a different way and therefore you made this house?"

"I don't know what came first," she replied. "Perhaps a little of both—the environment mirroring who we are, and in turn assisting us to evolve into who we want to be. By the time we moved up here, we were starting to not avoid things, not going into our separate rooms and shutting the doors."

Beverly's mushroom house in the forest thus became a symbol for a new way of relating, and its very form nurtured the relationship and Beverly's evolving sense of self. Beverly had chosen to project an evolving self-image onto a particular building-type, one that, in her case, personifies how she sees herself—solid, round, centered, and yet flowing. It is a house where "everything is a continuation of everything else."

In listening to Beverly and reflecting later on her words and images, I was reminded of the work of French psychoanalyst Olivier Marc in which he discusses how early man took possession of space in an unconscious imitation of the creation of the universe: "It is through self-expression that man [sic] sets out on the road back to unity. It is a road which passes through the exterior to reach interior unity. By building his circle-house, man expresses his connection with the cosmos, and the symbol, which he thus created reminded him that the unity existed inside himself, since he was able to produce its image." [13]

Although most of us might not choose, as Beverly did, to move into a dome in the forest, there *are* ways in which we all can modify or nurture aspects of our current environment in order to support our personal growth. No particular style of being is more "correct." We each have to find the balance that feels right and comfortable for us at the stage of development in which we find ourselves.

Home is not only a literal place but also a place of deep contentment in the innermost temple of the soul. *Home is where the heart is* runs the familiar saying. It has, I think, two levels of meaning. Heart or love is our connection to family and friends, to places and persons familiar and nurturing. But heart is also our innermost being, our soul. In this latter sense, *home is where the heart is* refers to that way of being, that place, that activity in which we are most fully and deeply ourselves. For Pat, it was her tree house and the desert. For Anita, it was her state of being when jogging or meditating. For Sara, it was writing in her journal and wandering the earth. For Beverly, it was living in a round house and pursuing her calling as a stained-glass artist. Each of them, in her own way, had come home to herself.

What I have learned from the many profound, often soul-searching dialogues recounted in this book is that the human spirit is constantly in process, constantly on a journey of discovery. Every culture has myths of the hero's or heroine's journey, of leaving the familiar home and of exploring fearful, sometimes dangerous dimensions of life. Like Odysseus, we all—on our own individual paths—take a journey. And like his son, Telemachus, and his wife, Penelope, we all have portions of our psyche that long for the return of the father/husband/adventurous spirit so that life can be restored in the image of the perfect family and home. Without the journey, there may be stagnation, frustration, disempowerment. Thus, like it or not, we all have to leave home to find ourselves. However, the self we are seeking is not literally "out there" somewhere in some remote geographic location; it is always within, seeking to reveal itself through life experiences, both mundane and dramatic. The paradox is that while our latent higher Self or soul is always present as seed or dream, we still need to go on a journey—geographically and psychologically—to allow it to flower. We are each and every one of us always/never leaving home. To leave it is to grow through adventure, risk taking, danger, excitement; to return is to find stability and strength at the still center of our being. Leaving home—and returning—is something we do every day and throughout our lives. The home is the pivot point of these journeys—the beginning and the end. To never leave home is to avoid risks, to refuse to grow. To always leave home is to reject some aspect of self that resides there and which needs to be embraced. As we stumble toward maturity, we learn that both are necessary—leaving and staying, security and danger, stillness and movement, at home and away. The secret is to find the balance and to recognize when to leave and when to stay. Each stage of our life, each passage of our growth, will reveal what is right for us.

Sometimes it is scary to make this journey to the Self. To be fully true to ourselves may mean making changes in our lives. And for many of us, change is problematic, anxiety-provoking. But through change—whether self-consciously willed or thrust upon us—we restructure our lives and our psyches; we start to see other possibilities, new directions for our lives. It takes courage, humor, self-reflection, time, and patience. We can ignore the call of the soul and still live a fulfilling life, or we can heed its wisdom and experience times of deep joy and contentment.

While we go through that process, home remains, whether in our hearts or in reality, the place of security and nurturance necessary for our psyche. It remains the envelope into which we retreat for privacy and intimacy, which reflects who we are as individuals and as members of society; *that* is essential for our well-being. But it may not be enough. The garden may beckon us also, or the wilderness, the ocean, the landscape, wildlife. We must heed that call too, for deep within it, the soul is asking for attention. Home-base and journey, home and away, inside and outside—we all need to experience and embrace this dialectic of life's polarities to be fully ourselves, to be deeply integrated in the rich complexity of who we are meant to be. As Thomas Merton so beautifully expressed it, we need sometimes to escape the enveloping peace of home to experience the deep contentment that is our birthright: "My chief joy is to escape to the attic of the garden house and the little broken window that looks out over the valley. There in the silence I love the green grass. The tortured gestures of the apple trees have become part of my prayer. . . . So much do I love this solitude that when I walk out along the road to the old barns that stand alone far from the new buildings, delight begins to overpower me from head to foot and peace smiles even in the marrow of my bones."[14]

BEYOND THE HOUSE-AS-EGO: EXERCISES YOU CAN DO YOURSELF

Soul Nurturance at Home

How can we nurture our souls within the homes we have made for ourselves? For myself, it means allowing a place and time for reflection, for my inner imagination to be set free. Sitting alone by a fire, feeling the warmth, watching the flames darting, the embers glowing, the gift of tree being slowly transformed into light—that is a time and place for soul. Sitting under an avocado tree in my garden, my eyes grazing over ferns and azaleas, ocean-tossed pebbles and a small statue of Buddha; picking raspberries, planting winter lettuce, placing bulbs in the damp November soil, picking spring flowers for the dining table. I find that my garden is preeminently a place for my soul—a place that has nothing to do with ego-projection or social standing, but everything to do with a yearning to acknowledge connectedness with all matter, with the *anima mundi,* the soul of the world.

Take Time to Do What Brings You Delight

What can you do to assist yourself in nurturing your soul in your daily life, in the home where you live? One way to nurture your soul is to be aware of what brings you peace and a centeredness in your daily activities. It may be something as mundane as dusting the furniture: feeling the soft fabric in your hands, touching the rocking chair, the polished wood of an antique chest. If that's what brings you pleasure and a time of quiet reflection, keep doing it your way and resist the pleas of TV ads or family members to buy a noisy "DustBuster." For one man I interviewed in his rather austere and colorless converted-factory home, it was the ritual of watering and misting his many plants early each morning before starting work. For another man, it was feeding a family of ducks that had taken up residence on the deck of his houseboat-home. For writer and poet May Sarton, it was the arranging of flowers cut from her garden. For the contemplative monk and writer Thomas Merton, it was many of the rituals of simple daily living at the Abbey of Gethsemane in Kentucky, which included walks in nature and the art of photography. He recognized that contemplative time need not be sought in special places or at special times. "Solitude is not found so much by looking outside the boundaries of your own dwelling, as by staying within. Solitude is a deepening of the present, and unless you look for it in the present you will never find it."[15]

Whatever you are doing—chopping carrots, raking leaves, sweeping the floor—be present in the moment, fully aware of what you are doing. Gestalt therapist Fritz Perls once said: "Anxiety is the gap between the 'now' and the 'then.'" The more we are truly present in whatever we do, the less we concern ourselves with "what if . . ." and the more we nurture the soul. Vietnamese Zen master Thich Nhat Hanh, now living and teaching in the West, suggests simple breathing and awareness exercises to bring us into the present moment, however mundane an activity. Here is what he has to say about washing dishes:

"To my mind, the idea that doing dishes is unpleasant can occur only when you aren't doing them. Once you are standing in front of the sink with your sleeves rolled up and your hands in the warm water, it is really quite pleasant. I enjoy taking my time with each dish, being fully aware of the dish, the water, and each movement of my hands. . . .The dishes themselves and the fact that I am here washing them are miracles! . . . I must confess it takes me a bit longer to do the dishes, but I live fully in every moment and I am happy. Washing the dishes is at the same time a means and an end—that is, not only do we do the dishes in order to have clean dishes, we also do the dishes just to do the dishes, to live fully in each moment while washing them."[16]

If you are not sure what it is that brings you delight, notice what you observe—that is who you are. If you pay close attention to your houseplants and ignore the cobwebs catching dust in the corner of the ceiling, don't judge yourself, just notice it. If you keep looking at one picture in your house and ignoring the others, notice it. When the rooms dedicated to the body's needs—kitchen, bathroom—are kept ordered and beautiful, but the room where you file your papers and work is a mess, could you be telling yourself something? If the housework seems a chore but gardening is a joy, pay close attention. Rather than chastise yourself for ignoring the house, ask yourself: What *is* this joy I feel in the garden? Be aware of your state of mind when you are there; spend *more* time in the garden! What you pay attention to is who you are—and who you are yearning to be more fully.

In the short story "The Yellow Wallpaper" by Charlotte Perkins Gilman, a married woman yearned to write; she took her notebook everywhere with her, noting down things she saw, feelings she had. But this was in the patriarchal era at the turn of the century, when women were supposed to devote themselves only to husband and family. Her husband—ironically, a doctor—diagnosed her as neurotic, took her away to the country, put her on a strict regimen of rest, exercise, and eating and forbade her to write. When she did, surreptitiously, he took the notebook away. In the end she went mad.[17]

We live in a different era. After childhood, there is not usually another person telling us what to do—or what not to do. But most of us carry around an equally punitive internal judge: "You *ought* to clean up the front room." "You *ought* to like this wonderful home your husband has worked hard to provide." "You *ought* not to fritter away time staring into the fire when there are papers from the office that need to be seen to."

Yes, the day-to-day chores need to be accomplished, but it is critically important to notice what *is* a chore—and do it as efficiently and painlessly as possible—and what is a delight. Can we not give ourselves the gift of devoting as much time as possible to whatever it is that brings us happiness? When we do what delights us, we feel whole, we feel centered, we radiate. Those around us see and feel the difference. Be aware of what brings you delight in and around your home—and go do it!

Another way of recognizing the call of your soul is to be aware and open to any particular object or picture that captures your attention and which pulls you into its being. Place it where you can see it every day. It may be something you found—a stone, a pine cone, a shell—or something you were given, or a picture or photograph you bought. Several years ago, I bought a card for my mother—a color photograph of a springtime scene in an English wood, a narrow path winding its way amid a profusion of bluebells. It looked remarkably like a place of my childhood. I never sent it to my mother. I wedged it into the corner of a mirror I look at every day in my bedroom. I am not sure what it means—perhaps it does not "mean" anything. All I know is that I gain immeasurable pleasure from looking at it. I love to hike through woodlands such as that, with everything I need on my back, following a narrow trail that seems to beckon me forward. Perhaps it is urging me to greater freedom.

A Place for the Soul

Most of us find it hard to make time in our lives to become deliberately self-reflective. We've heard about the value of relaxation or meditation, but haven't yet fit it into our lives. One way we can assist ourselves is by creating a special *place* in our home that is designated for quiet meditation or contemplation. You can think of it as your sanctuary, your personal sacred space. Set up a small table and arrange on it a special selection of objects that seemed to "speak" to you when you picked them up—a shell, a rock, a pine cone, some pebbles, a piece of driftwood. Perhaps you'll want to add a small vase of flowers, a candle, and some incense. You could think of this as your personal altar, or if this word jars you, use a different term—sacred table, meditation corner. Whatever its name, this is a place just for you. And whether you spend five minutes there each day or an hour, it is a place for you just to sit and to be; no agenda other than being quietly by yourself, breathing deeply, being conscious of images and feelings that arise, and then letting them go.

Meditation is to be fully present in the moment. To assist in stilling the mind, imagine that your thoughts are like leaves floating by on a clear stream of water; you notice them and they float away, then another comes and floats on downstream. By practicing this simple—though admittedly difficult—exercise, you are quieting the ego-self and allowing your transpersonal Self or soul to receive air and nurturance. The ego is threatened by silence, hence the proclivity of the mind to keep up a ceaseless chatter, even when not actually engaged in conversation with another person. In periods of silence—both inner and outer—the soul starts to reveal itself.

The purpose of the assemblage of found objects in your sacred space is as a mnemonic device to remind you of your connection to the world beyond material possessions, however important and comforting the latter may be. It is a reminder each day that you are more than this personal or social identity living in this particular house. You are both more—and less. You are connected to all living and nonliving matter and, in that sense, you are simultaneously as insignificant as a molecule and as all-encompassing as a galaxy. *And* you are also the personal ego-self who chose and furnished this dwelling-place.

Reflecting on her Catholic upbringing, Patricia Hampl recognized that its greatest gift was the nurturing of contemplation. "Observing it all, noting it, seeing it—this was the real point not only of literature but of Life itself. Life, fundamentally, was neither active nor passive. It was contemplative. Pondering was the highest vocation . . . a special kind of thinking. It was not done in the mind, that chilly place, but in the heart, where the real mystery of intelligence—intuition rather than thought—lay catlike and feminine, ready to pounce. Life was a scurrying mouse, amusing in its way but ultimately hapless before the fixed bead of the contemplative gaze."[18]

Most of us need reminders to bring us back from our usual state of busyness, anxiety, stress, and tiredness, to a condition of "contemplative gaze." Your meditation corner or altar can be just such a reminder.

Engage in a Dialogue with the Environment

Part of a deep sadness we carry with us as a species is the barely conscious loss of a loving relationship with the world around us. While we may be quite aware of a lack of community in our lives, we are less conscious of how much we grieve at some deep level for that close connection with nature we once experienced in an earlier period of our history, or, perhaps, in our own personal childhoods. In nature, we encounter not noiselessness—for there are always the sounds of birds, wind, water, footsteps—but wordlessness. In outdoor natural places, lacking words, our own silence may have the freedom to be heard. One way to reconnect with your soul-level is to spend time alone in an outdoor place; give yourself time to settle into that environment; and, if it feels comfortable, engage in a dialogue with some feature of that place that seems to beckon you. It doesn't necessarily entail a trip to the wilderness. Sitting in an urban park during your lunch hour from the office, you may feel yourself attracted to a flowering tree, a patch of sunlight, a rock. No one need know what you are doing! Ask this rock or tree what it has to tell you; try not to censor yourself or judge what happens. Because I enjoy writing, I usually write down this dialogue in my journal—not stopping to bother about punctuation, spelling, or making sense. In fact, it often helps to silence the inner judge or critic by writing nonstop, not taking pen off paper until you feel done. This is not a paper to be graded! It is just for you, and you may be amazed at what you put down.

Be Conscious of Listening

In ancient Chinese mythology, it is said that the eye is young, male, rational, and analytic whereas the ear is old, female, spiritual, and receptive. What we see often triggers thought, associations, memories, connections. But what we hear—especially in the form of music or natural sounds—may, if we let it flow over and through us, activate some level of our soul. The art of soft listening draws on the feminine side of our psyche, regardless of whether we are biologically men or women. It is said that before birth, the average fetus hears twenty-six million heartbeats; listening is the first sense to develop before we are born and the last to leave us before we die.

Take time—in your house or garden or in a favorite outdoor place—to fully *listen*. If you find yourself, unexpectedly, paying attention to a bird singing, or music on the radio, stop and fully listen. Don't try to figure out what it means; this isn't a time for rational, linear thinking. Let it flow through you—and move on. The soul speaks quietly and slowly; once it has your ear, it will return. As an old Indonesian saying puts it, "The eye is the mirror—but the ear is the gate—to the soul."

Imagining a Home for the Soul

An interesting way of contacting that part of yourself we call soul or spirit is to imagine a fantasy place where you would feel totally at ease, completely at home. This is not your ideal neighborhood or house—not a place for day-to-day family living. Rather, this is a place where you'd be happy to be alone, where you would feel inspired, nurtured, stimulated—in short, alive!

One way to contact this home for the soul is to make yourself very comfortable, perhaps in your favorite chair or hammock, close your eyes, and allow yourself to breathe very deeply. When you've exhaled all the air in your lungs, pause for one or two seconds before you inhale again. When you are feeling very relaxed, ask yourself the question: What would a home for my soul be like? Let your imagination run wild! Sometimes we treat our imagination like an unruly child—something to be reined in, to be disciplined. But our imagination is one pathway to the soul. Give it permission to create a wonderful fantasy setting just for you. Explore it in your mind's eye, walk through it, touch it, and smell it. Perhaps you will meet someone there. If you do, ask them what they have to tell you. Or, if there is a big question facing you in life right now, ask their advice.

When you have spent enough time exploring this place in your imagination, use some crayons or felt-tipped pens and draw it. Maybe it will turn out as a picture, maybe a map or plan with words attached. Do whatever feels right for *you*—this is not an art class! As Carl Jung once wrote, "The hands will often reveal the mystery that the intellect has struggled with in vain."

Your soul-place may contain images or echoes of real places, or it may be a total fantasy, like the setting for a fairy tale. In either case, try not to figure out why it is this way or that; the analytical or rational part of your brain probably has plenty of exercise in other segments of your life. Your imagination is a rich source of intuitive wisdom rather than learned knowledge. It is not irrational, but rather arational. If nothing much happens the first time you try this exercise, don't give up! Try again in a few days. If your imagination has had little exercise since childhood, it may take a while for you to access it. Like the muscles we need for various sports, the frame of mind for imaginative daydreaming needs to be exercised and fine-tuned. If you have small children or grandchildren, try making up stories for them—a wonderful way to exercise your imagination and communicate at the same time. If a real-life environment is especially supportive of daydreaming—for me it is the ocean or a quiet garden setting—spend time there, and take your journal, notebook, and crayons with you. When we are in a contemplative state of mind, we are most deeply and truly ourselves—not who we think we ought to be, not who our parents expected us to be, not what our education trained us to be. The important point is to give yourself time and be patient. Eventually, an image, a feeling, a sensation will emerge. Explore it, get to know it, fix it in words or an image, and, if you like, engage it in dialogue, for it undoubtedly has something to tell you.

As Buddha taught, "There is only one time when it is essential to awaken. That time is now."[19]

Chapter One: House as a Mirror of Self

1. William Goyen, *The House of Breath* (New York: Person Books, 1947), p. 42.
2. Carl Jung, quoted and paraphrased by Ralph Metzner in *Opening to Inner Light* (Los Angeles: Jeremy P. Tarcher, Inc., 1986), p. 5.

Chapter Two: The Special Places of Childhood

1. Janet Frame, *Living in the Maniototo* (London: The Women's Press, 1982), p. 222.
2. David Malouf, *12 Edmondstone Street* (Ringwood, Victoria, Australia: Penguin Books, Ltd., 1986), pp. 8-9.
3. Edward Edinger, *Ego and Archetype* (New York: Penguin Books, 1972), p. 295.
4. Carl Jung, *Memories, Dreams, Reflections* (London: Fontana Library, 1969), pp. 48-9.
5. Richard R. Merrifield, *Monadnock Journal*, p. 60.
6. Helena Worthen, "How Does Your Garden Grow?" *Landscape*, vol. 19, no. 3, May 1975.
7. Carl Jung, *op. cit.*, pp. 182-3.
8. *Ibid.*, p. 184.
9. Louise Bogan and Ruth Limmer, *Journey Around My Room: The Autobiography of Louise Bogan: A Mosaic* (New York: Penguin Books, 1981), p. 30.
10. Emilio Ambasz, *The Architecture of Luis Barragan* (New York: Museum of Modern Art, 1976), p. 77.
11. Stuart Miller, "Designing the Home for Children," *Children's Environments Quarterly*, vol. 3, no. 1 (Spring 1986), pp. 55-62.

Chapter Three: Growing Up: Self-Expression in the Homes of Adulthood

1. Olivier Marc, *The Psychology of the House* (London: Thames and Hudson, 1977), p. 80.
2. Carl Jung, *op. cit.*, p. 250.
3. *Ibid.*, pp. 251-2.
4. E. Prelinger, "Extension and Structure of the Self," *Journal of Psychology* 47 (1959), pp. 13-23.

5. Janet Frame, *Scented Gardens for the Blind* (London: The Women's Press, 1964), p. 215.

6. George Herbert Mead, *Mind, Self, and Society: From the Standpoint of a Social Behaviorist* (Chicago: University of Chicago Press, 1934).

7. Witold Rybczynski, *Home: A Short History of an Idea* (New York: Viking, 1986), p. 17.

8. Carl Jung, *op. cit.*, p. 228.

9. William James, *The Principles of Psychology*, vol. 1 (New York: Henry Holt, 1890), p. 115.

10. Rick Talcott, "Three Analogies" in Patricia Adler (ed.) et al. *Fire in the Hills: A Collective Remembrance* (Berkeley, CA.: Adler, 1992), p. 131.

11. F. Baekland, "Psychological Aspects of Art Collections," *Psychiatry* 44 (1981), p. 46.

12. G. McCracken, *Culture and Consumption: New Approaches to the Symbolic Character of Consumer Goods and Activities* (Bloomington: Indiana University Press, 1988).

13. May Sarton, *I Knew a Phoenix* (New York: Rinehart, 1959), p. 65.

14. *Ibid.*, pp. 80-81.

15. Carolyn Verheyen, "The Therapeutic Function of the Home and Personal Objects" (M.A. thesis in Environmental Psychology, San Francisco State University, 1990).

Chapter Four: Always or Never Leaving Home

1. Joan Colebrook, *A House of Trees: Memoirs of an Australian Girlhood* (London: Penguin Books, 1988), p. 190.

2. Donald Winnicott, *The Child and the Outside World* (New York: Basic Books, 1957).

3. Michael Balint, "Friendly Expanses—Horrid Empty Spaces," *The International Journal of Psychoanalysis*, vol. 36, part 4/5 (1955), p. 228.

4. *Ibid.*, p. 235.

5. Nancy Mairs, *Remembering the Bone House: An Erotics of Place and Space* (New York: Harper & Row, 1989), p. 77.

6. David Seamon, *The Geography of the Lifeworld* (New York: St. Martin's Press, 1979).

Chapter Five: Becoming More Fully Ourselves: Evolving Self-Image as Reflected in Our Homes

1. Janet Frame, *op. cit.*, p. 155.

2. Anaïs Nin, *The Diary of Anaïs Nin* (New York: Swallow Press, 1969).

3. Kamo no Chomei, "Record of a Ten-Foot-Square Hut," trans. by Burton Watson, in *Four Huts: Asian Writings on the Simple Life* (Boston: Shambhala, 1994), pp. 60-106.

4. Thomas S. Moore, *Care of the Soul* (New York: Harper Collins, 1992), p. 186.

Chapter Six: Becoming Partners:
Power Struggles in Making a Home Together

1. Jill Ker Conway, *The Road from Coorain* (New York: Vintage Books, 1990), pp. 24-5.
2. Louise Mozingo, *Women and Downtown Open Space* (M.L.A. thesis, University of California, Berkeley, 1984).
3. Chuan-Sheng Chiao, "Teenage Hang-Out Places," (unpublished student term paper, University of California, Berkeley, Fall 1985).
4. E. Mackintosh, R. Rosen, and W. Wentworth, *The Attitudes and Experiences of the Middle Income Family in an Urban High-Rise Complex and in the Suburbs* (New York: Center for Human Environments, City University of New York, Graduate Center, 1977).
5. Susan Saegert, "Masculine Cities and Feminine Suburbs: Polarized Ideas, Contradictory Realities," *Signs: Journal of Women in Culture and Society*, vol. 5, no. 3 (1980), suppl., pp. S96-S111.

Chapter Seven: Living and Working: Territory, Control,
and Privacy at Home

1. Virginia Woolf, *A Room of One's Own* (New York: Harvest/HBJ Book, Harcourt Brace Jovanovich, Inc., 1961), p. 91.
2. Thomas Merton, *New Seeds of Contemplation* (New York: New Directions, 1961).
3. Glenn Robert Lym, *A Psychology of Building: How We Shape and Experience Our Structured Spaces* (Englewood Cliffs, NJ: Prentice Hall, Inc., 1980), p. 10.
4. *Ibid.,* p. 21.
5. *Ibid.,* pp. 108-9.
6. Rachel Sebba and Arza Churchman, "The Uniqueness of Home," *Architecture and Behavior,* vol. 3, no. 1 (1986), pp. 7-24.
7. Sherry Ahrentzen, "A Place of Peace, Prospect and . . . a P.C.: The Home as Office," *The Journal of Architectural and Planning Research*, vol. 6, no. 4 (Winter 1989), pp. 271-88.
8. Penny Gurstein, *The Electronic Cottage: Implications for the Meaning of the Home.* Paper presented at a symposium on "The Use and Meaning of Home and Neighborhood," Alvkarleby, Sweden, September 1989.
9. Sherry Ahrentzen, *op. cit.,* p. 282.
10. *Ibid.*
11. *Ibid.*
12. *Ibid.*
13. Penny Gurstein, *op. cit.,* p. 13.

Chapter Eight: Where to Live? Self-Image and Location

1. Kimberly Dovey, "Home and Homelessness" in *Home Environments, Human Behavior and Environment, Advances in Theory and Research,* Irwin Altman and Carol M. Werner, eds. (New York: Plenum Press, 1985), p. 46.

2. Roberta A. Feldman, *Settlement Identity and the Life Course.* Paper presented at the international workshop, "The Home Environment: Physical Space and Psychological Processes," Instituto di Psicología of Italian National Research Council, Cortona, Italy, May 1991, pp. 4-5.

3. H. S. Maas and J. M. Kuper, *From Thirty to Seventy* (San Francisco: Jossey-Bass, 1974).

4. E. Mackintosh, et al., *op. cit.*

5. Susan Saegert, *op. cit,* p. S104.

6. E. Mackintosh, et al., *op. cit.*

7. E. Mackintosh, et al., *op. cit.*

8. Sylvia Fava, "Women's Place in the New Suburbia" in Gerda Wekerle, Rebecca Peterson, and David Morley (eds.), *New Space for Women* (Boulder, CO: Westview Press, 1980).

9. Susan Saegert, *op. cit.*, p. S105.

10. William Michelson, "The Place of Time in Longitudinal Evaluation of Spatial Structures by Women," University of Toronto Center for Urban and Community Studies, research paper no. 81 (Toronto, 1973).

11. Susan Saegert, *op. cit.*, p. S110.

12. Deborah Tannen, *You Just Don't Understand: Women and Men in Conversation* (New York: Ballantine, 1991).

13. Roberta Feldman, *op. cit.*, p. 17.

14. James S. Duncan Jr., "Landscape Taste as a Symbol of Group Identity," *Geographical Review* (July 1973), p. 355.

15. *Ibid.*, p. 343.

16. *Ibid.*, p. 344.

17. Sydney Brower, *The Function of the Near-Home Spaces.* Paper presented at the international workshop, "The Home Environment: Physical Space and Psychological Processes," Instituto di Psicología of Italian National Research Council, Cortona, Italy, May 1991, pp. 7-8.

18. *Ibid.*, pp. 7-8.

19. *Ibid.*, p. 15.

Chapter Nine: The Lost House: Disruptions in the Bonding with Home

1. E. M. Forster, *Howard's End* (New York: Vintage Books, 1994), p. 268.

2. U.S. National Census Data.

3. Katherine Anthony, "Breaking Up Is Hard to Do: The Meaning of Home to Parents and Children of Divorce." Paper presented at a symposium on "The Use and Meaning of Home and Neighborhood," Alvkarleby, Sweden, September 1989.

4. Anderson-Kweif, 1982, cited in Katherine Anthony, *op. cit.*

5. Cited in the San Francisco *Chronicle.*

6. Jeremy Larner, "Deal with It" in Patricia Adler et al. (eds.), *op. cit.,* pp. 30-33.

7. Tobie Helene Shapiro, "Fire Journal" in *Ibid.,* pp. 118-20.

8. Nancy A. Pietrafesa, "Song" in *Ibid.,* p. 57.

9. Marc Fried, "Grieving for a Lost Home" in L. J. Duhl (ed.), *The Urban Condition* (New York: Basic Books, 1963), pp. 151-71.

10. Nancy Mairs, *op. cit.,* p. 35.

11. Tadashi Toyama, *Identity and Milieu: A Study of Relocation Focusing on Reciprocal Changes in Elderly People and Their Environment* (Stockholm, Sweden: Department for Building Function Analysis, The Royal Institute of Technology, 1988).

12. *Ibid.,* p. 50.

13. *Ibid.,* p. 178.

14. *Ibid.,* p. 179.

15. E. M. Forster, *op. cit.,* pp. 98-9.

Chapter Ten: Beyond the House-as-Ego: The Call of the Soul

1. Martin Buber, *Tales of the Hassidim* (New York: Schocken Books, 1961).

2. June Singer, *Boundaries of the Soul: The Practice of Jung's Psychology* (New York: Anchor Books, 1972).

3. Edward C. Whitmont, *The Symbolic Quest: Basic Concepts of Analytical Psychology* (Princeton: Princeton University Press, 1967), p. 62.

4. Thomas Moore, *op. cit.,* pp. 120-22.

5. *Ibid.*

6. Suzanne Owens, "House, Home and Solitude: Memoirs and Journals of May Sarton" in Constance Hunting (ed.), *May Sarton: Woman and Poet* (Orono, ME: The National Poetry Foundation, University of Maine, 1982), pp. 62-3.

7. May Sarton, *The House by the Sea* (New York: W. W. Norton & Co., 1977), p. 17.

8. Thomas Moore, *op. cit.,* p. 86.

9. Edward Edinger, *op. cit.,* p. 166.

10. Thomas Moore, *op. cit.,* p. 120.

11. Edward Edinger, *op. cit.,* p. 17.

12. T. S. Eliot, "Little Giddings" in *Four Quartets* (New York: Harcourt, Brace and World, 1971), p. 62.

13. Olivier Marc, *op. cit.,* p. 51.

14. Thomas Merton, *The Sign of Jonas* (New York: Harcourt Brace and Co., 1953), p. 288.

15. *Ibid.*, p. 262.

16. Thich Nhat Hanh, *Peace in Every Step: The Path of Mindfulness in Everyday Life* (New York: Bantam Books, 1991), pp. 26-7.

17. Charlotte Perkins Gilman, *The Yellow Wallpaper and Other Writings* (New York: Bantam Books, 1989).

18. Patricia Hampl, *Virgin Time: In Search of the Contemplative Life* (New York: Farrar, Straus and Giroux, 1992), p. 62.

19. As quoted in Jack Kornfield, *Buddha's Little Instruction Book* (New York: Bantam Books, 1994), p. 33.

REFERENCES

Adler, Patricia, et al. (eds). *Fire in the Hills: A Collective Remembrance.* Berkeley, CA: Adler, 1992.

Ahrentzen, Sherry. "A Place of Peace, Prospect and . . . a P.C.: The Home as Office." *The Journal of Architectural and Planning Research,* vol. 6, no. 4, Winter 1989, pp. 271-88.

Altman, Irwin, and Carol M. Werner (eds.). "Home Environments." *Human Behavior and Environment: Advances in Theory & Practice,* vol. 8. New York: Plenum Press, 1985.

Ambasz, Emilio. *The Architecture of Luis Barragan.* New York: Museum of Modern Art, 1976.

Bachelard, Gaston. *The Poetics of Space.* New York: Orion Press, 1984.

Baekland, F. "Psychological Aspects of Art Collecting." *Psychiatry* 44 (1981) pp. 45-49.

Belk, R. W. "Attachment to Possessions" in I. Altmann and S. M. Low (eds.), *Place Attachment.* New York: Plenum Press, 1992, pp. 37-62.

———. "Possessions and the Extended Self." *Journal of Consumer Research* 15 (1988), pp. 139-68.

Bogan, Louise, and Ruth Limmer. *Journey Around My Room: The Autobiography of Louise Bogan: A Mosaic.* New York: Penguin Books, 1981.

Brower, Sidney. *The Functions of Near-Home Spaces.* Paper presented at the international workshop, "The Home Environment: Physical Space and Psychological Processes." Instituto di Psicología of Italian National Research Council, Cortona, Italy, May 1991.

Cather, Willa. *The Professor's House.* New York: Vintage Books, 1973.

Chomei, Kamo no. "Record of a Ten-Foot-Square Hut," Burton Watson (trans.), in *Four Huts: Asian Writings on the Simple Life.* Boston: Shambhala, 1994, pp. 60-106.

Cooper Marcus, Clare. "Remembrances of Landscapes Past." *Landscape,* 22 (3) Summer-Fall, 1978.

Dovey, Kimberly. "Home: An Ordering Principle in Space." *Landscape,* 22 (2), 1978.

Duncan, James S., Jr. "Landscape Taste as a Symbol of Group Identity." *Geographical Review,* July 1973, pp. 335-55.

Edinger, Edward. *Ego and Archetype.* New York: Penguin Books, 1972.

Fava, Sylvia. "Women's Place in the New Suburbia" in Gerda Wekerle, Rebecca Peterson, and David Morley (eds.), *New Space for Women.* Boulder, CO: Westview Press, 1980.

Feldman, Roberta A. *Settlement Identity and the Life Course.* Paper presented at the international workshop, "The Home Environment: Physical Space and Psychological Processes." Instituto di Psicología of Italian National Research Council, Cortona, Italy, May 1991.

Forster, E. M. *Howard's End.* New York: Vintage Books, 1994.

Fried, Marc. "Grieving for a Lost Home" in L. J. Duhl (ed.), *The Urban Condition.* New York: Basic Books, 1963, pp. 151-71.

Gay, P. "Introduction" and "Freud: For the Marble Tablet" in Edmund Engelman (ed.) *Berggasse 19: Sigmund Freud's Home and Offices, Vienna 1938: The Photographs of Edmund Engelman.* New York: Basic Books, 1976, pp. 13-54.

Goyen, William. *The House of Breath.* New York, Penguin Books, 1947.

Gurstein, Penny. *The Electronic Cottage: Implications for the Meaning of the Home.* Paper presented at a symposium on "The Use and Meaning of Home and Neighborhood," Alvkarleby, Sweden, September 1989.

Hampl, Patricia. *Virgin Time: In Search of the Contemplative Life.* New York: Farrar, Straus and Giroux, 1992.

James, William. *The Principles of Psychology,* vol. 1. New York: Henry Holt, 1890.

Jung, Carl. *Memories, Dreams, Reflections.* London: Fontana Library, 1969.

Korosec-Serfaty, P. "The Home from Attic to Cellar." *Journal of Environmental Psychology* 4 (1984), pp. 303-21.

Lym, Glenn Robert. *A Psychology of Building: How We Shape and Experience Our Structured Spaces.* Englewood Cliffs, NJ: Prentice Hall, Inc., 1980.

Mackintosh, E., R. Rosen, and W. Wentworth. *The Attitudes and Experiences of the Middle Income Family in an Urban High-Rise Complex and in the Suburbs.*

New York: Center for Human Environments, City University of New York, Graduate Center, 1977.

Mairs, Nancy. *Remembering the Bone House: An Erotics of Place and Space.* New York: Harper & Row, 1989.

Malouf, David. *12 Edmondstone Street.* Ringwood, Victoria, Australia: Penguin Books, Ltd., 1986.

Marc, Olivier. *The Psychology of the House.* London: Thames and Hudson, 1977.

McCracken, G. *Culture and Consumption: New Approaches to the Symbolic Character of Consumer Goods and Activities.* Bloomington: Indiana University Press, 1988.

Merton, Thomas. *New Seeds of Contemplation.* New York: New Directions, 1961.

———. *The Sign of Jonas.* New York: Harcourt, Brace and Co., 1953.

Miller, Stuart. "Designing the Home for Children." *Children's Environments Quarterly,* vol. 3, no. 1, Spring 1986.

Moore, Thomas S. *Care of the Soul.* New York: Harper Collins, 1992.

Prelinger, E. "Extension and Structure of the Self." *Journal of Psychology* 47 (1959) pp. 13-23.

Rosenblatt, P. C., R. P. Walsh, and D. A. Jackson. *Grief and Mourning in Cross-cultural Perspective.* New Haven, CT: Human Relations Area File, 1976.

Rullo, Giuseppina. *Experience of the Home Among Young Adults: Territorial Behaviors and Attitudes of Young Adults in Different Living Arrangements.* Paper presented at the international workshop, "The Home Environment: Physical Space and Psychological Processes." Instituto di Psicología of Italian National Research Council, Cortona, Italy, May 1991.

Rybczynski, Witold. *Home: A Short History of an Idea.* New York: Viking, 1986.

Saegert, Susan. "Masculine Cities and Feminine Suburbs: Polarized Ideas, Contradictory Realities." *Signs: Journal of Women in Culture and Society,* vol. 5, no. 3 (1980), suppl., pp. S96-S111.

Sarton, May. *The House by the Sea.* New York: W. W. Norton & Co., 1977.

———. *Journal of a Solitude.* New York: W. W. Norton & Co., 1973.

———. *Plant Dreaming Deep.* New York: W. W. Norton & Co., 1968.

———. *Recovering.* New York: W. W. Norton & Co., 1980.

Seamon, David, and Robert Mugerauer. *Dwelling, Place and Environment: Towards a Phenomenology of Person and the World.* Dordrecht, Netherlands: Martinus Nijhoff, 1985.

Seamon, David (ed.). *Dwelling, Seeing and Designing: Toward a Phenomenological Ecology.* Albany, NY: State University of New York Press, 1993.

———. *The Geography of the Lifeworld.* New York: St. Martin's Press, 1979.

Sebba, Rachel, and Arza Churchman. "The Uniqueness of Home." *Architecture and Behavior,* vol. 3, no. 1 (1986), pp. 7-24.

Tannen, Deborah. *You Just Don't Understand: Women and Men in Conversation.* New York: Ballantine, 1991.

Whitmont, Edward C. *The Symbolic Quest: Basic Concepts of Analytical Psychology.* Princeton, NJ: Princeton University Press, 1967.

Worthen, Helena. "How Does Your Garden Grow?" *Landscape,* 19 (3), May 1975.

About the Author

Clare Cooper Marcus, retired University of California at Berkeley professor of architecture and landscape architecture, has written several books on architecture and community, including *Housing as if People Mattered* and *People Places*, and numerous articles published in academic and architecture journals. She has consulted for the Department of Housing & Urban Development in Washington, DC, the San Francisco Housing Authority, New Zealand Department of Public Works, and the Canadian Housing Design Council, as well as many private architecture and engineering firms. Marcus has received NEA grants and awards, a Fulbright Travel Grant, Guggenheim Fellowship, and numerous other awards and fellowships. She lives in Berkeley, California.